Gender, Schooling and Global Social Justice

Elaine Unterhalter

 Routledge
Taylor & Francis Group

LONDON AND NEW YORK

First published 2007
by Routledge
2 Park Square, Milton Park, Abingdon, Oxon OX14 4RN

Simultaneously published in the USA and Canada
by Routledge
270 Madison Ave, New York, NY 10016

Routledge is an imprint of the Taylor & Francis Group, an informa business

© 2007 Elaine Unterhalter

Typeset in Galliard by
HWA Text and Data Management, Tunbridge Wells
Printed and bound in Great Britain by
MPG Books Ltd, Bodmin

British Library Cataloguing in Publication Data
A catalogue record for this book is available from the British Library

Library of Congress Cataloging-in-Publication Data
A catalog record for this book has been requested

ISBN10: 0–415–35921–X (hbk)
ISBN10: 0–415–35922–8 (pbk)
ISBN10: 0–203–46584–1 (ebk)

ISBN13: 978–0–415–35921–4 (hbk)
ISBN13: 978–0–415–35922–1 (pbk)
ISBN13: 978–0–203–96584–9 (ebk)

To Beryl and Jack

Contents

Tables

Series editors' foreword

One of the most remarkable transformations over the last 200 years has been the universal development of mass education. With each successive decade, provision has expanded to encompass more learners at more stages in their lives. The ambitions for education systems have also expanded to encompass objectives as diverse as personal fulfilment and wellbeing, cultural transmission, active citizenship, social cohesion and, increasingly, international economic competitiveness.

The broad range of ambitions and the sheer pace of change have created a climate in which it is sometimes difficult to stand back and make sense of what education is for and where it should be going. *Foundations and Futures of Education* provides an opportunity to engage with these fundamental issues in new and exciting ways. The series adopts a broad and inter-disciplinary stance, including historical, philosophical, sociological, psychological and comparative approaches as well as those from within the fields of media and cultural studies. The series also reflects wider conceptions of education embedded in concepts such as 'the knowledge economy', 'the learning society' and 'lifelong learning'.

In each volume, the academic rigour of the arguments is balanced with accessible writing which we hope will engage the interest of those working in and for education, as well as a wide range of undergraduate and postgraduate students. Although it will be clear that there are few 'easy answers' to many of the questions currently being asked, we hope that you will find the debates and dialogues exciting and thought-provoking.

This book explores the relationship between gender, schooling and social justice. In recent years, much attention in the UK has been focused on the relative underperformance of boys rather than girls. However, if we take a global perspective, the lack of educational opportunities for girls and women remains an enduring problem. Almost two-thirds of those who receive little or no schooling are female.

In this book, Elaine Unterhalter provides a compelling and carefully argued analysis of the various ways in which gender inequalities have been conceptualized and addressed. Scholarly and unpolemic in its approach, the book shows how successive movements and policies designed to promote 'education for all' have been based on quite different conceptions of the nature and causes of gender inequalities. Unravelling these conceptions, and the principles on which they are based, provides at least a partial explanation for the limited progress of gender equality programmes.

The book's unusual and original combination of philosophical critique and empirical illustration not only reveals the limits of particular approaches, it also points to new ways of tackling this enduring issue. It is essential reading for those who wish to broaden their understanding of gender, schooling and global social justice on a theoretical level and for those who are actively working to promote gender equality in education.

Preface

In 2005 it was estimated that of the one billion people in the world with little or no schooling, 64 per cent were women and girls.[1] Disquiet and distress at the scale and form of this injustice is widespread but no clear consensus has yet emerged on how best to confront the inequalities entailed. This is a book about gender equality in education as an aspiration of global social justice, looking particularly at the ethical and conceptual language in which this aspiration has been framed, and some of the policy and practice developed to turn aspirations into action. In a world where divisions between rich and poor have widened, economic globalization has not been met by equivalent advances in global social justice. The realpolitik of much international relations makes for an unstable political context to review ideas and build alliances to support social justice. In this context this book attempts to bring together two streams of discussion usually held separate, on the one hand a critical engagement with debates in political and social theory which frame some global initiatives concerning gender and schooling, and on the other descriptions and analysis of activities to deliver change.

The book is structured to examine discussions about global justice, gender and schooling at three levels. Part I provides an overview of the extent and form of gender inequalities in schooling worldwide distinguishing different meanings of gender (Chapter 1). It describes some of the major international gatherings that have sought to address gender inequality and schooling and introduces some of the key actors who have taken forward conference resolutions through global alliance building. This section also outlines some of the debate about global justice and cosmopolitanism in relation to gender and schooling (Chapter 2). Part II of the book (Chapters 3–6) examines a number of different arguments that have been made with regard to why gender equality in education is an appropriate issue for global justice. Why and on what terms have concepts associated with global social justice addressed the large numbers of girls and women without education and the gendered experiences in school of all children? Part III (Chapters 7–9) describes and analyses different kinds of action on the global stage to address gender and schooling highlighting their connection with the form of ethical discussion outlined in Part II and different approaches to global social justice examined in Part I. The conclusion (Chapter 10) highlights the significance of the inter-relationship between different forms of the ethical argument for global social justice and approaches to addressing gender and schooling in practice.

In summary, the argument concerns three different dynamics regarding how the aspiration for gender equality in education as a matter of global social justice has been expressed and given effect. Three contrasting approaches to understanding gender, global social justice and associated forms of action are outlined. The first understands gender in terms of the problems of girls. Global social justice is understood as instrumental for achieving valued outcomes worldwide, whether linked to economic growth, political stability or cultural diversity. Girls and women are seen as key to this process. In this framing global social justice may also be understood as what is required to address a minimal level of need, that is being schooled. This instrumental orientation has been the most widely used and is associated with the programmes of powerful countries and organizations to deliver development assistance.

A second approach is concerned with gendered relations in education and society. Global social justice is linked to ideas about the intrinsic importance of gender equality and human rights specified either legally in a number of Conventions and Declarations or through a particular moral conception of universal rights. This approach has been associated with actions that have concentrated on institution building and forms of regulation to deliver more gender equitable schooling. They have tended to focus on the legal meanings of rights and thus have been open to criticism regarding their limited specification of the ethical demands that underpin rights, lack of attention to the question of distribution, and concern that rights, which are formally justiciable, fail to capture or address the complexity of many informal gender inequalities. Thus their approach to gender equality through institution building does not fully secure equality.

A third approach is amenable to understanding gender as multifaceted, characterizing both forms of inequality but also forms of interaction. Gender in this approach is alert to diverse circumstances. Global social justice here is oriented to secure rights and capabilities, that is entitlements to particular outcomes or forms of flourishing. The combination of positive and negative freedoms which support capabilities give rise to substantive claims on others. Thus diverse interactions and a very wide range of obligations are entailed, not just those framed by existing institutions and juridical procedure. A challenge for this approach is how to understand the nature of the freedoms, forms of regulatory mechanism and public accountability that support it and how these articulate with interventionist and institutional forms of action. This approach attracts criticism for being too thick a notion of global social justice enjoining more from states than they can reasonably agree to and placing a huge onus on civil society and non-government organizations (NGOs) to articulate freedoms and engage with forms of regulation without access to appropriate accountability structures. The instances we have of this approach in action are all fragile, and have not as yet realized the potential for change ascribed to them.

In the chapters that follow I examine all three dynamics in some depth, looking first at the arguments about global social justice, and the different forms this takes, then turning to discussions of needs, rights and capabilities as foundational ideas which provide a rationale for different kinds of global justice project. Lastly, I consider how putting ideas into action raises new kinds of questions about the three different conceptual framings.

The book has developed out of my work in teaching education, gender and international development and my association with advocacy work in this area over 15 years. My ideas have been influenced partly by debates in feminist theory and education, partly by my interest in the capability approach, and its application in education. Since 2003 I have linked these academic interests with work as one of the co-ordinators of the *Beyond Access: Gender, education and development* project. In its initial phase this project was a collaboration between the Institute of Education, University of London, Oxfam GB and the UK Department for International Development (DFID). The project worked to develop and circulate new knowledge concerning gender, schooling and global social justice to researchers, policy makers, practitioners and campaigners. A major focus of the project was to build connections between these different constituencies. This book is not a description or evaluation of *Beyond Access*, but is informed by discussions in the project with representatives of governments, inter-government organizations (IGOs), international and national non-government organizations (NGOs). It draws on insights gained through participation in meetings where policy on gender and schooling was considered, debates engaged and positions defended. This is not, however, an empirically based account of institutions, forms of global regulation, or the strategies of international non-government organizations (INGOs). It is a work of synthetic analysis based primarily on reading in development theory and development ethics, analysis of selected policy documents, and conversations in the course of practice with key informants.

My warmest thanks to the many people who have helped me think about this book and complete it. Unfortunately, my very long personal thank you list has had to be pared down, but the particular contribution of a few people deserves special mention. This book has grown out of my work with the *Beyond Access* project largely funded by DFID. I am very grateful to close colleagues – Sheila Aikman, Chloe Challender, Amy North and Rajee Rajagopalan – and the wider project community who have talked through ideas, helped with requests, and made our collaboration richly rewarding.

Many discussions with students and staff at the Institute of Education, University of London have shaped my ideas. I have learned an enormous amount from them and particularly want to acknowledge their impact and the insights they have generated.

Some sections were presented as conference papers and invited lectures between 2003 and 2006. My thanks to participants in the following events who have helped me improve my arguments: Conferences of the Human Development and Capability Association, Pavia (2003 and 2004), Paris (2005), BERA (2004), Gender and Education (2005), UK Forum for International Education and Training Oxford (2005), Philosophy of Education Society Great Britain (2006), and lectures and seminars delivered at the Human Sciences Research Council, Pretoria (2004), the National Education Conference, Nairobi (2004), and the University of KwaZulu Natal (2005).

Sally Power initially suggested I prepare an outline of this book. She and Peter Aggleton have overseen its progress and given detailed written comments on drafts. I am immensely grateful for this thoughtful and supportive criticism. Harry Brighouse and Joe Crawford most generously read the whole manuscript. I am particularly grateful for their incisive written comments and overall appreciation of what I was trying to do

The first draft of the book was completed during 10 weeks' study leave from the Institute of Education. Thanks are due to Senior Management for agreeing this. Deborah Gaitskell covered my teaching during this period. Her friendship, encouragement and wide knowledge opened up valuable new directions.

Excellent research assistance helped keep a complex task more or less on schedule. I am very grateful to Rajee Rajagopalan, who meticulously gathered the information for the Tables, Rosa Crawford, who skilfully helped assemble references, and Anjali Kothari who patiently helped format the final draft.

At different times I have been inspired, contradicted, motivated and sustained by friends: Madeleine Arnot, Leontine Bijleveld, Linda Chisholm, Bob Cowen, Ireen Dubel, Sally Gear, Anne Gold, Diana Leonard, Terry Lovell, Louise Morley, Rob Morrell, Louisa Polak, Janet Raynor, Ingrid Robeyns, Gertrude Shotte, Caroline Suransky, Melanie Walker, and Michael Young. As I was completing the final draft of Chapter 3, Terry McLaughlin died suddenly. His wisdom and warmth were a resource I turned to often.

My family – Richard, Joe, Rosa, Oliver, Sophie – each in his or her way, has given me enormous support, understanding, and reassurance that have sustained me over months of work.

Abbreviations

ADEA	Association for the Development of Education in Africa
ASPBAE	Asian South Pacific Bureau of Adult Education
AWID	Association for Women's Rights in Development
CAMPE	Campaign for Mass Primary Education
CEDAW	Convention on the Elimination of Discrimination against Women
CEF	Commonwealth Education Fund
CRC	Convention on the Rights of the Child
DAC	Development Assistance Committee
DAWN	Development Alternatives with Women for a New Era
DFID	Department for International Development
DPEP	District Primary Education Programme
EDI	Education Development Index
EFA	Education for All
EMIS	Education Management Information System
EU	European Union
FAWE	Forum of African Women Educationalists
FTI	Fast Track Initiative
GABLE	Girls' Attainment in Basic Literacy and Education
GAC	Global Advisory Committee
GAD	Gender and Development
GADN	Gender and Development Network
GAP	Gender Achievements and Prospects
GCE	Global Campaign for Education
GEM	Gender Empowerment Measure
GENIA	Gender and Education Network in Asia
GER	Gross Enrolment Ratio
GEEI	Gender Equality and Education Index
GEI	Gender related EFA index
GETT	Gender Equity Task Team
GEU	Gender Equity Unity
GMR	Global Monitoring Report
GMS	Gender Management System

GRB	Gender responsive budgeting
HDCA	Human Development and Capability Association
IGO	Inter-Government Organization
ILO	International Labour Organization
IMF	International Monetary Fund
INGO	International Non-Government Organization
MDGs	Millennium Development Goals
NEPAD	New Partnership for Africa's Development
NER	Net Enrolment Ratio
NSM	New Social Movement
NGO	Non-Government Organization
PROMOTE	Programme to Motivate Train and Employ women teachers in rural secondary schools
PRSP	Poverty reduction strategy programme
SAARC	South Asian Association for Regional Cooperation
SAPs	Structural Adjustment Programmes
SIDA	Swedish International Development Cooperation Agency
SSA	Sarva Shiksha Abhiyan
UDHR	Universal Declaration of Human Rights
UEE	Universal Elementary Education
UN	United Nations
UNAIDS	Joint United Nations Programme on HIV/AIDS
UNDP	United Nations Development Programme
UNESCO	United Nations Educational, Scientific and Cultural Organisation
UNGEI	United Nations Girls' Education Initiative
UNICEF	United Nations Children's Fund
UPE	Universal Primary Education
USAID	United States Agency for International Development
WID	Women in Development
WTO	World Trade Organization

Part I

Context

History and concepts

Introduction

Throughout the world, gender often linked with injustice, marks life in schools. This book examines gender inequalities in schools and the forms of challenge to this mounted by global social justice, as an idea and form of practice. The chapters in this section set out some features of gender inequality in schooling worldwide, briefly introducing the history of attempts to tackle this. They go on to examine debates about global social justice and how some of the ethical discussions bear on the question of gender and schooling.

Several different meanings of the term global underpin the argument. Aspects of injustices associated with gender inequalities and schooling can be found in every country of the world so at one level this book is descriptively concerned with a meaning of global that signals 'all countries'. However, historically, United Nations (UN) institutions and international non-government organizations (INGOs), two of the key players in this field, have given more attention to work on gender in developing countries. In some of these, very large proportions of the population of women and girls receive no schooling. Thus many of the examples are drawn from the field of international development. A second meaning of global is associated with the extensive discussions of globalization. Despite many differences, these have in common an acknowledgement that the contemporary era encompasses a significantly different phase of economic, political and social inter-relations across the boundaries of states and peoples. Against this background 'global' is used as a shorthand for heterodox relations which signal new forms of inter-connectedness across the globe. This book is not about the globalization debate, but it is concerned with a wide range of global relationships across national boundaries. A third meaning of global is often linked with discussions of global justice and signals normative concerns with the form of morality and ideas about justice that may be appropriate for people who do not share citizenship or other forms of readily recognized affiliation. In this form the term global is sometimes used interchangeably with universal. Chapter 2, which deals with the theme of cosmopolitanism, considers this in greater depth.

1 Gender and Education for All

Setting the scene

From 1990 the Education for All (EFA) movement has been a loose term for the global mobilisation amongst disparate actors to advance demands for increased provision of schooling. Different meanings of gender and education can be discerned in this history (Unterhalter 2005a). The uneven presence and absence of girls and boys in schools has entailed a concern with gender as a noun, for example how many girls and boys attend school or pass a certain grade. A second meaning of gender is associated with changing social processes. Here gender is an adjective which describes a range of social relations and institutional forms which structure social relations leading to particular forms of action in school and as a consequence of school. This is sometimes termed the gender regime. An example is the way a gendered curriculum makes it difficult for girls to succeed in mathematics and provides openings to certain boys. The relational dynamic between men and women in particular social settings is also signalled by this meaning of gender which is alert to the ways in which, for example, assumptions about girls' innate propensity to care for children and express emotions is in relational tension with assumptions about boys' innate propensity to act rationally. A third meaning highlights the way gender can be a verb. This signals a process of being or becoming 'girl' or actions in accordance with particular forms of masculinity. Social actions entailed in performing gender and forming the self entail different actions in different settings. Changing social circumstances might mean that people of the same sex are required to act gender in different ways. For example in a society segregated by race white women and men might have more similarities in the way they consume resources. White and black women might perform gender in markedly different ways.

As the following chapters highlight, the emergence of gender and education as a theme in global social justice debates has been associated with tension and contestation. The main dispute has entailed differences between a focus primarily on girls, boys and schools, that is using gender as a noun, and a focus on gender as an adjective which entails looking at gendered relations within schools, households, and the broader political economy. Conceptions of gender as a form of action and identity formation – gender as a verb – have had somewhat less impact in social justice debates about gender and schooling, although they have been utilized in thinking about gender, sexuality and schooling, particularly in the context of the HIV epidemic. They also have particular salience in thinking about how poverty has diverse effects.

Expanding access: girls and schooling since 1945

The expansion of education to all citizens was an objective of nationalist movements in Asia, Africa and Latin America and of many social reform movements in Europe and America from the beginning of the twentieth century. Decolonisation and post-war reconstruction from the 1940s saw many new governments establishing mass systems of schooling linked to projects of national development which aimed to include all citizens. In newly independent states these expanded the limited provision of the colonial era when education had been largely provided for men and women from elites and was only sporadically available to the rest of the population in under resourced schools (Carnoy and Samoff 1990; Fagerlind and Saha 1989). The Universal Declaration on Human Rights (UDHR) of 1948 contained passages on universal rights to education irrespective of gender. Concerns to implement this were a part of the early years of the work of the United Nations Educational, Scientific and Cultural Organisation (UNESCO). However in the 1950s gender equality in education as a separate policy area had little prominence in the work of global institutions. On the whole, girls and women benefited from the expansion of education provision within nation states, concerned with reaching all citizens, rather than specific groups.

The expansion of access to schooling and adult literacy was not uniform. Regional and social inequalities within countries were reflected in who did and did not enrol in school, magnifying existing social divisions. Table 1.2 (Appendix 1) shows the growth of enrolment in primary school by gender in different parts of the world since the 1960s. Although the proportion of girls and boys in primary school over the last 40 years has risen in every region, a gender gap, that is the difference between the enrolment rate or progression of girls and boys in school, persists. A gender gap was evident in all regions in the 1960s – except North America, Western Europe, Latin America and the Caribbean. By 2000 it had only been eradicated in East Asia. It had narrowed in the Arab States, South Asia and Sub-Saharan Africa, but it had not been eliminated. The proportion of girls and boys at primary school in Africa fell in the early 1990s, and then started to rise again at the end of the decade. From the 1980s the restrictions on public sector growth demanded by Structural Adjustment Programmes (SAPs) meant that fees were often charged for schooling, teachers were not appointed and sometimes irregularly paid, and schools fell into disrepair. These conditions contributed to a slow growth in enrolments or a reversal of gains made in previous decades. They were associated with the persistence of the gender gap in three regions – Africa, South Asia and the Arab States.

Table 1.3 (Appendix 1) gives figures for the growth in enrolment for girls and boys in secondary schools from 1965–2000. There has been considerable expansion of access to secondary school for girls and boys worldwide from the 1960s, but it was only in the mid-1990s that roughly equal proportions of girls and boys were in secondary school in the Arab States, East Asia and the Pacific. Here and in Latin America between 20–30 per cent of girls and boys were not in secondary school in 2000. The picture was much bleaker in South and West Asia and Sub-Saharan Africa. Here, while the gender gap in secondary school narrowed as the twentieth century progressed, at its end only a quarter of girls in Africa were in secondary school and under half of all girls in South Asia. The gender gap in secondary school enrolments has narrowed more dramatically than in primary, because, by the 1990s if families could afford to educate children to secondary level, they tended to support girls and boys. Indeed in some regions – Arab States, East Asia and the Pacific and Latin America and the Caribbean – by the mid-1990s the gender gap at secondary level was in favour of girls, as boys from poorer families left school to work.

Table 1.4 (Appendix 1) shows changes in enrolment and retention in selected countries where there is time series data since the 1960s. This shows up some of the differences within regions that the aggregated data in Tables 1.2 and 1.3 (Appendix 1) mask. In many countries in Africa, steady rises in girls' and boys' net enrolment ratio (NER) from the 1960s started to be reversed in the mid-1990s. Countries suffering the effects of HIV/AIDS, structural adjustment, and war were the hardest hit. However, in a small number of countries – Uganda, Malawi and Mozambique – this reversal did not happen, or a downward trend in the mid-1990s was halted and turned around by the end of the decade.

All the countries included in Table 1.4 (Appendix 1) from South, Central and East Asia show an increase in girls' and boys' primary NER and retention, with the exception of Afghanistan. All show increasing proportions of girls and boys enrolled in secondary schools with a pronounced gender gap in most countries, with the exception of the Philippines and Sri Lanka. A similar trend with increasing levels of primary enrolment and retention for girls and boys is evident in the countries listed from Latin America and the Caribbean, although in the 1990s Jamaica and Trinidad show falling rates of enrolment for girls, and more dramatically for boys. There are much higher proportions of girls and boys enrolled in secondary school in Latin America and the Caribbean, and considerable increases over the 40 years surveyed. Here, the picture is generally of equal proportions of girls and boys enrolled, but, in a number of countries, e.g. Chile, Columbia, and Nicaragua, a considerably larger proportion of girls.

Table 1.5 (Appendix 1) selects the countries with the highest, lowest and median girls' NER in each region in the mid-1960s. Here we see that countries with high levels of girls' NER in the 1960s were generally able to maintain this to the end of the century, while countries with low levels of girls' NER in the 1960s increased this sporadically over the next 40 years, with acceleration taking place mainly in the 1990s.

There has been an accelerating rate of increase in enrolments in primary and secondary school in many countries since 1990, but for a large number this acceleration has been from an extremely low base. Table 1.6 (Appendix 1) lists 26 countries where there were increases in girls' primary NER of more than 25 per cent between 1990 and 2000. In a number of countries – Guinea, Mali, Mauritania, Eritrea, Chad and Ethiopia – starting from a very low NER for girls in 1990 there has been a huge percentage increase. Ethiopia, notable for a Minister of Education, who was in post for many years and was particularly committed to increasing girls' enrolment, had a percentage gain of 95 and Malawi, with a similar high level of political focus on this issue had a percentage gain of 126. Girls' NER in Chad doubled over the period and in Mali, where the government instituted extensive programmes supported by large development assistance programmes, there were similar huge increases (Ahouanmènou-Aguey 2002).

By 2005, despite this growth in enrolments and retention since 1960, millions of children remained out of school. Girls comprised a significant proportion. In 2005 UNESCO estimated there were 100 million children out of school, 55 per cent of whom were girls. Worldwide approximately 771 million adults were illiterate as a result of never accessing or completing school. Only 88 women were considered literate for every 100 men. In some countries this was much lower, with 60 or fewer women literate for every 100 men. The proportion of adults without literacy represented one-fifth of the world's adult population (UNESCO 2005a: 17). Thus, despite some energetic programmes, education was still denied in the poorest countries and for the poorest sections of the population. Gendered social relations were a feature of this injustice, simultaneously helping to shape and maintain it.

Gendered schools and societies: education and injustice

Gender has been implicated in forms of exclusion and discrimination which have denied millions of children access to school, regular attendance, conditions to learn appropriately, or progress beyond a few years of instruction. Gender structures the political economy and social conditions surrounding schools. The gender politics of power have particular consequences for children's wellbeing and gender dynamics often mean the outcomes of schooling are distributed unfairly.

The exclusion of girls from school takes a number of forms that are different to those entailed in the exclusion of boys. Some girls are never enrolled because the financial and social costs of schooling are too high, the quality of learning too low, or there is no school available locally (Colclough *et al.* 2004; Kane 2004). In some regions there are cultural prohibitions or cautions about girls' schooling linked to assertions of particular cultural identities under certain circumstances. Sometimes these conditions are political, for example with the break-up of the USSR in Tajikistan (Waljee 2005). Cultural affirmation which shapes gendered ideas about schooling and households can be associated with strategies about livelihood and economic hardship as was the case for pastoralists in Northern Kenya in the 1990s (Leggatt 2005). Sometimes cultural identification, which entails the withdrawal of girls from school, is linked to violent and repressive regimes as in Afghanistan under the Taliban. It is generally in the poorest communities that gendered social relations have particularly harsh consequences for girls' schooling. Some girls attend school infrequently because of work obligations, or inadequate facilities, for example no running water or long distances to travel to school. Some girls attend school but under-nourishment means they are unable to participate fully. Some girls leave school after a few months or years because of changes in the economic circumstances in a family, a fee increase, repeatedly failed grades or persistent lack of teaching (Vavrus 2003; Bista 200; Page 2005). Some leave because they experience a form of gender-based violence (Mirsky 2003; Leach *et al.* 2006). Sometimes armed conflict forces girls out of school and girls recruited as child soldiers have enormous difficulties in reintegrating once they return to school (Machel 1996; McKay and Mazurana 2004). The HIV/AIDS epidemic has meant girls are the family members generally preferred to leave school to look after relations who are ill, or orphaned (Zoll 2006). Girls, like boys suffering from HIV, have to abandon school because they are too weak to study further (UNAIDS *et al.* 2004).

Poverty is a major factor in the denial of schooling to girls. The poorest parents wish to educate their daughters, but cannot because of want and other dimensions of discrimination. Sometimes there are no schools available in the poorest communities because there has been no infrastructural or social development by the state or private organisations. Sometimes school fees or the costs associated with schooling, for example uniforms, books or transport, are economically and socially unaffordable for the poorest families. Sometimes the quality of learning and teaching in schools for the poorest is low which means parents see no reason for children to attend. While all these factors can result in the denial of schooling to boys as well as girls, the gendered dynamics in households and communities generally entail that where resources are restricted they go to boys before girls. This is the result of a complex interplay of relations. The financial costs of schooling for boys are somewhat lower for families than those for girls as the clothing boys wear to school is cheaper and they are perceived to be less vulnerable and therefore not in need of additional transport (Kingdon 2005). The social costs of schooling poor boys are also lower as there are fewer restrictions on their mobility post puberty. In most poor households children work, but the sexual division of labour generally entails girls' responsibility for childcare and work inside the home can mean protracted periods when they are not in school, taking care of siblings, adults who are ill, and social obligations relating to the maintenance of the community. Boys' responsibilities for work outside the home have more flexibility around time and can often be more easily combined with school attendance.

Within schools, gendered assumptions about what girls should learn, whether they can learn, and what the outcome of their learning will be often means that girls do not get adequate support from teachers, do not have knowledge in subjects that attract status and do not proceed to secondary school (Heward and Bunwaree 1999). Ames' work in rural villages in Peru documents how teachers assumed girls were less clever than boys, required girls clean the school and perform domestic work for teachers, and did not support girls to proceed to secondary school (Ames 2005). Page's study of schools in a small town in Northern India showed how many teachers did not pay sufficient attention to what girls were learning and assumed their parents did not support their education, findings corroborated by Sarangapani through an ethnographic study in another state (Page 2005; Sarangapani 2003). Vavrus' work in Tanzania shows how there is a complex interplay between the changing socio-economic circumstances of parents linked to structural adjustment, the employment opportunities for girls post-secondary school, girls' views of their own identity and sexuality and conditions in schools which have a bearing on whether or not girls remain in school (Vavrus 2005). On the other hand, some schools have supported girls, even the most marginalized, to learn. Sometimes this is in extremely difficult circumstances, such as post-conflict Afghanistan (Kirk 2004) or a city divided by caste in India (Doggett 2005).

The absence of women from decision-making bodies concerning curriculum, learning and teaching helps maintain the gendered form of institutions. Although there are examples of women who maintain gender discrimination in schools, in a number of instances when women gain access to power in education, very dramatic changes have been recorded with regard to learning and teaching for all children. In 2003–4 women's presence on local school committees in Uganda led to improved monitoring and evaluation of schooling at village level as women attended to whether teachers performed their jobs, how budgets were spent and whether children progressed (Garrow 2004). Integrated social development planning in Brazil linked with higher levels of women's political visibility, resulted in the provision of direct cash grants to women whose children attend school and consequently better enrolment and retention (Palazzo 2005). Improvements in the quality of learning for adults and children has been noted in particular programmes which mobilize women as teachers and encourage them to reflect on their own histories as a means to enhance their teaching (Oomen 2005). Thus the politics of women's presence in decision making and shifts in gendered power seem to correlate with expansion of access to school, enhancement of retention, learning and progression. This suggests a connection between changing gendered power in decision making *about* education and changes in gendered social relations *within* education.

The gender dynamics of households, schools, economic and political relations can intersect to reproduce gendered relations of inequality. But these are not fixed. While gender can be a powerful form of discrimination it has been successfully challenged in many settings. Empirical studies note that women who have disposable income and work in economic sectors with a more equal sexual division of labour can dispute gendered relations in schools and bargain within households for the education of their children, arguing on behalf of girls (Quisumbing *et al.* 2004; Kabeer 2002). They use their own income for their children's education. Women working together in saving schemes draw collective strength to challenge gendered relations in schools (Unterhalter and Dutt 2001). A number of studies document more equal household relations and men contributing to daughters' schooling or challenging forms of violent masculinity (Morrell 2005; Mgumya 2004).

Gendered social relations inside and outside schools make access and progression difficult for large numbers of children, but the effects weigh especially heavily on girls.

Where is gender equality in education the largest challenge?

Gender inequality in access to school and progression takes a number of forms, not all of which are amenable to clear documentation. In 2005 UNESCO's Global Monitoring Report recorded 72 countries that had less than 90 per cent of girls of primary school age in school (see Table 1.6, Appendix 1). These ranged from some of the poorest countries in Africa – Niger and Mozambique – to countries within the European Union (EU) like the Czech Republic which had only 88 per cent of primary school age girls in school. The largest number of countries with low NER were in Africa, but countries with large populations in South Asia – India and Pakistan – had low girls' NER as did a number of countries in the Middle East. While many countries in Eastern Europe had nearly 90 per cent of girls in school, a handful had surprisingly low NER for girls – Serbia, Moldova and Ukraine.

In a number of countries enrolments have fallen. Table 1.8 (Appendix 1) lists the 15 countries for which there is data where the proportion of girls of school age in school fell between 1990 and 2000. Some of these are countries which have experienced the devastations of war – Angola, Serbia and Iraq – and others are associated with military regimes and high levels of repression – Myanmar and Equatorial Guinea. In some, the effects of HIV/AIDS have been acute – Zambia, Botswana, Zimbabwe, Kenya, and Namibia – and in some, this has been coupled with economic crisis.

In a large number of countries, girls do not remain at school over five years to complete a minimal primary cycle. Table 1.9 (Appendix 1) lists the 50 countries which in 2002 had less than 90 per cent of girls who enrolled in primary school remain over five years. Many countries with a high proportion of the population living on low incomes are on this list, for example Mozambique, Malawi, Ghana, Bangladesh, India and Lao. Unsurprisingly, countries which have experienced conflict are here too, such as Rwanda, Ethiopia, Eritrea, and Iraq. The list also includes a number of middle income countries with long histories of education reform like Columbia, South Africa, Morocco, Philippines and Vietnam. This suggests that social change has not adequately addressed this social division. Table 1.10 (Appendix 1) lists the 47 countries for which there is data where less than 80 per cent of girls enrolled in primary school progressed to secondary school. These range from middle income countries like Ecuador and Israel to some of the poorest countries, such as Mozambique, Tanzania and Nepal.

The challenges of girls' access to schooling and equality within school are compounded by the lack of women's representation in decision-making bodies and women's low income. Table 1.11 (Appendix 1) lists 59 countries out of 87 for which there is data where women comprised less than a third of managers and legislators between 1995 and 2004. Although women are incorporated into the labour force in diverse ways, generally only very highly educated women employed in the formal sector are likely to earn 80 per cent or more of men's pay. Data for 2003 available for 154 countries showed that in only two – Switzerland and Kenya – was the overall level of women's earned income 80 per cent or more of men's (Chen *et al.* 2005: 50; UNDP 2005: 299–302).

Table 1.12 (Appendix 1) combines available information on countries with low levels of girls' enrolment and retention in primary school, progression to secondary school, limited opportunities for women to take part in decision making and discrimination in women's pay as a proportion of that of men in the formal sector. The table presents one picture of the countries where gender equality in education is the greatest challenge. There is data for these countries on a combination of at least two forms of gender inequality in education and low levels of representation of women's views in decision-making bodies plus a large gender gap in earnings. The 32 countries listed in Table 1.12 (Appendix 1) are not the only countries where these injustices exist. The table notes only combinations of injustice, while a single injustice with regard to access, participation or outcome are all matters for concern. The aggregation of data means that regional injustices within a country or injustices to specific groups do not show up sufficiently. The lack of data in some fields means that certain countries are not listed not because there is no combined injustice, but because there is no data. The table is presented to give an indication of some of the scale of the global challenge regarding gender, social justice and schooling, not as a definitive marker of which countries do and do not 'score well'.

The challenge of global justice with regard to gender and schooling has been compounded by poverty and debt. Table 1.13 (Appendix 1) links information on low girls' NER, the proportion of the population living below $1 per day and the level of debt service. It can be seen that countries with a very low proportion of girls in schools have either a very high level of debt service as a proportion of GDP – more than 3.5 per cent – or more than one-fifth of the population living on less than US$1 per day. Of the eight countries where this pattern is not evident, there are gaps in the information for all except one. There is thus a strong indication that the poorest people are unable to afford education for girls and those governments, unable to invest in education because of high levels of debt service, have not developed programmes to address this.

In 2005, a debt forgiveness package was agreed by the G8 summit and confirmed by the international financial institutions in nine out of the 25 countries listed in Table 1.12 (Appendix 1). A subsequent deal with Nigeria later in the year meant that 10 countries with high levels of debt and low levels of girls' enrolment in school gained some financial support. Of the 10 countries benefiting from debt relief, four – Niger, Nigeria, Mali and Burkina – had only approximately one-third of the school age population of girls at primary school. Part of the argument for debt forgiveness was that without a debt burden these countries would be able to institute some quick improvements in access. Others – Benin, Ghana and Mozambique – had nearly two-thirds of school age girls in primary school. Some of the debt forgiveness, it was hoped, could help fund improved access for poorer families and general improvements in school quality. However, some of the countries with the lowest levels of girls' enrolment – Afghanistan, Angola, Djibouti, and Somalia – and some of the poorest populations were not yet in line for assistance in this way.

Gender in the EFA movement: some key actors and events

Declines in school enrolment during the 1980s and anxieties about the effects of structural adjustment were part of the impetus for convening The World Conference on Education for All, hosted by four UN agencies in 1990 at Jomtien, Thailand. This launched the EFA movement. The Jomtien Conference, attended by 155 governments, 20 IGOs and 150 NGOs, adopted the World Declaration on Education for All. The Declaration noted the high incidence of girls amongst the children out of school.

When EFA was launched at Jomtien in 1990 it included some of the first signals that the education of girls was important for a global social justice project. The World Declaration highlighted that girls and women comprised two-thirds of the large numbers of children without access to primary school and the large numbers of adults without literacy. It set out 'an expanded vision' and a renewed commitment to basic education to address the 'scale and complexity of the challenge' (World Declaration 1990: 74). The exclusion of girls and women from education was thus part of the problem EFA set out to tackle. Their inclusion was seen as part of the solution which was to be supported by policies for universal access, a focus on learning rather than just enrolment, a concern to utilize a range of different forms of delivery, and to strengthen the international solidarity that would underpin a common and universal human responsibility.

The movement became associated with some of the initial optimism of a peace dividend that flourished after the fall of the Berlin Wall and the break up of the USSR. Reforming governments, elected in many countries in the 1990s, gave an explicit commitment to the expansion of education and instituted innovative programmes. Many NGOs and researchers began to advocate for EFA. But the confidence of the new era was crosscut with the hardship and suffering associated with structural adjustment policies, imposed because of beliefs in the inherent virtue of market liberalisation in place of state provision. The harsh consequences of structural adjustment helped drive the EFA agenda with regard to access, built up consensus for support and generated some of the resources needed to realize EFA goals (Mehrota and Jolly 2000; Colclough 2004). From the late 1990s new geopolitical forces came into play driven by interlinked processes which included the attenuation of peace initiatives in Israel and Palestine, the emergence of the 'war on terror' as a major preoccupation of some governments, new conflicts over scarce resources, the growth of China's economy and the emergence of new regional political and economic formations. Flows of development assistance were often linked with shifts in G8 countries' foreign and economic policy associated with these unfolding events and new alliances. But development assistance also had elements of its own particular dynamic rooted in specific histories and old collaborations

In the meetings of the EFA movement, gender was given some attention. However, 'gender' generally meant a concern with girls. Gendered relations in schools and the formation of gendered identities had little leverage on policy (Aikman and Unterhalter 2005a).

In parallel with the EFA movement, the global women's movement was working for gender equality demands in a rather different manner. A huge worldwide mobilization of women inside and outside government has taken place from the mid-1960s to advocate for women's rights and gender equality in policy and practice, drawing particular strength from global connections between organisations and regional alliances (Ashworth 2000; Antrobus 2004). Between Jomtien and the second EFA conference at Dakar in 2000, the third World Conference on Women took place in Beijing in 1995. Attended by virtually all governments, and IGOs and accompanied by a huge mobilisation of 2,600 NGOs working on women and gender, the conference adopted the Beijing Declaration and Platform for Action. This document is the fullest statement regarding gender equality and women's rights yet produced by an international meeting. It acknowledges 'the diversity of women and their roles and circumstances', commits itself to the social and political project of promoting 'the goals of equality, development and peace for all women everywhere in the interests of all humanity' and identifies a number of key priorities in terms of the eradication of poverty, social development, environmental sustainability and the inclusion of women in the design and delivery of policy and programmes to achieve this (Beijing Declaration 1995). Key passages of the Platform of Action were concerned with education, which together with poverty, health, violence and the promotion of women in decision making were flagged as the major areas for future work. Disappointingly, over the next decade, there were to be few links made between the global women's movement, oriented to realising the vision of the Platform of Action, and the EFA movement, oriented to implementing the Jomtien Declaration.

Limited progress worldwide on the expansion of education during the 1990s led to the second EFA conference in Dakar in 2000 which mobilized much wider support from governments, IGOs and NGOs compared to those who had gone to Jomtien. The Dakar conference adopted an expanded Framework which placed particular stress on financing EFA and education within broader poverty reduction programmes. Dakar saw a pledge by donor governments that money would be available to fund well-developed national education plans to achieve EFA. In 2002, the Fast Track Initiative (FTI) was established as a partnership between donors and developing countries to co-ordinate donor funding for EFA and facilitate increased financial flows. Governments applying for FTI funding had to demonstrate commitment to EFA through a process of developing national plans (Fast Track Initiative 2005). By 2004, disbursements had been relatively slow, although in 2005 these started to accelerate (for a more detailed discussion of the FTI see Chapter 9).

At Dakar, the focus was on delivery of the Jomtien vision and six specific goals were identified. While gender was implicit in all six, there was explicit mention of girls and women in three. The six goals were:

- the expansion and improvement of early childhood education;
- access to free, compulsory education of good quality for all children;
- all learning to be appropriate for children and that life skills to be included in learning;
- an improvement in levels of adult literacy;
- gender disparities in primary and secondary education to be removed;
- all aspects of the quality of education to be improved including measurable learning outcomes (Dakar Framework 2000: 15–17).

Goal two on access specifically mentioned girls amongst the children for whom access was to be assured. Goal four on adult literacy emphasized the importance of improving literacy levels for women. Goal five was the 'gender goal'. Gender equality was largely described in a restricted form as eliminating gender disparities, that is the gender gap between girls and boys, thus ensuring equal proportions of a population of girls and boys in any phase of education. In the commentary on the goal there is both a narrow focus on girls' access and participation and some delineation of the need to change aspects of conditions in school to 'eliminate gender discrimination' (Dakar Framework 2000: 17). This phrasing points to some wider dimensions of gender equality beyond access, but they are not well specified.

Some of the aspirations associated with the EFA movement and the Beijing Declaration came to be articulated in the Millennium Declaration adopted at the Millennium Summit of the UN in New York in 2000. This expressed a number of founding values which included freedom, equality, solidarity and tolerance in which the specific rights of women and men were affirmed. These were placed within a context of tackling poverty, advancing the UDHR and the Convention on the Elimination of Discrimination against Women. This was a fuller statement of global aspiration than the documents of the EFA movement. But the Millennium Declaration combined hopes for human rights and gender equality with concerns about the conduct of war, terrorism, reform of the UN and the harnessing of globalization for positive ends. Some of these aspirations united a broad consensus behind them, but others did not.

An approach to the distribution of costs and burdens of addressing global challenges was laid out. A form of redistributive global justice was expressed thus. 'Those who suffer, or who benefit least, deserve help from those who benefit most' (Millennium Declaration 2000). Eight Millennium Development Goals (MDGs) were set out. Each MDG had specific targets and indicators that were intended to set a time by which there would be evidence that the target and the goal might be met. Table 2.1 (Appendix 2) lists the MDGs, targets and indicators. Gender and schooling were explicitly mentioned in two targets and formed part of five indicators. Under MDG 2 for Universal Primary Education (UPE), the target was to 'Ensure that by 2015, children everywhere, boys and girls alike, will be able to complete a full course of primary schooling' (Millennium Project 2000). The indicators here were that there was 100 per cent NER for boys and girls, 100 per cent pupils starting grade 1 should reach grade 5, and that the literacy rate for young men and women from 15–24 was increasing. MDG 3 was concerned with the promotion of gender equality and the empowerment of women. The target here was to 'Eliminate gender disparity in primary and secondary education, preferably by 2005, and to all levels of education by no later than 2015' (Millennium Project 2000). Among the indicators for this target were an equal ratio of boys to girls in primary, secondary and tertiary education (gender parity) and an equal ratio of literate women to men among 15–24-year-olds.

The gender parity indicator for MDG 3 was not very demanding. A country could have complete gender parity, that is with the same ratio of boys and girls in school, but low overall enrolment. While MDG 2 provided a counterweight for this signalling a vision that all children should complete primary school, the indicators for MDG 3 focused on enrolment in primary schooling. They did not signal a concern with increased access of girls to secondary school and of young women to tertiary level education. Moreover, other indicators associated with MDG 3 – increasing women's share of wage employment and of seats in parliament – did not speak to the fuller understanding of gender equality articulated in the Beijing Declaration with its comprehensive vision addressing all aspects of poverty, reproductive rights and violence.

In 2005, when progress on the MDGs was reviewed at the World Summit in New York in September, the target for MDG 3, that is to have equal proportions of girls and boys in primary school by 2005, had been missed in 94 out of 149 countries with data (UNESCO 2005b). Countries in Sub-Saharan Africa and South Asia, according to UN agencies' statistics, were far from meeting the target, while countries in West Asia and Oceania were closer and might achieve this by 2015 (UNStats 2005a).

At the World Summit it was clear that much greater momentum was needed even to attain gender parity in education and UPE. The 2005 World Summit Outcome Document contained a commitment by summit leaders to take 'quick impact' actions in countries where achieving the MDGs was unlikely. These included expansion of school meal programmes and the elimination of user fees for primary education (World Summit 2005: Point 34). There was a reaffirmation of the Dakar Framework for Action, an undertaking to strive for expanded access of girls and women to secondary and higher education, and a promise of enhanced resources for compulsory primary education. On gender and compulsory schooling, the Summit document stressed a commitment 'to eliminate gender inequality and imbalance and to renew efforts to improve girls' education' (World Summit 2005: Point 44). An uneasy balance between different meanings of gender and whether these entailed minimal remedies for girls' access or maximal strategies for a wider meaning of gender equality was apparent.

The challenge for activists and analysts was partly to hold government and IGOs to account for the promises on gender equality and education made at Beijing, Dakar and New York. The growth of civil society organisations concerned with global dimensions of education became an important space in which lobbying and debate on these issues occurred A significant group of women and gender campaigners were concerned to defend and advance the vision of the Beijing Declaration, while working to implement the MDGs and the Dakar Framework (Dubel 2005; Subrahmanian 2005a; Unterhalter 2005c). Some of these concerns with expanding the understanding of gender justice and building connections between the global women's movement and the EFA movement have been part of the thinking that has shaped this book.

Regional and global networks for gender equality and schooling

At Jomtien, the institutional underpinnings for a global commitment to EFA and gender were sketchy. They were to strengthen over the next 15 years. The period saw the development of a distinctive institutional base to take these forward. UN agencies formed different kinds of partnership concerning gender and schooling, with first one agency and then another setting the pace. A particular lead was given through the Development Assistance Committee (DAC) of the OECD which in 1995 demanded measurable targets for global development, a demand that was later to be endorsed in the Millennium Declaration and result in the eight MDGs with their targets, indicators and particular emphasis on gender and women. Other IGOs and supra government organisations like the Commonwealth and the EU made particular kinds of intervention to give gender a higher profile (Commonwealth Secretariat 1999; Brine 2001; Staudt 2003). Some governments put in place particular programmes focused on the education of girls, explicitly grounding these in the language of Jomtien or Dakar (Kwesiga 2003; Muito 2004). The Gender and Education Network in Asia (GENIA), co-ordinated by UNESCO, brought together education officials in Asia who had a special gender brief – termed gender focal points – to share experiences This group held training sessions, produced guides on gender and planning, briefing papers, undertook research, and acted as a mobilising group within Ministries (Jensen and Rajagopalan 2004).

It is beyond the scope of this study to examine the extent to which programmes in a particular country were an explicit response to the EFA agenda or whether response in terms of EFA was mediated through more local political and economic aspirations. In Bangladesh, for example, implementing programmes concerned with girls' access to school was partly a matter of defining the nation and thus providing education to all. But it was also linked to the particular concerns of elite groups with remaining in power, a response to widespread popular mobilisation in which women figured prominently, and an engagement with global agendas (Hossain *et al.* 2002; Ahmed 2003; Unterhalter *et al.* 2003). In Kenya the education network *Elimu Yetu* developed after key NGOs returned from Dakar and campaigned for the right to education stressing issues about gender. As a result of their campaigning all the political parties fighting the election in 2002 included rights to education in their manifestos. The global EFA movement thus had a particular local resonance (Elimu Yetu 2005: 123–5).

In the months preceding the Dakar conference, development NGOs had begun to turn their attention to education and to strategize as to how to influence the international agenda. The Global Campaign for Education (GCE) emerged out of these networks and lobbying. Founded in 1999 as an alliance of NGOs and trade unions active in more than 150 countries, GCE became a key body holding governments accountable for the promises made at Dakar. It obtained a seat on the high level group monitoring the achievements of EFA,[1] became enormously respected amongst donor bodies and was able to combine the production of high quality briefing material with campaigning work. One of its remits was to lobby for more money for EFA. While GCE did not have a specific focus on gender, when it took up gender issues it gave them a particularly high profile. A campaigning tactic GCE developed was to have a week of co-ordinated action on EFA in a large number of countries. In 2003 this focused on gender. GCE published a review of case study material from nine countries with a global overview of some of the general features of gender discrimination in education and the kinds of actions governments could take to overcome this (GCE 2003a). The material was used by GCE in lobbying governments, the EFA High Level Group and the FTI. Popular mobilisation drew on this in co-ordinating a teaching session across the world involving more than 1 million children and teachers as part of the 2004 week of action (Beyond Access 2004; GCE 2004). In 2005 GCE developed a briefing paper for the UN Beijing plus Ten meeting called to review progress ten years after the Beijing conference. This called for a strategy for girls' education, demanded an end to all debt and the expansion of the FTI to countries ready to accelerate progress on girls education. It demanded an eradication of the worst forms of child labour, an increase in government spending on basic education, the introduction of free and compulsory schooling for nine years. Girls' needs, it argued, should be addressed through teacher training, school buildings, and management that would ensure an end to gender-based violence. The paper concluded with a call for attention to gender equality issues beyond education (GCE 2005a). Throughout 2005 GCE gave prominence to the gender aspects of the MDGs. At the end of the year, when it was clear the MDG target had not been met, GCE issued a forthright press statement in conjunction with UNESCO noting with dismay that the target for 2005 had been missed (GCE 2005b). Although GCE did not make formal links with the global women's movement between 2003 and 2005, it came to express wider concerns with gender than just a focus on girls' access to school.

The gender equality lobby within the EFA movement was enhanced through the work of the Forum of African Women Educationalists (FAWE) launched in 1992 in direct response to Jomtien. FAWE was initially a network of prominent women working in education across Africa, comprising women education ministers, senior civil servants, vice chancellors of universities and professors. Over the decade the number of FAWE chapters increased and diverse structures emerged in different countries. In 2005 there were 33 FAWE chapters organized in four regions – Southern, Eastern, Western Anglophone and Francophone – with each chapter aiming to develop appropriate and innovative strategies to address issues concerning girls' education (FAWE 2004). FAWE's range of activities encompassed research, advocacy, training, policy development capacity building, direct interventions and technical assistance. FAWE Centres of Excellence were schools created in

Senegal, Rwanda and Tanzania that aimed to establish girl-friendly learning environments. These gave particular attention to the quality of teaching, the relations between learners and teachers and the hidden curriculum. In a number of schools, FAWE helped develop *tusumene* clubs, where girls could speak out about their experiences and gain support to counter gender inequality (Mlama 2004). In Kenya, the FAWE chapter worked with community groups to help mobilize a campaign for access to school (Muito 2004). In a number of countries, FAWE was active in encouraging girls to study maths and science. FAWE was a key member of the African regional advocacy networks of GCE. At a country level FAWE was often the focus for action on gender in local advocacy networks, some of which were supported by the Commonwealth Education Fund (CEF).[2]

In South Asia, despite some very strong national campaigning groups for EFA and women's rights a similar organisation to FAWE did not emerge. The largest regional lobbying group was the Asian and South Pacific Bureau on Adult Education (ASPBAE) which, although not primarily concerned with girls' schooling or gender equality, had women's empowerment and education as one of its strategic objectives. As a campaigning network of organizations and individuals involved with formal and non-formal education ASPBAE brought together a wide range of concerns encompassing trade unions, women's movements and government agencies. It produced high quality research and made focused inputs into global strategies and advocacy developing a clear line on education, rights, empowerment and government accountability. ASPBAE did not face a burden of provision, like FAWE, and was thus a clearer and more consistent voice for advocacy within South Asia and the GCE.

From the late 1990s INGOs, New Social Movements (NSMs) and looser formations of the women's movement, have often been grouped together by analysts and activists, and termed global civil society. A range of gatherings by these groups at national, regional and international level took place to develop alternative positions on gender and education to those advocated by the development business (Stromquist 2000; Eccher 2004; Aikman and Unterhalter 2005a). Global civil society was associated with calls for the reform of aspects of the UN to make it more accessible to women's organizations, which were increasingly active on the global stage (GADN 2005). One form of activity was to take seats in key committees of UN agencies concerned with gender and/or education. The UN Girls' Education Initiative (UNGEI), which is described in detail in Chapter 10, is one example of an opening that became available to global civil society.

Conclusion

This brief introduction to historical trends, key events and organisations engaged with EFA highlights three orientations concerning gender and girls' schooling. Firstly, there has been a focus chiefly on girls' access and participation in schooling. This can be seen in the MDG targets on gender parity and UPE and programmes, such as those supported by FAWE, which focus on girls and school. Secondly, there has been an orientation to achieve gender equality as a dimension of the quality of schooling. This has entailed confronting some of the social relationships that undermine quality and equality in schools. This view is articulated in the Jomtien and Dakar documents. It can be seen in programmes and research concerned with schools as gendered institutions such as the UNESCO programme to establish gender focal points in Asia through the GENIA network. Thirdly, there have been wider aspirations regarding gender equality in all areas of life and the ways in which education more generally, not just schooling, can be part of this social transformation. This is the vision contained in the Beijing Declaration, but few of the education programmes linked to the EFA movement were able to give this effect although particular civil society organisations and coalitions have struggled to advance these demands through gender mainstreaming initiatives and alliance building with women's movements. The next chapter considers how these three orientations within the EFA movement connect to discussions of global social justice.

2   Debating global social justice

The global movement to secure EFA works form a variety of starting points about global social justice but generally these have not been examined in detail. Cosmopolitanism is a term that has been linked with global justice. Initially used by the early Greek philosophers the Stoics, it meant literally 'citizen of the world'. In its original context it connoted concerns and duties attached to a space that was common to all, not just bounded by locality.

In its contemporary form, however, cosmopolitanism is usually understood as a commitment to take the wellbeing of individuals wherever they are located in the world as central and is concerned with distributive justice across nation states and through transnational institutions (Beitz 2001; Moellendorf 2002). Thus, it is concerned with how justice regarding schooling is secured for individuals in every country of the world and how this might be achieved across different political settings by people who may not share obvious ties of affiliation.

Debates about cosmopolitanism are concerned with normative explorations of the content and weight of obligations we owe to those who are not citizens of the same state, but whose lives are affected by our actions, and who in turn affect our lives. What kind of education, for example how many years in school or with what form of instructional materials, do we owe to people with whom we share no ties of common citizenship? How much account must we take of their gendered lives? How must we consider their interests in social justice in relation to those of our fellow citizens?

Nowadays, cosmopolitanism is frequently criticized as an empty 'grand idea' which ignores giving appropriate attention to local concerns (McKim and McMahon 1997; Beck 2006). However, contrary to the views of its critics much contemporary writing on cosmopolitanism does recognize the existence of states, communities, and different languages which exert ties of affiliation. Indeed, a major discussion concerns the nature of obligations owed to a particular state or set of institutions. The growth of globalization lends discussions of cosmopolitanism a particular edge. The global restructuring of the past 15 years has been associated with a sharp increase in the speed and intensity of economic globalization, new forms of mobility of capital, labour, technology and information. Shifting political formations nationally and regionally, like the EU, the New Partnership for Africa's Development (NEPAD) and the South Asian Association for Regional Cooperation (SAARC), have sought to recast global, national and local power relations. New cultural articulations, expressed in debates about location and belonging, have been associated with intense contestation over beliefs, efforts to forge or disrupt connection across difference and the emergence of particular gendered identities. The poverty and lack of access to education of people who grow coffee, cotton or cocoa beans, for example, has a particular bearing on the lives of people who process, distribute and consume these – although the frames of meaning used by the latter groups do not recognize the nature of this shared experience.

Largely unacknowledged until recently, climate change has progressed implacably. This has consequences for people in high income countries bound by a common citizenship and culture of energy use and those in low and middle income countries, who may have been responsible for minimal carbon emissions, but who will suffer loss of land and livelihood through flooding or other natural disasters. Climate change bears on a global future to be inhabited by generations we will never see. Generally, we have a vague apprehension of global connection now and to come, in part because of the communication technologies associated with the emergence of globalization. But we have less clarity concerning how global justice might shape this link.

Cosmopolitanism: thick and thin

Miller distinguishes between what he calls thick and thin notions of cosmopolitanism. Common to both is the view that in deciding on an institutional form or a particular action, for example with regard to gender equality as a foundational value in legislation on schooling, the claims of each person affected should be weighed equally. For strong or thick versions of cosmopolitanism

> all moral principles must be justified by showing that they give equal weight to the claims of everyone, which means that they must either be directly universal in their scope, or if they apply only to a select group of people they must be secondary principles whose ultimate foundation is universal.
>
> (Miller 1998: 166)

Thus, for thick cosmopolitans, gender equality as a key component of legislation on schooling must apply in *every* country of the world. The overarching universalism of strong versions of cosmopolitanism is contrasted with a weaker meaning of the term which entails that

> We may owe certain kinds of treatment to all other kinds of human beings regardless of any relationship in which we stand to them, while there are

other kinds of treatment that we owe only to those to whom we are
related in certain ways, with neither sort of obligation being derivative
of the other.

(Miller 1998: 167)

For thin cosmopolitans, regardless of our citizenship, we owe concern to
redress certain aspects of gender discrimination worldwide, for example that
girls should encounter no barriers in access to school, but our interest in gender
equality as the foundational dimension of legislation on schooling as it applies
to curriculum, teacher training, the management of sexual harassment, and
decisions about levels of expenditure, is something we owe only to those with
whom we share a common legislative system. Thick cosmopolitans therefore
might argue for institutions that deliver gender equality in education globally
because they are governed by principles that give equal weight to the valued
lives of each and every man and woman. Thin cosmopolitans might argue
that we owe opportunities to access to a bounded package of a set number
of years in school to all people in the world, regardless of whether or not
we are citizens of the same country, because this is entailed by a notion
regarding equal claims of everyone to what is considered an appropriate
amount of schooling that will protect against harm. These claims entail some
obligations to help girls gain access to schooling, but this obligation might
be met through a donation to a charity which supports a girl at school or
our government contributing some form of aid. It does not place obligations
on us to make arguments to the governments of countries in which we are
not citizens about the content and form of schooling or gender relations
within and outside school. These are arguments we can legitimately make
to our own governments. Thus thin cosmopolitans have more affinity for
meanings of gender and education concerned not with the gendered power
relations of institutions but with girls' and boys' access to schooling. Thick
cosmopolitanism characterizes the stronger demands of gender equality as a
global aspiration articulated in the Beijing Declaration.

David Held has outlined a position between the thick and the thin forms,
writing that cosmopolitanism denotes an 'ethical and political' space which
lays down 'regulative principles which delimit and govern the range of
diversity and difference that ought to be found in public life' (Held 2005:
18). He is concerned here to link together a thick and thin cosmopolitanism.
Thus he affirms certain principles from thick cosmopolitanism about the
nature of persons, the form of institutions, and processes of prioritisation in
decision making. He considers these can with work with a particular form
of thin cosmopolitan support for local interpretations, a plurality of value
sources, and different ethical forms of institutions (Held 2005: 18–19).
Held seems to be arguing for gender equality in education as a matter of
global social justice ethically entailed by a form of thick cosmopolitanism
which rests on particular notions of the person – that is equal worth and
dignity, active agency and political accountability. Institutions, such as

schools and education departments and ideas about curriculum must allow for the consent of participants, collective decision making and inclusiveness. These principles also address the processes entailed in decision making about education on a global scale, and can be interpreted as enjoining the avoidance of serious harm through all children being given access to school and attention to the sustainability of initiatives given the fragility of the changing climate.

Elsewhere, Held characterizes this approach as promoting the values of social democracy in a global context (Held 2004: 16–17). He suggests that social democracy offers an alternative global policy agenda to neoconservatism, neoliberalism and radical anti-globalisation. He sees this approach based on reformulated global rules for security which will entail new aspects of international human rights law and a regulation of global markets. This will entail democratization of national and suprastate governance, for example incorporating concerns with global justice into national legislation and reforming global institutions like the UN and the World Trade Organisation (WTO). But Held stresses that these strong meanings do not entail any particular injunction about the form of agency, accountability, and collective decision making or a particular form for the delivery of welfare.

The implication of this is that there is no particular pre-given commitment to gender equality in education. In a particular society, all women and men may consent to women being excluded from decision making about curriculum or school finance or access to the labour market. They do this because they consider it is consonant with ideas about equal worth and dignity arguing that women's worth lies in looking after children at home. Providing serious harm is avoided because all children have a minimum of, say, five years in school,[1] Held's version of the cosmopolitan aspiration would have been satisfied because principles regarding the dignity of all persons would have been upheld, all would have participated in deciding on the form of institutions, and the process of whether to prioritise the rearing of children at home over women's participation in politics and economics outside the family. Local meanings about family and women's worth would have been given value.

The central divisions between thick and thin cosmopolitanism concern the relative ethical weight of different spaces of justice and the significance of competing values. For thick cosmopolitanism, family, community or national spaces for justice operate no differently to the global space; and they see cosmopolitan principles as especially weighty. Thin cosmopolitanism draws a sharp distinction between the spaces of justice and see cosmopolitan principles as having no more weight than other, sometimes competing values. Held attempts to bridge the divide between thick and thin cosmopolitanism. He argues that interpretations of cosmopolitan principles, for example regarding the equal worth of each person, will be made locally. A revamped system of global governance will regulate and advance global social democracy which will protect these values by regulating markets and enhancing security.

While on some level this is an appealing vision, it leaves out any concern with advancing equalities. It is primarily concerned with establishing rules and building institutions. One such rule affirms the importance of local interpretations. But local value pluralism in relation to gender or education can be in tension with the universalism of strong cosmopolitanism which argues for gender equality in all institutions. If it is considered good in some communities that girls do not receive more than minimal education and are taught nothing of mathematics and science, while cosmopolitan principles affirm it is right that they should be given as much education as boys with the same curriculum, Held's global covenant cannot secure this equality. Thus, it is not clear how Held's position can be distinguished from that of thin cosmopolitanism.

In the next section I look at this discussion from a different angle. By examining approaches to global gender justice articulated by feminist writers the question of value pluralism is cast in the context of descriptions of context and forms of prioritisation that pay particular attention to the gender inequalities of society. I want to look at the ways this might advance the argument with regard to the division between thick and thin cosmopolitanism and the different paths with regard to global action on gender and schooling they point to.

Approaches to global social justice and gender

Martha Nussbaum, in addressing the question of how to think about global social justice, defends a version of thick cosmopolitanism.[2] She questions the starting point of contemporary global social justice theory, that is the assumption of a social contract made freely between rough equals who are not tied together as the subjects of kings or positioned in a particular relation because of a religious faith. She argues that there are limits to the attempt to apply such a contractarian method in social justice to global inequalities as these cannot be considered through a thought experiment entailing a bargain made to mutual advantage by rough equals. There is too much history of colonial conquest and its consequences, too many effects of past wars, and changing political economies. These make for real difference in human flourishing. Instead, she suggests returning to older ideas of natural law which turn on a notion that all the peoples of the world want to live with others.

> A central part of our own good, each and every one of us, is to produce and live in, a world that is morally decent, a world in which all human beings have what they need to live a life with human dignity.
>
> (Nussbaum 2005: 210)

On the basis of this, global justice does not begin with fair procedures for bargain, as in the work of Rawls, Pogge and Beitz (Rawls 1999; Pogge 2002;

Beitz 1999), but rather with a goal of entitlements or outcomes secured to each and every citizen regardless of whether those who have the obligations to provide for those entitlements have been identified. Education is one such entitlement. Nussbaum asserts

> Humanity is under a collective obligation to find ways of living and cooperating together so that all human beings have decent lives.
>
> (Nussbaum 2005: 211)

Decent lives implies much more than basic schooling. It suggests a meaning of education in relation to a valued life.

Nussbaum's notion of the person situated in relation to global justice in many ways can be seen as the same notion of the person related to the cosmopolitan principles Held outlined. These ensure equal worth and dignity, agency and political accountability to all. But Nussbaum goes further. She argues for strong positive freedoms and conditions for achieving personally modulated wellbeing and agency. It is unlikely that the rather minimal provision for schooling and women's participation in decision making, even if obtained through inclusive processes suggested as the form of global governance in Held's vision, would meet these requirements of justice.

Nussbaum then turns to look at institutions which she sees as essential to ensuring that individuals can live their lives without being excessively burdened with providing for the wellbeing of others (Nussbaum 2005: 213). She does not consider a world state desirable, as it would be impossible to make it accountable to all its citizens, impractical to translate across multiple languages, and provide no recourse if it became unjust. She thus suggests that ethical reflection entails the establishment of decentralized global institutions and global non-government organisations working with set principles. These are that national governments do everything to promote the fulfilment of wellbeing internally, even though justice will also require global obligations of non-national agents in this regard. National sovereignty is to be respected while global justice will work towards promoting entitlements. Rich nations are to give a substantial proportion of GDP to poorer nations and multinational corporations should promote human freedoms. The structure of the global economy should be fair to poor countries and a thin yet forceful global public sphere should be established for pollution controls and some limited form of global taxation. All institutions and individuals should give attention to the problems of the disadvantaged in each nation and region. Care for the ill, the elderly and the disabled should be a prominent focus. The family should be treated as precious, but not private. Her last principle is that all institutions and individuals have a responsibility to support education as a key to empowerment (Nussbaum 2005: 214–18). Education is thus positioned, not as a set of practices which flow from realizing cosmopolitanism through institutions, but as one of the principles that will guide the practice of forming just institutions.

These principles of cosmopolitan justice entail regulation and governance, as Held's do, but in Nussbaum's version they go further by enjoining specific obligations on institutions and individuals to promote the fulfilment of freedoms at home and abroad, to enhance the lives of the poorest and the most neglected, and specifically to fulfil a responsibility to 'education as a key to empowerment' (Nussbaum 2004: 325). The implication here is that global social justice requires not just support for girls' access to school – thin cosmopolitanism. Held's layered cosmopolitan is also inadequate. It entails recognition of the equal worth of girls and boys with regard to their experience of education, but this coexists with a relaxed view of whether or not there is gender equality in decision making and lack of attention to how girls and boys make use of school. Nussbaum's version of thick cosmopolitanism requires global institutions to deliver gender equality and education in all forms. This is a principle equivalent in weight to ideas concerning national sovereignty and the levelling of global taxation. Gender equality in education is not the outcome of global social justice, but is enmeshed in its rationale.

Amartya Sen interprets global social justice in ways that are consonant with Martha Nussbaum's thinking (Sen 2001, 2004, 2005a). But Sen does not start with natural law and the institutions that must deliver it, rather with a particular view of social action as framed by valuing substantive individual freedoms. Adequate basic education across gender and race is one of these freedoms. These freedoms give rise to claims or ethical demands on others, wherever they are located, to respect and support these. This is achieved partly through non-interference – negative freedoms – and partly through defending and promoting these through positive action and substantive opportunities. Realizability, that is whether or not institutions currently exist to underpin these freedoms, is not a condition of their admissibility. Obligations are thus claims on states which may or may not have the capacity to develop appropriate institutions. They are also claims on other forms of association – families, households, civil society – and on individuals. Sen's approach entails both perfect obligations, that is global and national institutions have a closed and delimited set of obligations to fulfil, and imperfect obligations, which are broader and more diffuse in scope, and take in the widest meanings of global, entailing relations between countries, organisations and institutions (Sen 1999, 2000, 2004). Imperfect obligations do not demand a prescribed action from a particular organisation or individual as perfect obligations do, but enjoin a vaguer, yet no more compelling, requirement to take action because of a form of human relationship and responsibility. For example, a teacher may be under a perfect obligation, stipulated in a contract, to inform local education officers if she is aware a child has experienced gender-based violence at school. Fellow pupils, support staff, parents or onlookers may have no such contractual obligations to report such an incident, but we consider it appropriate they take some action in fulfilment of imperfect obligations to prevent harm.

Sen's version of strong cosmopolitanism is thus not only rooted in institutions, as Nussbaum's is, but suggests an ethical system which does not depend only on specifying precise links between rights and obligations or on codifying particular prescriptions into international law. While he considers duties and counter-party rights are enforceable, they are not only enforceable through law but also through processes of dialogue, discussion, critical examination, and associated actions. Human rights are thus linked to imperfect, that is very widely diffused obligations, as well as perfect obligations located within particular institutions.

Polly Vizard has highlighted how Sen indicates what actions might be required with regard to the diffuse form of imperfect obligations (Vizard 2006). This has particular salience in thinking about obligations with regard to gender equality, education and global social justice. Vizard sees certain rights as goal rights, which require 'reasonable actions' to be fulfilled. Gender equality in education may be viewed as one such goal right. As such it is associated not only with strict claims against particular institutions – perfect obligations laid down in contracts or laws – although these may exist in specific contexts where gender equality has been legislated. But where this has not happened gender equality in education might require general obligations to promote this goal – imperfect obligations – through 'reasoned actions' which can be specified and agreed. This version of thick cosmopolitanism is compatible with Nussbaum's principles for regulation and governance but does not only depend on the institutional architecture they enjoin as these reasoned actions may be taken by individuals working inside or outside specific forms of institutions.

Sen and Nussbaum's route to this thick cosmopolitanism is very different to that taken by Onora O'Neill, but there are some surprising similarities in the implication of their ideas for thinking about gender, education and global social justice (O'Neill 1993, 2000). O'Neill proceeds by considering two main critiques raised in discussion of women, gender and international justice. Firstly, there is the view that analyses of justice, and by implication global justice, are based on an idealized version of a male political subject, engaged in rational choice, paying no attention to obligations of care or connection. Secondly, much work on gender and global justice requires a level of abstraction that gives no attention to particular contexts, for example the particular histories of political or cultural communities.

In response to these two critiques, O'Neill argues for the importance of 'abstract principles of universal scope' which she distinguishes from 'unargued idealizations of human agency, rationality, and life, and of the sovereignty and independence of states' (O'Neill 2000: 150). She points out that the confrontation between abstract principles and context sensitive judgements, a confrontation Held tries to mediate with the notion of layered cosmopolitanism, is so strong because advocates of universalism on the one hand and context specificity on the other draw on particular assumptions and idealizations of human agency, rationality and the sovereignty of states.

One critique draws on examples of views of schooling held by women relayed through ethnographic study (Aikman 1999; Robinson Pant 2004). The argument runs that discussions about global justice which require gender equality in school worldwide do not pay sufficient attention to women's relation to their families or to their histories, which may mean some women do not wish to attend school. O'Neill points out that this form of analysis takes particular instances and elevates them to fundamental principles. Analyses based on particular instances of women valuing their history or tradition become idealizations when they are interpreted as indicating something about how all women are assumed to act. These are just as questionable as idealizations based on assumptions that all men always act rationally. She distinguishes between idealization and abstraction. Idealization contains a number of unexamined assumptions and these can be justifiably critiqued. On the other hand, abstraction entails a process that strips away the detail of particular instances and the interpretations that underpin these. Abstraction entails delineating only the very general outlines of a process. Through this process of distancing it provides an appropriate method through which the claims of justice can be adjudicated:

> We do not have to hinge liberal arguments for rights or for the limits of government power either on the *hypothetical* consent of those who meet some *ideal* standard of rationality and mutual interdependence, or on the *actual* acceptance of an outlook and its categories that *relativizes* consent to an establish order. We could instead begin simply by abstracting from existing social orders. We could consider what principles of action must be adopted by agents who are numerous, diverse and *neither* ideally rational *nor* ideally independent of one another.
>
> (O'Neill 2000: 156)

O'Neill comes to the conclusion that justice is a matter of the principles that could be adopted by all agents, 'a plurality of potentially interacting beings' (O'Neill 2000: 162) who share a world they must all live in and she suggests that there could be universal adoption of the principle that action of individuals and institutions should not be based on deception, violence and coercion (O'Neill 2000: 159). In answer to the question of how this view of justice might be operationalized she suggests we ask, in designing policy and practice, whether the 'arrangements that structure vulnerable lives are ones that could have been refused or renegotiated by those they actually constrain' (O'Neill 2000: 163).

In other words, when we look at the arrangements for the provision or denial of education to poor women and men we consider whether they have *all* had opportunities to refuse particular policies and practices or renegotiate the terms on which education is provided. Nomadic pastoralist communities of Northern Kenya are often mentioned as examples of cultural opposition to schooling, because in these districts very few girls and boys are enrolled (Leggatt 2005). Yet projects like the Wajir girls' primary school in North Eastern Province, which have expanded girls' access, were based on consultation and negotiation with these communities over a long time, in ways suggested by O'Neill (Unterhalter *et al.* 2005c: 13–17). These meetings in which teachers and members of the community with different attitudes to girls' education took part, offered opportunities for policies on increasing girls' access to school to be refused or renegotiated by women and men who might lose labour that was important to household survival when girls went to school. Discussions took place household to household accompanied by extensive talk in other local forums which allowed for a full examination of all the issues concerning girls' schooling. This process resulted in significant increases in the enrolment of girls because a single sex primary school was provided (Unterhalter *et al.* 2005c). This seems an example of education officials working with teachers, NGOs and an IGO providing opportunities for all the adults in Wajir to refuse particular policies and renegotiate the terms on which schooling is provided by requesting a single sex primary school for girls. Similar changes in overcoming objections to school for girls have been noted in Northern Ghana. When traditional leaders have been involved in discussions with women and men of all ages about expanding girls' schooling after a long process of local discussion their objections have been countered (Challender 2003). Offering opportunities to refuse and renegotiate the form and content of schooling as the examples from Kenya and Ghana describe depends on open conditions for information exchange, and discussion. In both instances there was examination of a proposition concerning girls' schooling using the perspective of outsiders. These were women teachers in Wajir, and young women who had successfully completed school in Northern Ghana. Taking forward discussion appears a key dimension of building the conditions for justice.

In contrast to Nussbaum's thick cosmopolitanism with its detailed vision of how it is desirable to live and the principles that will make this happen, O'Neill suggests a very refined, abstracted notion of global justice. This contains no idealizations regarding particular assumptions about subjects, situations or forms of action. Justice is a matter only of a single principle that can be agreed by very different peoples. While Held asserts thick cosmopolitan principles to be achieved through thinly cosmopolitan institutions, O'Neill presents a more highly abstracted version of global cosmopolitan principles.

Moving from an abstract cosmopolitan principle to judgements in particular settings requires building institutions or conditions for action where deception, violence and coercion can be confronted and changed. Thus O'Neill takes issue with the libertarian position, which affirms the importance of non-interference with the person. Instead, she argues that universal positive obligations of assistance and aid are possible and necessary to establish appropriate conditions for justice. This makes a powerful case for gender equality in and through education. While gender equality in education is not itself a principle, as Nussbaum makes it, it becomes essential to realising the abstracted principles regarding avoiding deception, violence and coercion, as without gender equality in education it is hard to see how these principles would be achieved. In the examples from Wajir and Northern Ghana, it was educated women from outside the community who were able to make the arguments and help build the institutions for more gender equitable schools. However, underlying O'Neill's argument for cosmopolitan concerns with gender equality in education in this way is her conviction that these universal imperfect obligations are not enforceable by external sanction. Imperfect obligations deal with undetermined maxims that are ethically but not legally binding, and are relatively general and relatively indeterminate. These obligations require action but do not specify who should act (Vizard 2005: 8, 28).

Thus, O'Neill from a position that appeared like a version of thin cosmopolitanism, admitting value pluralism and diverse institutional spaces for engaging global social justice, ends up with a strong defence of gender equality in education that would have effects more similar to those envisioned by Nussbaum and Sen than by Held.

At the time of her death in 2004, Susan Moller Okin was working on issues concerning gender, economic development and human rights. Apart from her review of work by Amartya Sen and Martha Nussbaum on this theme (Okin 2003) no full argument relating to global social justice has yet been published. Here, I want to review some of her arguments about gender and justice to consider what some of their implications are for the debate about cosmopolitanism. In *Is multiculturalism bad for women?* Okin argues that to make liberal arguments for the protection of group rights requires that special attention should be given to examine the inequalities within those groups, particularly cultural practices relating to the subordination of women. Much of this discrimination is hidden in the private sphere. The tendency of male cultural leaders or older women to speak on behalf of a group obscures the needs and interests of other members, particularly younger women (Okin 1999a: 9–24).

In response to some critical commentaries on this essay, Okin outlined her views on global inequality and human rights:

> Liberalism's central aim, in my view, should be to ensure that every human being has a reasonably equal chance of living a good life according to his or her unfolding views about what such a life consists in. This requires vastly more socioeconomic equality than exists in the world today. In particular it requires that no child go without adequate food, housing, healthcare, or education, that no person who is sick or disabled, or who is prepared to work (including child care as work), be in need and that governments aim at full employment, high minimum wages, and whatever redistribution of wealth is required to satisfy the needs I mention. It also requires that richer countries help poorer ones rather than, as they often do now, require of them that they cut social programs even while arming

themselves expensively. I am by no means only concerned with gender equality, though I think … there is a particularly sharp tension between it and cultural group rights.

(Okin 1999b: 119–20)

Okin is arguing here for a form of thick cosmopolitanism drawing on ideas about entitlements similar to Nussbaum. She refers to ensuring 'that every human being has a reasonably equal chance of living a good life according to his or her unfolding views about what such a life consists in' (Okin 1999b: 119). 'Liberalism's central aim' is thus inevitably a global aim requiring states to attend to 'a reasonably equal chance of living a good life' for each and every citizen and for rich countries to help poorer countries to achieve this.

In response to the question whether she saw herself as a political or comprehensive liberal Okin said she positioned herself in the middle of this debate:

Many parents belonging to religions or cultures that do not respect autonomy would (and do) very strongly resist their children's being exposed to any religious or cultural views but their own. But … I do not believe that liberal states should allow this to happen. I believe that a certain degree of nonautonomy should be available as an option to a mature adult with extensive knowledge of other options, but not thrust on a person by his or her parents or group, though indoctrination – including sexist socialization – and lack of exposure to alternatives. But such hybrid liberalism puts strict limits on the extent to which children's education can be confined within the framework of any single religion, and prohibits it from being sex discriminatory in any way.

(Okin 1999b: 129–30)

These are statements about gender and education in states and cultural groups, so we do not know whether Okin supports a version of thick cosmopolitanism, requiring concern with education and empowerment in every country in the world regardless of the boundaries of citizenship, or whether she endorses the more limited obligations hinted at in the first extract quoted above. What is clear, however, from the general body of Okin's work is her concern with listening to what women say, particularly the poorest and most marginalized, and this was the theme in her work with Brooke Ackerley. While both writers are sceptical of a general lack of democracy in transnational organisations, they highlighted how women's rights activists around the world made use of women's diverse and dispersed experiences in working to achieve women's rights as human rights. Both saw this process as a form of democracy in action (Ackerley and Moller-Okin 1999). Concern with autonomy and transnational democracy provides another inflection of how to think about cosmopolitanism and global social justice linking gender equality and education. It is autonomy producing education that enables women to engage in these dialogues and to be attentive to the views of other women.

Nussbaum saw gender equality in education as a principle of cosmopolitanism, Sen as a form of social action in diverse settings, O'Neill as a means to put more abstract principles of cosmopolitanism into practice. Okin and Ackerley seem to suggest gender equality in education is one component of cosmopolitanism from below, made in the relations between individuals who are educated to become alert to each other.

Transnational feminist perspectives

A number of feminist commentators have approached the question of global social justice, not primarily on the basis of principles and procedures, but rather in terms of processes. They are thus neither thick nor thin cosmopolitans, but concerned with cosmopolitanism as a form of lived social action. They talk to aspects of Sen's interest in imperfect obligations, O'Neill's acknowledgement of the wide differences between people, and Okin's apprehension of the importance of dialogue. These writers have theorized the generative process of people making links across difference and thus building a new kind of politics. Nira Yuval Davis has referred to this process as transversal politics, 'A model of feminist politics which takes account of national as well as other forms of difference among women, without falling into the trap of identity politics' (Yuval Davis 1997: 4). Transversal politics engages a process of dialogue which entails rooting and shifting. Rooting encompasses recognizing one's own historical and national specificity. Shifting requires an alertness to the needs and histories of others, an appreciation of different perspectives. Transversal politics is thus alert to both processes, but not entirely one or the other (Yuval Davis: 1997). Iris Young outlines the potential of a politics of inclusion and public discussion as part of democratizing. She critiques the secretive processes of decision making in the institutions of global governance (Young 2002: 272–3). Judith Butler has identified how particular frames of meaning in the world post-September 11 cut off the possibility for Americans to see themselves as vulnerable in a world connected by human frailties. While the potential for forms of cosmopolitanism from below have been severely circumscribed, their potential remains in language and action (Butler: 2004).

What is suggested in all these different accounts is that claims for gender equality in education are made not by principles, procedures or formal institutions, but through processes of political connection which translate and negotiate meanings. In this way it is implied cosmopolitanism is both linked to values and descriptions of actions. Gender equality in education as an objective of global social justice is thus an open global dialogue which entails practice.

Nancy Fraser points out that it is no longer obvious that we should base justice claims on the Keynsian-Westphalian state, that is a territorial state in which politics and economics reinforce territorial integrity. This form of the state associated with the past three centuries entails sharp differentiation between citizens inside borders and those located outside in an 'international' space. But this form of the state is now intermixed with new political formations. In the contemporary period socio-economic redistributive justice claims and legal cultural claims for recognition are made both within states and across borders. As a consequence, Fraser argues for a third dimension of justice, in addition to redistribution and recognition, concerned with representation, that is the principle of who is included and excluded from making justice claims (Fraser 2005).

The implication of Fraser's analysis is that claims for gender equality in education are both distributional relating to meeting equal needs of all children for schooling and recognitional relating to the particular status of women in the education provided. Both forms entail justice claims which are made against states and in transnational spaces where multiple actors bear obligations. Demands for gender equality in education thus entail dialogue and forms of democratic justice at every level. This is another version of cosmopolitanism as process, although it pays more explicit attention to institutions than Yuval Davis or Butler. Terry Lovell notes how democratic deliberation and the dialogic method underpins Fraser's work (Lovell 2003), and this is particularly apparent in her work on global social justice where there are more connections than differences with other feminist theorists working in this field, despite some of the sharp disputes between them on other issues.

Gender equality, education and global social justice

What are the implications of these discussions and differences of emphasis for thinking about gender equality and education in relation to global social justice? All the writing I have reviewed argues for forms of thick cosmopolitanism but there are differences between those who tend to see this as implying an institutional architecture to deliver rights and aid, and those who argue for looser forms of association, which will generate ethically informed actions, inside and outside institutions, guided by wide imperfect obligations. Some features of the demand for gender equality in education are not enforceable through laws and the judicial system, as so many gender inequalities in education touch on custom and practice in families or in civic association. Principles of global social justice, concerning say levels of distribution of education and forms of obligation apply to institutions but also go beyond these. Given these conditions, what is the content and weight of global social justice obligations? What is required of different actors?

Vizard provides some pointers towards answering this. She highlights how Sen, in emphasizing the development of 'subordinate principles of justice' in relation to 'reasonable actions' associated with imperfect obligations suggests how international legal obligations in relation to global poverty and human rights can be deepened (Vizard 2005: 25–30). A theory of justice might guide institutions, but subordinate principles of justice help orient actions to address injustices that are not only located within institutions. Poverty and gender inequality are examples of such injustices that require redress both through perfect obligations, attending to actions legally enjoined on us, and through imperfect obligations, that is actions which are ethically, but not necessarily legally required. Vizard argues for the extension of a theory of human rights to the domain of imperfect obligation through development of 'subordinate principles' for evaluating actions to promote general goals. This suggests a means to make a connection between the abstract principles relating to gender and global justice articulated by O'Neill, the institutionally located cosmopolitanism associated with Nussbaum and Held, and the rather fluid sphere of negotiating and translating meanings and imperfect obligations delineated by the other writers discussed. Specifying 'subordinate principles' can help guide decisions that seek to translate general ideas about global justice into particular actions and forms of education practice.

Conclusion

The multiple forms of gender inequality make all the theorists discussed so far, for different reasons, unsympathetic to the boundaries to justice provided by nation states and local communities drawn by thin cosmopolitans. They all, in different ways, acknowledge that people have diverse values. But they also argue value pluralism cannot trump some principle or process that engages the question of gender equality and education. Nussbaum, Sen and O'Neill delineate very different principles of global justice which entail gender equality and education. Nussbaum starts with assumptions about a natural law that should govern all human behaviour, Sen with ethical obligations that guide right actions, O'Neill with what might make actions right, that is principles that all could assent to. The other writers see a gender equitable process of education in its widest sense undergirding global justice as a process of negotiation and representation. Although for different reasons in each analysis, not one of the authors discussed accords any difference to the space of the family, the locality, the nation or the global with regard to claims of justice. All hold up to Held's global covenant a question regarding whether gender equality is prominent enough in the regulatory mechanisms for global governance he proposes. All suggest that unless an approach to global social democracy takes seriously the pervasiveness of gender inequalities in a range of settings, but particularly within states and in most existing transnational institutions, the processes by which millions experience lack of education, forms of miseducation and exclusions from decision making about education, global justice will not be realized.

Part II

Why address gender and schooling globally?

Introduction

David Held (2004) and Anthony McGrew (2004) have pointed to complementary silences in contemporary writing on global social justice. On the one hand a rich debate exists concerning cosmopolitan accounts of justice. This literature is largely silent on the institutional and political formations through which global social justice will be delivered. On the other hand the literature on how global institutions work generally does not comment on the ideas about justice that underpin these institutions and activities. This is evident in studies of the EFA process and some of the global institutions most closely concerned with this (Jones 1992; Chabbot 2003). This book is an attempt to bring these two strands of inquiry together by looking at some of the issues raised by political philosophers concerned with global social justice and cosmopolitanism and some of the obstacles governments, IGOs and global civil society have had to confront in their actions to effect global social justice relating to gender and schooling.

In the following chapters I outline different ways in which the demand for gender equality in education as a matter of global social justice has been articulated and some of the actions taken by governments, IGOs and global civil society. Three main forms of approach emerge. Firstly, there is an understanding of global social justice which stresses interventions to prevent gross insufficiency or harm, for example the provision of a basic five years of primary schooling to all children with little attention to the content of that education, the safety of children at school or the relationships built through schooling. I term this approach an interventionist form of global social justice in that it requires a bounded form of action by governments, IGOs, individuals or global civil society to prevent extreme suffering or want. Interventionist approaches are commonly associated with thin cosmopolitanism, because whether substantively or merely rhetorically this form of justice is done *to* citizens of other countries, to whom citizens outside believe they owe only minimal obligations. It is unlikely that gender equality will be addressed in any way that goes beyond parity. Questions of who is represented in decision making, what information they draw on, what level of coercion they experience, how they understand the process and what potential they have to effect changes, are unlikely to be addressed or considered as part of the assessment of global social justice.

A second understanding of global social justice and gender equality in education can be characterized as institutional. This sees efforts to secure global social justice based on building and deepening the alliances and institutions which shape the relations between governments, multilateral organizations and global civil society that have evolved thus far so that allocation of resources – financial aid, ideas – proceeds efficiently and is measured appropriately. This institutional approach is generally concerned to address elements of want and inadequate provision. It can point up how institutions require particular actions of states, transnational organizations and individuals. It often facilitates the smooth running of the interventionist approach. It is interested in gender for the way it impedes the institutional allocation of resources. The gender indicators laid out in the MDGs and in the Dakar Framework have become the shorthand that guides the concerns of those working with an institutional approach. This resonates with the framework offered by Held's layered cosmopolitanism. The institutions which deliver global social justice are there to secure interventions and to affirm some versions of a wider concern with removing gender inequality with regard to the quality of education. In this form the obligations of global social justice are met if the rules that govern it, as articulated for example in Declarations and frameworks of action, are fulfilled. Institutional forms of global social justice can incline towards thin cosmopolitanism with a light touch regulation or evaluation or thick cosmopolitanism as outlined by Nussbaum where institutions have global reach.

A third understanding of global social justice for gender equality and education is discernible, which I have termed interactive. This is a version of thick cosmopolitanism that places most emphasis on the dialogues about and actions for gender equality and education that take place criss-crossing all levels from the local to the transnational. Interactive approaches to global social justice use dialogue, discussion and education in conjunction with ideas about international obligations and institution building in relation to human rights. They articulate claims in terms of principles – be these strongly drawn by Nussbaum, highly abstracted by O'Neill, or filtered through ideas about reasonable action to promote positive obligations as suggested by Sen. These claims can be made within states by those who share citizenship and talk the language of voting, governance and budgetary accountability. They can be made by insiders who work in institutions and by those who have little judicial leverage at national and transnational level. Through interactive forms of global social justice, claims may be made by private associations and families and across the boundaries of states by those who do not share citizenship but who are concerned with gender issues in schools and through schooling. The source of these claims may arise from engagement with regional political and economic collaboration or through informal and more dispersed ties of affiliation. The global chain for the supply of commodities like flowers or clothing gives rise to claims for the education of workers across many countries. This interactive form of global social justice requires that questions of gender equality in education are a matter of global concern to all, not only those citizens who experience or pay for that education. They entail very wide imperfect obligations but these are mediated by forms of institutions or principles of reasonableness or levels of relative indeterminacy. Interactive global social justice is primarily critical of its own processes and those of other individuals, institutions and organisations. It is necessary, but not sufficient to deliver gender equality in education and generally recognize both the remit, but also the limitations of interventionist and institutional approaches.

3   Schooling women and girls

A means, not an end

Understanding global social justice in terms of interventions to provide a minimal level of schooling for all children is often associated with the descriptive use of the word gender identified in Chapter 1. In this usage gender has come to mean girls. Assumptions that schooling is instrumental for development often accompany this view. Three forms in which this argument has been made since the 1970s emerge: human capital theory, the basic needs approach and Women in Development (WID)

Seeing gender equality in education as an instrumental lever for the achievement of other valued aspects of global policy, for example economic growth or social development has had the longest history of appeal to policy makers. Articulated by advocates of human capital theory, influential from the 1960s to the present, it has contributed both to shaping the analytic field of education and development, and associated policy (King and Hill 1993; Unterhalter 2005a). The basic needs approach, important for a brief period in the 1970s, but later eclipsed by arguments for efficiency and marketization in the 1980s, suggested that need could be satisfied by a commodity – say five years of primary schooling (Gasper 2004). The linked notions of human capital theory and basic needs came to make a powerful case for gender equality in education understood in terms of provision of fixed amounts of schooling for women and girls without attending to wider dimensions of gender equality. Thus gender inequalities in property rights, political, economic and social participation, and gender inequalities associated with learning and teaching fell outside this frame of reference.

WID was a critique of human capital theory and basic needs that raised the question of whether women had disappeared in human capital theory's general concerns with cost benefit analysis and the focus on universal basic needs associated with the basic needs approach (Moser 1993). Despite its roots in feminism, from the 1970s, WID came to be appropriated by development planners as providing a rationale for the education of women to make them better mothers and more efficient producers of human capital. The WID assumption was that gender equality entailed including women in education institutions, employing them in certain jobs, and giving them positions on policy-making bodies. This entailed forms of monitoring and research that counted the numbers of women at certain levels of education and in certain occupations.

The instrumental argument for gender equality in education was a powerful combination of ideas founded in the economics of 'good sense' and cost benefit associated with human capital theory, a depoliticized notion of need extracted from the basic needs approach suggesting that need can be satisfied by a single commodity, and an approach to the advancement of women associated with WID suggesting counting their presence in education institutions, occupations and on decision-making bodies (King and Hill 1993). As such it shaped the thinking of most IGOs, some key governments and campaigning NGOs from 1990. It was to have particular affinities with the interventionist version of global social justice concerned to 'simply' address gross insufficiency and lack of girls' access to school through policies to 'get the girls in'[1] to school.

Human capital theory

Initial formulations of human capital theory which pointed to the importance of studying investment in humans through formal education, or on the job training and quantifying the rate of return on these investments made no distinction between men and women. Theodore Schultz, who was to win the Nobel prize in economics partly for his work on human capital, in setting out the background concerns that shaped his development of the theory used conventional language of the time:

> It is my contention that economic thinking has neglected two classes of investment that are of critical importance under modern circumstances. They are investment in man and in research, both private and public. The central problem … is to clarify the nature and scope of these activities.
>
> (Schultz 1971: 5)

He went on to elaborate:

> The distinctive mark of human capital is that it is a part of man. It is human because it is embodied in man, and it is capital because it is a source of future satisfactions, or of future earning, or of both. Where men are free agents, human capital is not a negotiable asset in the sense that it can be sold. It can, of course, be acquired not as an asset that is purchased in a market but by means of investing in oneself. It follows that no person can separate himself from the human capital he possesses. He must always accompany his human capital whether it serves him in production or consumption.
>
> (Schultz 1971: 48–9)

For a reader 35 years later, the absence of concern with differences of gender, race, global location and the conditions in which production and consumption take place is jarring. Schultz was more interested in the differences between human capital and other forms of capital, than he was in the differences between different types of human except with regard to levels of earnings. However, in a concluding chapter he raised questions about the rates of return from the education of women, given their lower levels of employment in the USA at that time. In passing, he acknowledged problems with agglomerating discussion of human capital and ignoring problems of inequality (Schultz 1971: 193–4, 196–8). Schultz thus signalled some of the key areas in which human capital theory was later to develop.

Human capital theory as it came to be applied to development underplayed the significance of gender issues (Krueger 1968; Psacharapoulos 1987; Blaug 1987; Psacharapoulos 1994). However, in the late 1980s special interest began to attach to rates of return from the education of women. Schultz's son, Paul, also an economist with an interest in human capital theory, became an important advocate of the significance of the high rates of return from the education of women. The arguments made by him and others engaged in the study of population statistics highlighted how the education of women seemed to provide 'a silver bullet' of protection in the face of the growing poverty of the 1980s (Jeffrey and Jeffery 1998). Lawrence Summers, Chief Economist at the World Bank condensed this view in 1993 into a statement of the instrumentalist approach to gender and schooling couched in almost law like terms:

> … recent research and concrete calculations show that educating females yields far-reaching benefits for girls and women themselves, their families, and the societies in which they live. Indeed, during my tenure as chief economist of the World Bank, I have become convinced that once all the benefits are recognized, investment in the education of girls may well be the highest return investment available in the developing world.
>
> (Summers 1993: v)

Summers' conclusions were based on the work of Paul Schultz and others at the World Bank who had looked at the costs and benefits of girls' education (King and Hill 1993). Paul Schultz's argument is worth examining in some detail because it highlights some of the nuance that later policy appropriations of the instrumentalist argument were to omit (Schultz 1993). Schultz noted that the rate of return on schooling differed by gender. In work published in the 1980s he had suggested this might relate to gender differences in pay and the differences in costs entailed in educating girls and boys (Schultz 1987). He went on to explore how family decision making might result in the education of a daughter being valued less highly than the education of a son. The private costs, for example costs associated with the removal of a girl from household duties, of her uniform and transport were not matched by private benefits. She was deemed unlikely to gain access to the labour market or the marriage market to generate an appropriate rate of return. Thus families were acting efficiently in keeping their daughters out of school if they did not have adequate access to the labour market or forms of public subsidy. Schultz reviewed research in developing countries on private rates of return to education by school level and gender and showed that, despite difficulties with sample selection and the method of calculating rates of return given local labour market effects, the general picture indicated that the private rate of return for the education of women was at least as high as that for men and sometimes higher.

Schultz then went on to look at non-market effects of women's education drawing on large-scale family surveys which showed statistically across different kinds of study and society that the higher the level of women's education the lower the rate of her fertility, the greater her concern with the education of all her children, and the lower the rate of child mortality. In this form the instrumentalist argument was to have enormous impact. But it was not based on data relating to the causal effects of the level of a women's education on the nutrition, health or future education of her children, but only that this effect was replicated across so many studies. Schultz acknowledged the puzzle as to why the mother's level of education should be so significant an explanatory variable, irrespective of access to health care, cost of health care or family income (Schultz 1993: 70). He points out how difficult it is to measure the inputs that will play an important role in producing a child who is well fed, has adequate access to water, good health care, and has the capacity to survive. It is because these other processes are so difficult to measure across societies that women's education, which is believed to be a constant and measurable factor, was given so much explanatory power (Schultz 1993: 70–1). The article concludes that the work of social scientists does not yet provide a full account of how better educated mothers produce healthier children with a greater chance of surviving into adulthood. Schultz then slips suddenly from the careful voice of academic appraisal to an exhortatory tone. He finishes with the injunction that the negative consequences of the gender gap in education requires governments, researchers and international agencies to pay attention to allocating resources to address this.

Schultz's argument builds carefully from an empirical base. But the caution he shows in drawing conclusion on whether data supports increased private rates of return from women's education, and the correlations between women's education, reduced fertility and the health of their children is not present when he considers policy. There are many variables in the studies he reviews. Yet the policy he distils sees women's education as a constant. This implied that interventions for what Summers had called the 'highest return investment in the developing world' need not be affected by the quality of the school, the knowledge and professional expertise of the teachers, the presence of absence of sexism, and allocation of esteem within families and peers. The strong implication of Schultz's conclusion was that women's education is instrumental to enhanced social benefits although the empirical base for this still needed developing.

While the gaps in the academic argument are interesting, what is significant about this form of the instrumentalist argument for gender equality in education is how women, and specifically poor women, were positioned. Basic education was not primarily *for* the specific needs of the poor, but the general enrichment of their societies, particularly through industrialisation and economic growth. Initial private and social costs of schooling would be offset by the benefits of reduced population growth and the health of children. The argument is only concerned with women's activity in the labour market and with non-market action as *mothers*. The analysis ignores women's other key non-market activities such as participation in social and political action, care for parents, siblings, more distant relatives and non-family members within broader social networks. In so doing it implies that these features of women's action generate no social benefits. The argument is silent on the structures that shape gender, race or caste discrimination and the forms and processes of power entailed in struggling with these forms of poverty. The earnings gap between women and men is naturalized; the family is portrayed as a site of fair negotiation with regard to decision making about investment in education. The terrain of global social justice is portrayed as a field of rational choice about investments, costs and benefits. Complex histories within and between countries, power blocs, global social networks and their gendered dimensions are not considered.

Policy appropriations

Policy appropriations of the instrumentalist argument were evident in the Jomtien Declaration (1990). This asserted that in 1990 two-thirds of the 100 million children and 960 million adults without access to formal schooling were girls and women. It went on to list the 'daunting problems' the world faced, notably mounting debt, 'the threat of economic stagnation and decline, rapid population growth, widening economic disparities among and within nations ... the preventable deaths of millions of children ...'. While these were not the only problems listed these were the problems that resonated with the focus of human capital theory on economic and population growth and child health. The Declaration implicitly linked the high proportions of women and girls without education with the shortfall in health and the increase in poverty (World Declaration 1990: 74).

The Declaration was not a simple restatement of human capital theory, but it included a number of assumptions drawn from these writings. In later policy pronouncements of key IGOs these assumptions came to take the form of hard-edged assertions. The early global social justice agenda concerning girls' schooling thus came to express the demand in instrumentalist terms. A key World Bank education policy document published in 1995 made this explicit. The argument was for increasing access to education for women and girls in terms of the benefits that would flow to their existing and future children's health and to the GDP of their countries.

> Mothers with more education provide better nutrition to their children, have healthier children, are less fertile, and are more concerned that their children be educated. Education – in particular female education – is key to reducing poverty and must be considered as much part of a country's health strategy as, say, programs of immunisation and access to health clinics.
>
> (World Bank 1995: 110)

The Bank's justification for educating women and girls at this point lay not in its benefit for women and girls themselves, but in its benefit to their children – actual and prospective – and the society they inhabited. If it did yield those benefits, then women and girls themselves may eventually partake in them, depending on how they were distributed. There is brief mention of the fact that the educated person has an enhanced ability to participate in the labour market. But the Bank paid little attention to how education might directly contribute to the autonomy of women and girls and to the choices they might make about arrangements within their families, decisions concerning work or forms of social and political organisation they would value. The benefits of women's education were to be realized in the household, often the site of the harshest discrimination women experienced.

Nearly 10 years later, UN Secretary General, Kofi Annan, writing in the United Nations Children's Fund's (UNICEF) *State of the World's Children* report for 2003 said:

> To educate girls is to educate a whole family. And what is true of families is also true of communities and, ultimately, whole countries. Study after study has taught us that there is no tool for development more effective than the education of girls. No other policy is likely to raise economic productivity, lower infant and maternal mortality, improve nutrition and promote health – including to prevent the spread of HIV/AIDS. No other policy is as powerful in increasing the changes of education for the next generation. Two of the Millennium Development Goals are focussed on education for girls and boys alike. They are not only goals in their own right, how we fare in reaching them will be crucial to our ability to reach all the others. Only by translating them into reality can our international family grow stronger, healthier, more equitable and more prosperous.
>
> (Annan 2003)

Here once again is the instrumentalism of the human capital argument, stripped of Schultz's careful qualification. The education of women, it is implied is the magic key to unlock the door to global good fortune and ensure a form of human security. But this vision of global social justice, which women are instrumental in, positions women's education as primarily for others. To educate girls is to educate a family and the next generation of the world. In this version of the instrumentalist view it is not necessarily a problem that women do not participate in decision making about education and assessments of the value of education. The inequalities in the labour market and political and social relations are not germane. The benefits of education accrue to societies first and individuals a long way second.

A Fair Chance published by GCE for the week of action on girls' education in 2003 repeated some elements of this:

> Failure to educate girls is holding back the wider push to halve global poverty by 2015. Education not only provides basic knowledge and skills to improve health and livelihoods, but it empowers women to take their rightful place in the development process. Education gives women the status and confidence to influence household decisions. Women who have been to school tend to marry later and have smaller families. Their children are also better nourished and are far more likely to do well at school. By contrast the children of women who have never received an education are 50 per cent more likely to suffer from malnutrition or die before the age of five ... Educating women is key to breaking the cycle of poverty.
>
> (GCE 2003a: 2)

The simplicity of these conclusions that the most significant place of women's empowerment and contribution to development is the household are drawn from human capital theory. This has guided much of the research agenda on the education of women and girls in developing countries. Large-scale surveys have looked at how household relations impact on decisions about sending girls to school and keeping them there (Hadden and London 1996; Alderman *et al.* 1996). Analysis has concentrated on quantifying the benefits of girls and women's schooling in terms of reduced fertility and improved uptake of immunisation (King and Hill 1993; Klasen 1999; Subbarao and Raney 1995). There has been a concern to synthesize 'what works' in girls' education, that is what the key strategies are that will increase attendance and yield nutrition, health and growth benefits to the society (Herz and Sperling 2004). This work has been undertaken by multilateral organisations, which employ international research teams generally led by economists.

Human capital theorists and the policy makers, researchers and campaigners who followed them, saw the education of women and girls as instrumental for economic growth. The process of global policy making took Schultz's somewhat tentative suggestions and turned them into certainties about how the whole world might operate as a single country. The slogan 'if you educate a woman you educate the nation' nicely captures the thinking. However, the global policy agenda on gender and schooling was not a simple statement of the assumptions of human capital theory. It drew on some normative ideas concerned with basic learning needs. These had the potential to expand the foundation of the demand for gender equality in education beyond a cost-benefit calculation. However, as will be shown, the exigencies of measurement meant that meeting basic learning needs came to be interpreted very narrowly in terms of providing a finite small amount of education (approximately five years) making a neat fit with some of the assumptions of human capital theory. The affinity between the cost-benefit dynamic of human capital theory and the notion that meeting basic needs entailed only the provision of a finite amount of schooling to prevent gross insufficiency was to constrain the social justice dynamic of the instrumentalist argument and make its focus primarily 'getting girls' into any kind of schooling regardless of how this meshed with broader notions of equality. In this guise, as will be shown, it supported an interventionist approach to global social justice.

A limited interpretation of basic needs

The basic needs approach was not initially associated with a narrow meaning of education limited to four to five years in school. The basic needs approach underpinned some of the activism of the first development decade (1965–75) with its stress on rural productivity, the growth of the informal sector and the acknowledgement that women were important producers for agricultural economies, not just consumers. Basic needs was a critique of mainstream development policy and implicitly also a critique of some assumptions in human capital theory, particularly that policy should be assessed primarily in terms of costs and benefits, growth and modernisation. The basic needs approach asserted the importance of a normative idea of need as the guiding idea for policy. Specifying basic needs of the poor was a means of identifying those living in poverty using broader parameters than just income and attempting to take account of specific local conditions (Stewart and Streeten 1976; Doyal and Gough 1991; Gasper 2004). In 1976 the International Labour Organization (ILO) developed key policy and a programme for a basic needs strategy for development. The World Bank followed suit developing approaches to establishing indicators that would measure the satisfaction of basic needs. The general understanding was that basic needs encompassed needs for food, shelter, clothing, health care, water, and on some lists basic literacy. A widely held view was that providing the commodities to meet these basic needs would work towards ending poverty (Doyal and Gough 1991: 153).

The basic needs approach emerged partly as a pragmatic response to extensive evidence of poverty. It expressed concern to address this in ways that were not simply linked to the growth of capitalism. Basic needs entailed an engagement with utilitarianism and an attempt to apply in the context of developing countries insights from debates in political philosophy criticising the view that that the metric of social justice was wants or welfare as suggested by human capital theory. The language of needs had certain clear advantages over preference satisfaction for the architects of post-war welfare states. Needs could be considered as objective, and not linked to problems of desire satisfaction associated with formulations of wants or preferences. Indeed, it was sometimes claimed that needs existed independently of wants or were related to the prevailing organisation of the world and not a belief or supposition about the world, as is implied by wants (Miller 1976; Wiggins 1985). Much of the force of this argument lay with the assumption that needs were linked to workings of the body. Needs were seen as more biological, as opposed to wants which were considered more social.

The claims for a scientific basis for needs that could be determined by expert assessment was problematic. Some critiques of basic needs took issue with the 'top–down' form of assessment of need and provision, not generally informed by participatory or critical analysis of the specification of the nature of needs. The provision of expert assistance in defining and providing for basic needs was often enmeshed in an unequal global hierarchy of power such as was evident when experts in agricultural extension or teacher training from high income countries arrived in developing countries with pre-packaged solutions to what were perceived as simple problems sometimes causing more harm that the problems they set out to solve (Chambers 1984; Rahnema and Bawtree 1996). In education, where the social dimension of need was evident, the question of the politics of assessing needs took the form of an engagement with a question of relevant learning, and sometimes a consideration of the trade offs between economic and cultural needs (Fagerlind and Saha 1989; Leach and Little 1999).

Extensive debates considered whether basic needs are absolute or relative, observed – by some external criterion – or expressed – by the person in need and therefore likely to yield sometimes unexpected demands. Could basic needs be satisfied by minimal levels or did they express broader entitlements? Can needs be conceptualized with or without regard to justifying the ends and obligations associated with those needs? How, given a pluralistic society with diverse ends, can one develop a single set of needs (Gray 1983; Doyal and Gough 1991; Gasper 2004)? Wiggins formulated the importance of needs with regard not so much to an objective notion of needs separate from desires, but a view of need in terms of a state of human flourishing, which if not achieved would entail harm (Wiggins 1998). This view was debated with regard to interpretations of what constituted harm (Brock and Reader 2002). A further line of discussion with regard to need related to the question of whether or in what ways need entailed agency. Did need imply passivity on the part of the needy suggesting that only another actor could satisfy needs, or was the concept of need fluid enough to encompass a sense that those in need did not lose their capacity to act (Alkire 2003; Hamilton 2003; Reader 2004)?

Despite these debates concerning general ideas about need, basic needs in education came to be defined, as Colette Chabbott has shown, not through rigorous empirical study or reasoned exploration of philosophy, but through the repetition of key aspirations with regard to basic learning needs in the conferences and meetings of the EFA movement (Chabbott 2003). The language of basic needs was part of the development discourse of the 1980s, and so became a key resource when the Jomtien Declaration was drafted in 1988 (Chabbott 2003: 58–9).

The Jomtien Declaration begins:

> Every person – child, youth and adult – shall be able to benefit from educational opportunities designed to meet their basic learning needs. These needs comprise both essential learning tools (such as literacy, oral expression, numeracy, and problem solving) and the basic learning content (such as knowledge, skills, values, and attitudes) required by human beings to be able to survive, to develop their full capacities, to live and work in dignity, to participate fully in development, to improve the quality of their lives, to make informed decisions, and to continue learning. The scope of basic learning needs and how they should be met varies with individual countries and cultures, and inevitably, changes with the passage of time.
>
> (World Declaration 1990: 75)

Specifying the objective of global policy to be 'basic learning needs' was an attempt to evade some of the difficulties the basic needs approach had encountered. The problem of absolute or relative levels of need, observed or expressed needs, and the issues raised by pluralism, entitlement and resource provision were simply not addressed.

The clauses in the Jomtien Declaration on expanding access to schooling for women and girls come in Article 3 on 'Universalizing access and promoting equity'. These set out:

> The most urgent priority is to ensure access to, and improve the quality of, education for girls and women, and to remove every obstacle that hampers their active participation. All gender stereotyping in education should be eliminated.
>
> (World Declaration 1990: 75)

Basic education services, although depicted throughout the document as diffuse processes of lifelong learning, are linked in Article 5 with primary schooling. Although a primary cycle – that is the period of schooling deemed to comprise the primary phase – varied from country to country, the importance of a standard measure across societies was to emerge as a key concern at the end of the decade. The more general condition of 'being educated' could not be measured. Thus needs came to be associated with the commodity, in this case five years of primary schooling, which was believed to bring satisfaction of need. Chabbott considers the importance of these

Declarations lies in the way they articulated aspiration, rather than pointed to specific actions (Chabbott 2003). As such it is instructive to see how framing the Declaration in terms of basic learning needs implied satisfying those needs through a minimally agreed form of schooling. 'Basic learning needs' is reminiscent of ideas concerning a set amount of schooling generating a particular rate of return which underpinned the cost-benefit analysis of human capital theory. The normative notion of need thus came to articulate with the mechanics of cost benefit in human capital theory. In this framing addressing girls' needs for schooling was important, not concern with wider ideas of gender equality.

Linking gender and education concerns to basic needs in this way raises similar problems to those posed by considering basic needs such as food and shelter. Is education a commodity of which a person, irrespective of gender, needs a certain number of units, say passing five grades, or does education signal a particular condition, for example being literate, being numerate, being aware of certain key facts as required in official high status school knowledge? If the latter, given social relations marked by gender and other social divisions, one cannot assume the same inputs, for example hours of teaching, numbers of books read, will yield an appropriate satisfaction of need. Some who are subject to race, class or gender discrimination will require different forms of provision to ensure they achieve the condition of being educated.

Is the basic need for education to be assessed relative to the resources available for providing this? Are these resources, local, national or international? For example if there are no trained teachers in a particular region and particularly no trained women teachers, whom some communities require to educate their daughters, can a government claim it does not have to satisfy that basic need? Or must the whole population of teachers in the world or the potential of a society to train sufficient teachers, particularly women teachers by a certain date in the future be considered as a resource available for meeting the need? If a government provided only four years of compulsory education, but no more, could this be said to meet basic needs, even though the possibility of a population to have more education or to have amounts of education relative to those of the elite was denied? Can we distinguish, as Michael Walzer has suggested for needs, two levels of education provision, a basic level, which can be derived through some normative philosophy, and a more particular form, say articulated through concerns with appropriate curriculum level of teacher provision, agreement with regard to the extent of compulsory education, which is distributed through political deliberation, partly with respect to the resources available (Walzer 1983)? If we distinguish between a basic and particular level of needs how could we protect against gender discrimination in the particular – non-basic – form given that it is in the curriculum and pedagogy, the conditions of teachers' work, and the composition of institutions where decisions about levels of provision for education are made that gender inequality has been well documented (Aikman and Unterhalter 2005c; Skelton and Francis 2003)? Basic levels of provision are not insulated from gender inequalities in delivery just because they are basic.

Policy formulated in terms of basic learning needs suggests that girls and boys have the same 'basic' learning needs. One of the problems is differing levels of need, assessments of what need is and how it can be satisfied. A very limited conception of difference in terms of homogenized groups, for example expressing 'women's needs' or the needs of children with disabilities as special education needs, might be able to respond to the demands for a plurality of viewpoints specifying conditions or resources to satisfy needs. But this homogenization of disadvantaged groups is extremely problematic suggesting all women or children with disabilities share the same needs and have similar views on their differences (Mohanty 1988; Terzi 2005).

Basic needs as a development paradigm fell out of favour in the 1980s not because of its analytical difficulties, but more because of shifts in the global political economy. The oil crises from the mid-1970s, the emergence of monetarism and the assertion of the supposed benefits of market-driven structural adjustment policies diminished international attention to specific needs in favour of concern with what were seen as state distortions of markets (Colclough and Manor 1993; Fine 2001). Writers on gender and development picked up the concept of basic needs in the 1980s and used it to differentiate practical gender needs – for access to food, water and the means of everyday survival – from strategic gender interests and concerns to change the social conditions in which they lived (Molyneux 1985; Moser 1993). Naila Kabeer looked at basic needs and pointed out women's needs could not be agglomerated with those of the household (Kabeer 1994). Basic needs are met not only through income or state services but also through resources ranging from subsistence production to claims on social networks (Kabeer 2003). Thus strategic gender interests, that is claims on the state or demands for long-term change, are often empirically intertwined with practical gender needs for day-to-day survival. The debate over two decades concerning this distinction was interestingly not concerned with education (Molyneux 1998; Molyneux and Razavi 2002; Kabeer 2003). Education can be seen both as a practical gender need akin to food or shelter and essential for women's survival, or as a strategic gender interest key to developing women's understandings, skill and networks to advance political and economic change. Largely because the debate concerning practical gender needs and strategic gender interests was conducted within gender and development circles where there was little engagement with state provision of education, the difficulties noted above with regard to how to conceptualize education as a need and how this might connect to strategic interests were not discussed.

The language of basic learning needs formulated in the Jomtien Declaration evaded some of the openings provided by the discussion of need in development ethics where questions of distribution, difference and justice were canvassed (Gasper 2004). The importance of standardizing measurement meant that an interpretation of meeting basic learning needs came to be reduced to providing a commodity of five to six years in school for girls and boys. A measurable input of education would provide the means to protect against a measurable level of poverty and realize outputs in relation to rates of return for the polity and the economy. This is a very attenuated meaning of needs that pays insufficient attention to its potential. It limits the meaning of equality to equal numbers of girls and boys. Education here is limited to schooling. These understandings had a neat 'fit' with human capital theory. What Schultz sought to keep constant across all studies and all societies was a notion of what women's education meant. Interpreting women's education in terms of meeting a basic need provided that constant. It was this easy dovetailing that was to result in gender equality in basic needs being interpreted in instrumentalist terms. Large-scale policy and programme provision became concerned with counting how many girls gained access to and remained in schools The concept of basic needs deals with a normative idea about need that is not inherently instrumentalist. But basic needs came to be interpreted in terms of the commodities that satisfied that need, four or six years of basic education. In this guise the notion of need for basic education for women was easily harnessed to human capital theory to make the instrumentalist argument for gender equality in education particularly powerful.

Women in development

Feminist campaigners viewed the first UN decade for women (1975–85) with optimism hoping that development programmes and economic planning would incorporate women. Disaggregated statistics and new research, it was hoped, would correct the biases and omissions of previous periods (Tinker 1990b). Giving women education would facilitate their access to the labour market and enhance their political participation (Rogers 1980). The economist Ester Boserup's 1970 work on gender divisions in agricultural production was the defining book for the decade indicating the mistakes that flowed from ignoring the productive work of women (Boserup 1970). The originality of her thesis regarding the importance of rural development planning taking account of women's work in agriculture and of women's significance for the economy precipitated the emergence of WID as a major new orientation in development planning (Tinker 1990b; Moser 1993).

Boserup's arguments about the effects of women's education have tended to be overlooked in the attention given to her more general thesis. The large numbers of women taught domestic science in school, she observed, was of limited use in the labour market. Women were excluded from access to agricultural extension training except where this provided training in domestic skills. The gender division of labour in agriculture was associated with different technologies; the shift to intensive agriculture was generally associated with increased work for men and women, but generally greater benefits in income and status for men. However, the recruitment of educated women into the wage sector, she argued accelerated economic growth for everyone, but increased tensions between older women who were not educated and younger women who were. It also exacerbated tension between young women in employment and male family members (Boserup 1970: 220–2).

The nuance of this work on education was not reflected in the WID programmes, units or research that followed. Although continuing discrimination against women in many spheres constrained the initial optimism for WID, its influence on education policy, programming and research was enormous (Rogers 1980; Tinker 1990a; Moser 1993; Saunders 2002). WID was a major influence on the Jomtien Declaration which noted the high proportion of women and girls without access to school (Chabbott 2003). Throughout the 1990s WID research in education was the most widely published and had the most influence on policy. The collection edited by King and Hill in 1993 for the World Bank was a pivotal text. This stressed the importance of counting girls and women, particularly the rates at which they enrolled in school, completed a period of study, and how this correlated with increases in GDP per capita and decreases in fertility and infant mortality. A major concern was how to overcome barriers to access realising the *social* benefits of girls in school (King and Hill 1993).

> Evidence from many countries … points to strong links between the education of women and national development. Most analysis of these links has focused on the *level* of women's education; the implication of the *gender gap* in education have yet to be fully explored. Our empirical research begins by assessing the considerable negative effects of gender disparities in schooling on economic and social development. We then seek to understand why these disparities nevertheless persist by considering the environment within which educational decisions are made.
>
> (Hill and King 1993: 1)

WID policy and practice was not concerned with the content of what girls learned, how they learned or whether gender inequalities faced them after their years in school. Generally, WID analysts commented on the content of schooling when it has a bearing on access, but not more generally. Quantitative work inspired by WID on gender, access, retention and achievement did not deal with other dimensions of inequality, particularly race, ethnicity, caste and disability. Some acknowledgement was made of differences between rural and urban girls (Hadden and London 1996; UNESCO 2003), but there was little engagement with the complexity of social division. Writers in the WID framework interpreted equality, generally in terms of equal numbers of resources, for example places in school for girls and boys, male and female teachers employed, or equal numbers of images in text books of men and women (Unterhalter 2005a). Thus little attention was given to gendered processes of learning, the conditions in which women and men teachers worked, the way their work was regarded by their societies, or the meanings children make and take from the images they see in textbooks.

These WID formulations articulated neatly with human capital theory and with interpretations of basic learning needs as a set number of years in school. WID set out to tackle the gender gap, noted as the most persistent brake on development. It was not focused on the general question of rates of return on schooling in general (Hill and King 1993). But like human capital theorists WID writers were concerned with enhancing women's economic productivity. Research using a combined WID and human capital theory framework led to very precise calculations of how much a year of schooling for a girl could offer her community in terms of increased income or productivity in farming (Dollar and Gatti 1999; Quisumbing 1996). The gendered processes of schooling, exploitation or subordination in work and the impact of social division were initially not considered. Appointing women teachers to encourage families to send their daughters to school became a key policy proposal that combined human capital attention to the education of girls with WID concerns with girls' education and the employment of women. Similarly, understanding opposition within families to daughters' education became a key area where WID and human capital theory overlapped (Colclough *et al.* 2003).

Monitoring global action on EFA drew on WID. The numbers of women in schools as learners and teachers became a key concern of UNESCO's Global Monitoring Reports measuring progress on the Dakar Programme of Action. This monitoring provided part of the agenda taken to the High Level Monitoring Group charged with overseeing the implementation of EFA. In applying for money from the FTI to expand basic education, provision countries were required to complete EFA assessments which documented gender gaps in access and achievement (Fast Track Initiative 2004).

The WID approach to the problem of gender and schooling became a key element in the development of programmes. These concentrated on improving access to school through giving girls stipends or abolishing school fees (Raynor 2005a; GCE 2005b). Sometimes teachers, learners and communities were mobilized to encourage girls into schools and ensure they pass examinations (UNICEF 2005b). Girls were allocated food for education through feeding programmes at schools or set amounts of grain or oil given to each girl who attended school regularly. Water was piped to schools and latrines were dug to improve retention with a particular concern with assisting girls to attend over the days they menstruated (UNICEF 2005a). In some countries the infrastructure for teacher training was enhanced and accommodation built in an attempt to ensure employment for more women teachers (Raynor and Unterhalter 2007 forthcoming). Learning materials were developed with more images of girls and women.

Herz and Sperling's study drawing on WID and human capital theory was to be widely used by IGOs and NGOs in 2005 in advocacy work on the missed MDG target (Herz and Sperling 2004). They concluded it was essential that governments make girls' schooling affordable, build local schools and make the timetable flexible to accommodate girls' household and income generating activities. Schools should be safer, healthier, and more welcoming to girls through improved facilities and teacher attitudes (Herz and Sperling 2004: 9–15). Familiar WID concerns with facilities – teachers, textbooks and water – are intermeshed with human capital analyses of overcoming private costs.

Instrumentalist arguments and interventionist global justice

The instrumentalist argument for gender equality in education that emerged from human capital theory, the basic needs approach, and WID worked with isomorphic assumptions about the family, the community, the nation state and the global stage. The private cost-benefit calculations of the family were considered similar in form to those of the nation and the global polity. The policy and practice issues entailed in a nation acting to provide for the basic needs of a girl through the commodity of primary schooling were considered to be similar in form to the issues confronting an Inter-Government organisation or an NGO engaged in delivery. Similarly the barriers to efficiency and equity WID planners sought to overcome through focusing on the problem of access were considered more or less the same from the local to the national level. This isomorphism raised particular problems about meaning and action.

The instrumentalist argument for gender equality in education as a matter of global social justice rests on four mutually reinforcing ideas. Firstly, that gender equality in education is economically efficient; secondly, that gender equality in access to schooling attends to a universal need that can be satisfied through basic provision; thirdly, that women's education provides an avenue for them to step out of constraining forces of 'tradition' or domination by male family members, community leaders or development planners and enter a more neutral terrain of opportunity marked out by the labour market or political participation; and fourthly, that social relations at the local level have a similar form to those at the national and global level. All four ideas work with aspirations for policy and practice that is efficient, rational, and at basic levels fair to all. These ideas thus work well with those approaches to global social justice that are concerned primarily with eliminating gross insufficiency and want but go no further in distinguishing or addressing different terrains of gender inequality in families, schools, communities, work or politics. There is thus an affinity between instrumentalist arguments for gender equality in education and interventionist approaches to global social justice. Instrumental approaches work well with ideas about society where schooling has an 'impact' on gender inequality. But they are open to critiques from approaches that view society as comprising complex and interlocking sites, where gender may be structured within and between institutions. These, together with frameworks which see society in terms of co-evolving processes where gender dimensions are diffuse demand more strategic and dialogic approaches to change. It is possibly in these very different views about gender and society, and not simply in failures of strategic connection, that the explanation of the lack of connection between the EFA movement and the women's movement lies.

Conclusion

Three forms of an instrumentalist argument for educating women and girls have been discussed in this chapter. Human capital theory, the interpretation of meeting basic needs in terms of providing a limited commodity – four to five years in school – and the argument to increase the access of women to all public spheres have in common a perspective that considers the schooling of women and girls as a means, not an end. Instrumentalist ideas are not concerned with problems of difference, value pluralism or difficult problems of distribution. Because so much is excluded from the analysis of education provision clear policy messages are generated, for example on abolishing school fees, providing food for school, and digging latrines. The instrumentalist argument for gender equality in education has underpinned large-scale programmes to disburse money for gender equality in education and led to provision of schooling for millions of children. This is the huge achievement of the instrumentalist approach and the interventions for global social justice associated with it. What interventionist approaches to global social justice lose in intellectual nuance they gain in policy direction. The approach, however, has considerable difficulty in dealing with issues regarding obligations that go beyond a bare minimum of provision, and which may not meet cost-benefit criteria. It was partly to engage with some of these criticisms that rights-based programming emerged in development practice discussed in the next chapter.

4 Gendered human rights in education

Some of the limits of instrumentalist views of gender equality and education outlined in the previous chapter contributed to a turn to approaches based on rights. Arguments about rights highlight the intrinsic value of gender equality in education. The language of rights has come to be associated with institutional and procedural approaches to global social justice. This chapter distinguishes between moral rights, that is rights we have as a matter of moral truth, regardless of what the law says, and legal rights, that is rights the law or an international declaration claims or recognizes, some of which we may not have morally.

Universal moral truths?

The use of rights to argue for gender equality in education can be traced back to the writings of Mary Wollstonecroft in the late eighteenth century. But despite a number of international declarations in this area many issues concerning rights and gender equality in education have remained rather unexamined, despite the high profile rights commands in the language of global social justice. Ramya Subrahmanian, drawing on a paper by Duncan Wilson, distinguishes three forms of rights which reinforce each other and thus create a circular process that supports gender equality in education (Subrahmanian 2005a). These are rights to education – access to school and progression through different stages of learning – rights in education – fair treatment with regard to learning, for example in subjects studied and teacher attitudes – and rights through education – fair access to the labour market and fair treatment with regard to economic, social and political development.

This analysis assumes a consensus with regard to the moral basis of rights, but there is considerable controversy in this area. Rights can be viewed as deriving from a sense of self-ownership in the libertarian tradition where rights are associated with obligations from others not to interfere or from forms of social contract in the social justice tradition where rights entail obligations to deliver some end state. Different approaches to rights emphasize different interpretations of equality. Vizard draws up a continuum for examining approaches to fundamental and human rights with regard to the extent to which they admit poverty as a freedom restricting condition on human rights (Vizard 2006: 26). The method helps illuminate how gender equality in education can be interpreted in relation to different emphases given to the moral truths associated with rights. At one end of the continuum are libertarian thinkers concerned with negative freedoms and procedures for arriving at rights, who consider the ends of rights are of no consequence for understanding the moral basis of rights. Thus a particular socio-economic state, such as gender quality in education, is not entailed by notions of rights concerned with self-ownership. At the other end of the continuum are social justice thinkers concerned with the connection between negative and positive freedoms and the relevance of substantive opportunities to liberties. For these welfare, primary social goods or capabilities – valued beings and doings in Sen's definition as discussed in the next chapter – are of particular relevance to rights. Thus gender equality in education could be understood for these writers as a form of welfare in the utilitarian tradition, as a dimension of social primary goods, as outlined by Rawls, or as an opportunity to advance capabilities as outlined by Sen and Nussbaum.

O'Neill outlines how the different streams in the thinking about rights are associated with different views about the claim obligations associated with those rights (O'Neill 2000: 102–4). Some libertarians argue that there can be no universal right to goods and services associated, say with education, because all those who bear the obligations to deliver cannot be specified. There can be special rights linked to specific institutions like schools where teachers are contractually obliged to develop learning for girls and boys. However, in the view of writers such as Hayek, there are no universal obligations other than those established by custom, law, or formal contract to support and develop the rights of all children to education, and concomitantly no obligations to be particularly active with regard to gender equality in education. However there are, in this argument, universal rights not to be raped where obligations are universally held. But O'Neill points out how doubts about who bears the obligations to deliver services like education which animate part of this libertarian critique can be dispelled if the argument is made that the universal obligation to deliver education for all is not understood to be held by everyone in the world. Not everybody can teach or develop education provision. If claims to gender equitable education are considered to be made of people or organisations who can appropriately deliver gender equality in education, this universal right to education can be understood not just as rhetoric but in terms of universal claims appropriately distributed and allocated to particular bodies. However, this clarification shows up the distinction very clearly between liberty rights, for example the right not to be tortured, where the obligations are held by everyone, and rights to education where the individuals or organisations that are obliged to deliver must be specified. In the latter case the rights of women and girls entail claims to the same entitlements as men, that is seeing gender equality in education entailing a right to the same education for girls and boys (O'Neill 2000: 106).

Rights theories are subject to a number of criticisms the most relevant of which in this context is that they neglect the value of caring and attachment. The criticism goes something like this. The language of rights does not adequately convey the ethic of care or concern with human vulnerability that women have been particularly sensitive to. A major critique of rights and social contract was that these concepts fail to take account of relations within families, the ethics of care, affiliation, and responsiveness to frailty (Noddings 1984; Okin 1989; Gilligan 1986, 1995; Code 2006). Although the arguments for the significance of women's rights emerged partly out of concern that their obligations of care prohibited them from participating politically, civilly, economically, socially or culturally, the critique about the lack of concern with forms of relationship within families in rights-based frameworks illuminate some difficult issues for argument about the intrinsic importance of gender equality in education framed through rights.

The argument about the conflict between rights and the ethics of care has partly been that the private space of the family is kept out of bounds of political philosophy's concern with the public sphere, that is the state, citizenship and the distribution of justice. Commentators point out how the ethics of the family operate in a different form to those assumed to shape the public sphere and how this raises some key questions for the meaning of rights. The obligations of care expressed within the family or through private social networks are generally based on inequalities, for example between parents and children, the sick and the healthy, the emotionally robust and the emotionally fragile. These are of a different form to the rights between equals assumed in liberal political philosophy. The problem for seeing an intrinsic universal value in gender equality in education is that this might indeed run against obligations of care within families where certain members may not have unlimited freedoms to pursue their entitlements to study without causing harm because they withdraw care from those who need it.

One response to the criticism is that, in fact, the ethics of care and rights are rarely in conflict. Kymlicka has argued that one can interpret the ethics of care to bring out a connection with the ethics of equality in political liberalism (Kymlicka 2002: 400–20). He considers three aspects of Gilligan's assertion of two moral voices, an ethic of care and an ethic of justice (Gilligan 1982). Firstly, the distinction between learning the moral principles of justice and the moral dispositions of care may not indicate a complete disconnection, as it may well be through learning moral dispositions and a sense of justice in families or early schooling that one becomes able to apply general principles of justice. Secondly, Kymlicka argues that conceiving the frame of justice in relation to solving problems that have universal applicability and highlighting a contrast with the frame of care and its attention to particularistic cases may also be too stark. Contextualizing a moral situation is not the same as not applying relevant considerations that are not given by a particular case, but may be extremely salient with regard to questions of equality and justice. Some children at secondary school interviewed during fieldwork for a study in Durban, South Africa were so hungry they had to take the crusts out of the rubbish bins after domestic science lessons so that they were able to concentrate in lessons. This level of poverty needs to be placed in the context of their Constitutional right to education. Attending to justice issues entails invoking some abstract principles concerning rights to education, not simply 'care' through providing food on an ad hoc charitable basis or lessons at home. Thirdly, Kymlicka points out that the contrast between the moral concepts attending to rights and fairness associated with justice have been over-contrasted with those attending to relationships and responsibilities through care. A number of care theorists admit that care must attend not only to those we know but also to strangers. In this guise maintaining the relationships that undergird care may not be so different from maintaining the universality of the equal worth of each person associated with justice. O'Neill considers that there might be universal obligations, for example to care and show concern for the vulnerable that do not have a corollary in rights (O'Neill 2000: 107). Kymlicka points out that universal principles of justice may be understood in terms of a very generalized other, but utilitarianism and Rawlsian approaches to justice both have a concern with some very particular features of the other.[1] While the assertion that rights theorists are only interested in self-protection while care theorists look to responsibility to others, might be an adequate characterization of libertarians, it is not an adequate characterization of rights theories based on attention to the welfare of others and positive obligations to provide goods and services.

While at the most formal level Kymlicka's critique that the distinction between care and rights does not take account of their many connections may be true, the ethics of care has an important and distinctive contribution to make to our evaluation of choices made within the private sphere, which have consequences both for the individuals involved and for the social environment more generally. Swift, in analysing the issues of school choice has considered how much weight to give parental partiality – a form of the ethics of care – in relation to questions of equality and education (Swift 2002). In the context of global justice, gender and education this is a question about how different rights might be weighted against each other. For example do we understand a girl's right to education to have moral standing because it protects her interests to live a more healthy life, to understand something of the society and the world in which she lives, and to enhance her capacity to communicate and defend her interests? Is this right to be weighted more heavily than the interests of the adults in the community in which she is growing up? Whether one suggests the ethics and political decisions made in the family are only different in location to those made outside this private space, as Kymlicka argues, or whether one considers the private space of the family or social network to be different from public spaces only up to a specified degree, as Swift suggests, it raises some key problems about rights in general and gender equality in education as an aspect of rights in particular.

Considering rights as universal structures, whatever the tactical advantage to the women's movement and the clarity provided to policy makers as detailed below, confronts three kinds of challenge from arguments about the ethics of care and aspects of affiliation. Firstly, what might be the process through which one could consider how to weight different kinds of rights? This requires a normative theory. Much talk in terms of rights proceeds as though that normative theory is well understood, when it is the very point where claims in terms of rights become difficult. Libertarian and social justice theorists and the approaches to cosmopolitanism discussed in Chapter 3 each work with different interpretations of normative theory regarding global social justice and this has implications for how they understand rights. However, the legal, tactical and institutional understandings of rights which have framed much discussion of gender equality in education as an intrinsic right, as discussed later in this chapter, have not engaged with these normative debates and thus have tended to relegate issues concerned with care and vulnerability to the private sphere, where they are considered either problematically outside the bounds of justice – in the view of legal positivists and institutionalists – but within the realm of patriarchy – in the view of the women's movement.

Secondly, the idealized conditions outlined in legal instruments which purport to describe the moral basis of rights necessarily ignore aspects of non-ideal circumstances. A girl might indeed be kept from some grave harm if her right to education is ignored. But in societies where it is considered appropriate that girls are married very young and taken out of school, it might be that a girl who does not observe this convention risks the stigma of not being married at an appropriate age, a substantial decline in income and wealth and social ostrascization for being 'too educated'. Sarah Nakaweza writes about growing up in Uganda as the daughter of an abandoned mother. Her determination to progress her secondary school studies meant she became completely financially reliant on her father and brother, but this exposed her to violence (Nakaweza 2005). Ignoring her right to education and continuing to work on her mother's farm might have protected her from this harm. Sanou and Aikman describe a young girl in Mali promised in marriage to an older man. Activism by village animatrices secured a commitment from her father that she could finish school and delay the marriage, but there is no detail of what costs this reprieve incurred (Sanou and Aikman 2005). In both these instances fathers have infringed negative freedoms – through violence, physical abuse or coercive marriage plans – but some women were complicit with this believing that keeping a girl from education and ensuring she was appropriately married would protect her from harm. The issues here are not about the separation of the sphere of justice and the sphere of care, but about the way in which they are connected very complexly.

This links with a further critique of universalist claims based in rights. The argument runs that rights are Western and do not take account of different values, particularly values located in membership of particular communities. The debate has been particularly sharp with regard to whether rights of all children to schooling under the UN Conventions should over-ride the values of certain communities who do not believe in educating their daughters, or who have need for the labour of children who work (Moghadam 1992; Okin 1999a; Kabeer *et al.* 2003). Commentators highlight how universalist claims to human rights undermine the diversity of local histories and contexts, which are particularly salient with regard to education. Universalists generally fail to take account of varieties of 'patriarchal bargain' women strike – albeit not as equals – in order to survive and flourish in some measure. The implicit question is how important are culture and history in formulating a theory of human rights and in considering gender equality in education as part of such a theory. The basis of the demand for equality in rights was much debated by feminist political theorists throughout the 1990s who drew attention to some of the silences in political, economic and social demands based on equality and rights. These silences were set against the transformative power of recognizing difference while not abandoning the important claims rights afforded (Jeffries and Miller 1999). This writing was engaged with the limits that needed to be placed on difference to ensure projects expressed feminist aspirations (Cornell 1993; Cook 1993; Freedman 2001; Fraser and Honneth 2003; Lovenduski 2005). Are local cultures always to be placed in binary opposition to universal values, inviting the deconstructive post-colonial critique discussed in Chapter 7, or can we see them as important only to a certain degree, similar to Swift's argument about parental partiality and the family? If we follow this line of argument respect for particular contexts where gender equality in education is denied are only permissible up to a certain degree, say to the level of articulation in old forms of prayer, or in family discussion or comment, but not where they substantially abuse the rights of girls or women to follow an education. That is the values may be preserved, but actions that are linked to the values and cause harm cannot be taken.

The legal basis of rights

Framing gender equality in education as a global aspiration first appeared in the UDHR in 1948. The UDHR was the product of a particular political moment when the urgency of producing a Declaration at the end of the war overrode the importance of settling many of the philosophical issues concerning the justification of rights, which derived neither from the laws of a particular country nor religious beliefs that all subscribe to (Freeman 2002). The UDHR asserted all human beings were free and equal in rights, and that rights were entitlements which paid no account to distinctions of race, sex, language, or political opinion. Article 26 specifies rights to education in the following terms:

1 Everyone has the right to education. Education shall be free, at least in the elementary and fundamental stages. Elementary education shall be compulsory. Technical and professional education shall be made

generally available and higher education shall be equally accessible to all on the basis of merit.

2 Education shall be directed to the full development of the human personality and to the strengthening of respect for human rights and fundamental freedoms. It shall promote understanding, tolerance and friendship among all nations, racial or religious groups, and shall further the activities of the United Nations for the maintenance of peace.

3 Parents have a prior right to choose the kind of education that shall be given to their children (United Nations 1948).

The UDHR can be understood at two levels, on the one hand as expressing the conclusions of a particular form of moral arguments about human rights, thus as a largely philosophical document, on the other hand it provided the template for further international declarations, frameworks and more binding conventions.

The intrinsic value of gender equality in education has been specified in a range of Declarations and Conventions since 1948. The existence of these texts, not the moral arguments about rights, is commonly asserted as the reason why gender equality in education is important and why global action should be advanced (Subrahmanian 2005a; Tomasevski 2003). The conclusions of key documents such as the UDHR, the Convention on the Elimination of Discrimination against Women (CEDAW) and the Convention on the Rights of the Child (CRC) are frequently citied. For example the UNESCO Global Monitoring Report for 2004 which focused on gender equality in education concluded that the Dakar goals for EFA:

> ... reflect the substance of government commitments contained in four core human rights treaties introduced by the United Nations over the years 1976 to 1990, which have subsequently been ratified by the great majority of the world's governments ... There exists clear sets of legal and political commitments to achieve gender equality in education, which have been freely undertaken by a majority of countries. Thus the right to Education for All is well articulated and accepted internationally. The moral basis for these provisions is compelling.
>
> (UNESCO 2003: 28)

In this analysis rights are not seen as providing a moral claim for securing goods and services that advance gender equality as a matter of justice. Rights are not associated with the tactics of advancing women's claims as intended by the global women's movement discussed below. Rather rights to gender equality in education are based on existing instruments. This is a form of legal positivism which considers because laws or treaties exist, the social order they describe is moral and real. While legal positivism may not appear problematic as an approach to gender equality in education it has inherent difficulties. For example it implies that because laws exist sanctioning the death penalty or minimal taxation for the richest these are moral and realist approaches to punishment or economic organisation. On the basis of legal positivism the argument as to why gender equality in education is an intrinsic human right is not explored but asserted. Because this argument does not open up any complex philosophical issues it has been the one most commonly used by policy makers. For example the DFID Girls' Education policy paper, published in 2005, rested its assertion on education as a right on the existence of a sequence of international declarations to this effect (DFID 2005: 3). A similar assertion was made by UNICEF in a report setting out the need to attend to gender parity and the large number of children out of school. This sequenced how a long history of international declarations had confirmed that these demands were based in children's rights (UNICEF 2003: 3–11).

There are evident advantages to claims to gender equality grounded in rights conceived in terms of overarching principles and legal documents over those grounded in basic needs. Firstly, the question of the level of needs and who assesses this drops away because rights exist independent of objective or subjective assessments; they derive from qualities of 'being human' that are 'self-evident' and intrinsic to human beings, deriving either from a social contract made between free and equal persons, from the natural rights of human beings or from legal documents that claim to set out to codify this. Secondly, the question of commodities or conditions also drops away because education is intrinsic to the advancement of human rights and is not therefore reducible to a commodity, although it may be signalled by a set number of years in school.

Critics point out that asserting the existence of the UDHR and the CRC as a justification for policy or projects based on rights does not itself settle the question of the moral basis of gender equality in, say, education (Brighouse 2002). Claims about rights are claims about an underlying moral reality, which the UDHR may not describe correctly. Furthermore, rights assertions which are as general as the UDHR's require interpretation. Knowing, for example, that there is a right to freedom of expression in and through education tells us that expression of certain kinds must be protected, but not without additional interpretation precisely what kinds of expression. Private prayer seems a prime candidate for protection; sexual harassment is not. For example, the demand of sexual favours linked to securing a job for a woman teacher, obtaining a pass mark or ensuring that school fees are paid, may all be acts of expression, but they do not seem worthy of protection. We need a more fundamental normative theory to tell us exactly what the scope, content, and weight of the right to freedom of expression is. The legal documents do not provide this.

A further problem with legal positivism as the major framing for the argument regarding the intrinsic importance of gender equality in education is whether public pronouncements match provision on the ground. Concentrating only on the legal or rhetorical dimensions of rights gives no attention to the ways in which people gain resources to make use of their rights. Formal acknowledgement of rights, including the right to education, does not mean either a state obligation to provide education of a certain quality, or the ability of poor women and girls to make their right justiciable in court (Chinkin 1999).

For example, although the Constitutions in India and South Africa guarantee rights to education, empirical studies show how the poorest, and disproportionately girls and women, have inadequate resources to make these rights education realities either by claiming their rights to schooling, possibly because there is inadequate provision, or by alerting officials to where they have been denied their rights, because officials are not receptive to representations by the poorest (PROBE 1999; Page 2005; Chisholm 2004; Porteus 2003). These studies are corroborated by fieldwork I have undertaken on two research projects in India and South Africa. Representatives of women's organisations in a state in Northern India in 1999 were thinking about legal action to demand their Constitutional rights to education. But they faced the threat that whoever brought the action would be in grave danger and would have to live in fear of his or her life. At a school in Durban, South Africa, in 2005, children described hunger and social isolation as aspects of poverty. One girl graphically recounted the months in which she had no money for soap or water, could not wash herself or her clothes, and was unable to come school because of shame. These instances show how the right to education, formally guaranteed to children in India and South Africa by Constitutions, was not substantive enough because the local political economy did not support the realisation of rights. The assertion of rights to education as laid down in documents like the UDHR or CRC side steps the question, so difficult for the basic needs approach, of whether needs are dependent or independent of a specification of who will satisfy them. International documents lay down that 'basic' or 'elementary' education shall be compulsory and therefore it is implied that obligations rest with the state or the international body. But the problem the legal approach to rights encounters is that, as the examples from India and South Africa show, institutions based on laws do not always fulfil all the claims made of them. Some circumstances, for example the existence of poverty so that a girl cannot wash herself, or the deadly hatred local political operators bear towards the poor when they claim their rights, may be beyond the immediate scope of institutions to address.

From 1990 it has been commonplace in the statements of IGOs, INGOs and development partners, such as DFID and UNICEF to remark that the aspirations for gender equality in education as a human right laid out in Declarations are not matched by concrete commitments to deliver gender equality on the ground (UNICEF 2005c; DFID 2005; Watkins 2000). But it is not clear if appeal is only made to the legal framing of rights in Declarations and Conventions what obligations by states, IGOs, INGOs, NGOs and looser formations of civil society, families and individuals are entailed. The institutions established to advance rights and global social justice are notoriously unaccountable. IGOs are formally accountable to governing bodies made up of governments, but those governments generally do not take their positions, for example with regard to UNESCO or the World Bank, back to their parliament or electorate (Shapiro and Hacker-Cordon 1999). Accountability is not much better in INGOs which respond in much more diffuse ways to public opinion while also having formal governance structures. It is indeed unclear that formally mandating positions to structures of governance in IGOs and INGOs is what is required in order to make rights substantive. It seems that some accountability regarding finite responsibility to deliver on certain forms of rights affirmed in Declarations, for example the provision of a set number of years in school might be necessary, but not sufficient to ensure gender equality in education globally. Reasonable actions to advance this require multiple arenas for discussion, debate and consideration of accountability. The legal instruments that codify rights cannot cover all these settings.

Rights as tactic

Whatever the limitations of relying exclusively on legal positivism to advance arguments for rights, the fact that global declarations and conventions expressed goals for gender equality in education grounded in rights was a huge advance on the situation before the Second World War where gender was barely noted as a matter of concern with regard to social justice. It was the tactical advantages that could be gained by using the language of rights to advance women's claims that led to development policy and practice attaching itself in the 1990s to the rhetoric and conceptual frames of women's rights (Braig and Wolte 2002). Christa Wichterich has pointed out that the move from a focus on women's needs, in the previous era to women's rights in the 1990s signalled a sea change in the self-image of women and their analysis of the injustices they suffered 'They now came on as champions of a claim to general rights, as individuals under law, no longer primarily petitioners and the needy' (Wichterich 2000).

The initial utilisation of the rights-based approach by women activists was not out of conviction of its philosophical or political robustness, but rather because of some of the tactical openings it provided. In 1993, Hilary Charlesworth had argued powerfully for what could be won on the world stage through tactically using the language of rights in the international arena. She was aware of the many feminist critiques of rights for failing to convey the complex forms of women's oppression, the difficulties of balancing between different forms of rights, and the androgyny and patriarchy encoded into much of the writing on social contract from which notions of rights derived. However, she believed that it was important to strengthen international human rights law to take on the oppressed position of women worldwide. Tackling issues relating to institutions and civil and political participation were important as were challenges to the distinction between public and private as they impacted on economic and social rights. The question of group rights and social subjugation was also pressing (Charlesworth 1993). What is significant about the turn to rights in this analysis is that it is made tactically, not philosophically. This form of action linked to an institutional dynamic in global social justice and procedural aspects of cosmopolitanism. There was a gamble that there was more to be gained from working within the legal framework of human rights than waiting to settle the philosophical questions relating particularly to the differentiation between public and private spheres and weighting issues of cultural identity. This view of gender equality in education as an intrinsic human right thus emerged from the conviction of feminist lawyers and activists in the global women's movement that the language of rights offered a more powerful form of engagement with institutions working for global social justice than the language of needs.

Huge optimism about social development flourished with the end of the Cold War. Discussion and mobilization by women's groups initially focussed on the World Conference on Human Rights in Vienna in 1993, where claims were advanced that women's rights underpinned all human rights (Walby 2002; Antrobus 2004). The text of the Vienna Declaration did not make such a comprehensive statement. It stressed the importance of all human rights and gave particular prominence to the human rights of women and girls. The premise of the Vienna Declaration was that human rights derived from the dignity and worth inherent in the human person, and that the human person is the central subject of human rights and fundamental freedoms, and consequently should be the principal beneficiary and should participate actively in the realization of these rights and freedoms (World Conference on Human Rights 1993).

The intrinsic importance of rights is that they derive from qualities of being human. This is not the language of cost-benefit associated with human capital theory and the instrumental arguments for gender equality in education. Rights are claims humans make because they are human, not because this is efficient or will result in growth.

The text of the Vienna Declaration makes particular mention of the importance of affirming the rights of women and girls. Education is central to this project:

> The human rights of women and of the girl-child are an inalienable, integral and indivisible part of universal human rights. The full and equal participation of women in political, civil, economic, social and cultural life, at the national, regional and international levels, and the eradication of all forms of discrimination on grounds of sex are priority objectives of the international community. Gender-based violence and all forms of sexual harassment and exploitation, including those resulting from cultural prejudice and international trafficking, are incompatible with the dignity and worth of the human person, and must be eliminated. This can be achieved by legal measures and through national action and international

cooperation in such fields as economic and social development, education, safe maternity and health care, and social support. The human rights of women should form an integral part of the United Nations human rights activities, including the promotion of all human rights instruments relating to women. The World Conference on Human Rights urges Governments, institutions, intergovernmental and non-governmental organizations to intensify their efforts for the protection and promotion of human rights of women and the girl-child.

(World Conference on Human Rights 1993)

The Declaration inclines towards a thick version of cosmopolitanism with obligations regarding rights resting with a wide range of organizations. Education is one key area identified where action to advance women's human rights can be taken by national and international action. The passage intermixes moral and legal dimensions of rights. Rights are 'inalienable' but they are also protected and advanced through global human rights 'activities' and through legal instruments. This suggests institutions for the protection of rights, but also gives some sense of the interactive form of global social justice discussed further in the next chapter.

From 1993 the global women's movement made advances through networking at local and regional levels and through engagement with the UN system arguing for the universal scope of women's human rights (Antrobus 2004). Women's groups took the rights-based concern with issues of justice as their starting point for participation in a number of conferences, most notably the World Summit on Social Development (1995). Here women's organizations argued that continued commitment to structural adjustment could not result in poverty eradication, employment creation and social security or the reproductive rights agreed in Cairo in 1994 (Walby 2002; Antrobus 2004: 95–107). At Beijing in 1995, women's rights and human rights were intertwined. In a key passage the Beijing Declaration asserts:

Women's empowerment and their full participation on the basis of equality in all spheres of society, including participation in the decision-making process and access to power, are fundamental for the achievement of equality, development and peace; Women's rights are human rights.

(Beijing Declaration 1995)

It is the moral dimension of human rights that are stressed in this assertion. Women's rights are inherent and immanent in human rights. No further philosophical foundation is provided. While the assertion had great cogency because this was so 'self-evident' it also meant the catchphrase lay open to being used merely rhetorically. Reliance on the legal basis of rights to gender equality in education often made these demands appear as nothing more than rhetoric.

Dakar and Jomtien compared

At the Dakar World Education Forum in 2000 rights featured much more prominently in the Programme of Action than they had in 1990 at Jomtien. There are some interesting shifts between the Jomtien Declaration and the Dakar Programme of Action regarding the relationship between needs and rights. The second section of Article 1 of the 1990 Declaration reads:

> The satisfaction of these [basic learning] *needs* empowers individuals in any society and confers upon them a responsibility to respect and build upon their collective cultural, linguistic and spiritual heritage to promote the education of others, to further the cause of social justice, to achieve environmental protection, to be tolerant towards social, political and religious systems which differ from their own, ensuring that commonly accepted humanistic values and *human rights* are upheld, and to work for international peace and solidarity in an interdependent world.
>
> (World Declaration 1990: 74; my italics)

The Declaration thus suggests that the satisfaction of needs enables people to act in accordance with human rights. Rights do not precede needs, as claimed by the Vienna Declaration but are respected because needs are met. The suggestion here, therefore, is that there is some hierarchy of needs and that having had basic needs satisfied human rights will be honoured. Empowerment and respect for human rights, the Jomtien document implies are returns from the provision of education and do not exist independently. Although this is not an instrumentalist argument on the lines of those discussed in the previous chapter, the implication that rights are a benefit derived from the satisfaction of needs is at odds with the universalist moral arguments regarding the foundation of rights expressed in the Vienna Declaration of 1993.

The Dakar Framework reaffirmed the vision of Jomtien. However, basic learning needs, the pivotal framing of the Jomtien Declaration, appear only twice in the Dakar Framework. At the first mention:

> ... all children, young people and adults have the *human right* to benefit from an education that will meet their *basic learning needs* in the best and fullest sense of the term, an education that includes learning to know, to do, to live together and to be. It is an education geared to tapping each individual's talents and potential, and developing learners' personalities so that they can improve their lives and transform their societies.
>
> (Dakar Framework 2000: 8; my italics)

It can be seen that here rights precede needs. This is the Jomtien position turned on its head. The concept of basic learning needs presented here takes in aspects of full moral agency. This is a step on from the notion of needs linked to tools, content and the means to survival outlined at Jomtien. This more expansive concept of learning needs in the statement of the moral basis of EFA drew explicitly on the formulations of the Delors Commission Report of 1995 which had reframed the economism of human capital theory within a republican version of citizenship, stressing the importance of active participation in and through learning (Delors 1995). The Dakar Framework, despite this nod to Jomtien regarding needs, was strongly influenced by Delors' thinking. Thus it gives a central space to rights:

> Education is a fundamental human right. It is the key to sustainable development and peace and stability within and among countries, and thus an indispensable means for effective participation in the societies and economies of the twenty-first century, which are affected by rapid globalization. Achieving EFA goals should be postponed no longer. The basic learning needs of all can and must be met as a matter of urgency.
>
> (Dakar Framework 2000: 8)

Needs, it is suggested, do not arise from biology. Meeting needs derives from rights. The notion of 'fundamental human rights' signals that the moral basis of rights is either something fundamental to humanness or can be presumed to be derived from a social contract between humans. Rights secure participation and ensure sustainable development and peace. Education is a right and in acknowledgement of this the EFA goals must achieve the satisfaction of 'basic learning needs'.

At Jomtien there had been a limited acknowledgement of the barriers girls and women faced. Implicit in the stronger rights language used at Dakar was an orientation of the EFA agenda towards some of the positions advanced by the global women's movement concerning women's rights. The Framework deals with gender issues on the following terms:

> We hereby collectively commit ourselves to the attainment of the following goals ... ensuring that by 2015 all children, particularly girls, children in difficult circumstances and those belonging to ethnic minorities, have access to and complete fee and compulsory education of good quality ... eliminating gender disparities in primary and secondary education by 2005, and achieving gender equality in education by 2015 with a focus to ensuring girls' full and equal access to and achievement in education of good quality ... implement integrated strategies for gender equality in education which recognize the need for changes in attitudes, values and practices.
>
> (Dakar Framework 2000: 9)

This statement holds out a vision of 'gender equality in education' suggesting this is wider than 'access to and achievement in education' and entails forms of social transformation in 'attitudes, values and practices'. While the language of rights is not invoked as part of this aspiration for gender equality these wider concerns with gender in Dakar are wholly consonant with the new placing of rights preceding needs. They thus go considerably beyond Jomtien, where access and the more limited vision regarding gender articulated there, linked to meeting the basic learning needs of girls.

The Dakar Framework appropriates a number of principles specifying the moral basis for rights and EFA. The concept of the person in this document is that of the individual rights bearer. Rights are realized in institutions where the Declaration asserts that girls and boys should have equal status. Institutions should develop 'integrated strategies' to change 'attitudes, values, and practices' to secure 'impartial treatment'. Rights therefore entail claims regarding quality and equality in institutions. The vision of global justice is one realized through institutions which give effect to a moral notion of rights. However, this was a problematic assumption. Legal institutions cannot address the very comprehensive notions rights cover. While laws can protect against inflicting bodily harm and forcing underage marriage, it is extremely difficult to maintain their reach within the family. Thus, the examples from Uganda and Mali quoted earlier in this chapter show how both the negative freedoms of the two young women were unprotected by rights, and the inadequacy of the protection of positive freedoms, meant that education provision was expensive and not compulsory. These examples do not dispel the importance of institutional protections but show how these need to be supplemented to ensure the protection and advancement of rights.

Rights, governance and the World Bank

The power of the argument regarding the intrinsic importance of gender equality in education framed through rights brought women's rights activists into discussion with UN institutions, such as the World Bank, which had, up to the mid-1990s, made the instrumental argument a key matter of policy. Rights language was to emerge from these discussions as an ambiguous feature of World Bank policy. It linked with strategies advocated by the Bank relating to reformations of government and governance as part of the realignment of global social relations (Rai 2004). This approach to rights thus became connected to and associated with some of the strategic and institution building dimensions of global social justice. In some contexts, entangled with visions of large global powers like the USA, it came to focus on aspirations to build the institutions of other nations in their image.

A key World Bank policy research report published in 2001 exhibits both the promise of the turn to rights-based language regarding the intrinsic importance of gender equality in education, while at the same time showing how such a project was enmeshed with older instrumentalist views and a new agenda about global institutional reform (World Bank 2001). The Bank argued that the effects of gender inequality and poverty were intertwined. James Wolfensohn, then President of the World Bank, in his Foreword, pointed out that poverty exacerbated gender inequalities and that development was hindered by gender inequalities in schooling, access to credit, jobs, and limits on the ability of women to participate in public life. The implication was that promoting gender equality would foster more effective development (Wolfensohn 2001: xi). What is striking is, firstly, the view that gender equality was intrinsic to overcoming poverty and not instrumental as the Bank had asserted in the 1990s. Secondly, the use of the language of rights intertwined with that of cost-benefit.

The team that worked on the Report included World Bank staff, consultants and commentators, some of whom were actively advancing the importance of rights in the global women's movement. The argument made in the World Bank policy for the intrinsic importance of gender equality in education as a right can thus be interpreted partly as a tactical move by key advocates in the global women's movement to use this document as a platform to advance a rights-based framework. But the report is also partly an intervention by the Bank in the emerging debate on the importance of governance and institution building as a key response to globalization and the repositioning of states. From the 1990s the view emerged in the Bank that free markets were not simply 'the answer' to development, but instead what was needed was advocacy and implementation of good governance, generally on terms sanctioned by the World Bank rather than spontaneously generated by locally formulated aspirations (Fine *et al.* 2001).

The argument made in the Report is that gender inequalities in 'legal, social and economic rights' were found throughout the world. While women and girls bore the heaviest costs of these inequalities, they harmed everyone. Therefore overcoming gender inequalities 'is a core development issue – a development objective in its own right' (World Bank 2001: 1). The case for the intrinsic value of gender equality in education, however, was advanced with clear reference to costs and benefits. The report argued:

> It [gender equality] strengthens countries' abilities to grow, to reduce poverty and to govern effectively. Promoting gender equality is thus an important part of a development strategy that seeks to enable *all people* – women and men alike – to escape poverty and improve their standard of living economic development opens many avenues for increasing gender equality in the long run. A considerable body of evidence around the world supports this assertion. But growth alone will not deliver the desired results. Also needed are an institutional environment that provides equal rights and opportunities for women and men and policy measures that address persistent equalities.
>
> (World Bank 2001: 1)

It can be seen that the rights-based approach does two kinds of work in the Report. Firstly, it provides a moral not a theoretical basis for policy. The moral argument, although philosophically underdeveloped, to some extent places the approach beyond question. Rights, like gender equality, are asserted by the Report as self-evidently valuable and therefore, it is implied, non-contestable (World Bank 2001: 2–3). The definition of rights used here is an expansive one taking in legal, social and political rights but paying little attention to some of the philosophical debates about rights claims.

Secondly, the assertion of rights to gender equality legitimates concern that a very generalized aspiration regarding economic expansion to overcome poverty is linked with political institutions. The language of rights puts concern with the form of social and economic relations associated with that economic expansion outside the frame and suggests they are beyond the reach of questioning as what is important is establishing institutions. The failure to make any philosophical arguments for the importance of rights means that the language of rights become a sanction for any form of governance reform that can be associated with real or promised economic growth. As will be shown in Chapters 8 and 9, global social justice in the form of interventions to secure girls' access to school and the weakness of many of the institutions and regulatory mechanisms to ensure strategic advancement of rights often meant there was little engagement with a wider understanding of gender equality as opposed to a minimal provision of school for certain women and girls.

The Report recommends three strategies to achieve gender equality and supports these with case studies and statistical material. Firstly, the reform of institutions such as the law, employment and political participation to give equal rights to men and women; secondly, faster economic development to reduce gender disparities in education, health and nutrition; and thirdly, active measures to enhance the political voice of women to help achieve legal reforms and the delivery of services (World Bank 2001: 2–3). These strategies mesh with interventionist and institutionalized approaches to global social justice. Generally, they lean towards endorsing a thin form of cosmopolitanism where the form of institution or economic growth can be seen as a principle weighted equivalently to those principles concerned with the equal worth of all.

The argument made about gender inequality in education in the Report, does not draw directly on the language on rights. It is generally made by reference to the more familiar framework of human capital theory pointing out how gender inequality in access to schooling contributes to low economic output (World Bank 2001: 11), how there are marked intergenerational benefits from mothers' education (World Bank 2001: 84), and how school costs affect families' decisions to send daughters to school (World Bank 2001: 166). The report is concerned not to lose a focus on growth and sets out to show that growth oriented views of development should not be set against rights-based approaches which it equates with 'institutional approaches':

> ... the evidence suggests that both economic development and institut-
> ional change are key elements of a long-term strategy to promote gender
> equality. For example, where per capita income and gender equity in

rights are low, increasing either equality in rights or income would raise gender equality in education levels. Improving both rights and institutions would yield even greater gain.

(World Bank 2001: 21)

Assessing this turns on statistical data, for example by looking a correlations between levels of rights understood as political participation, equality in employment, marriage and divorce, school enrolments, life expectancy and parliamentary representation (World Bank 2001: 115–17). This turn to empirical questions of measurement has the effect of forestalling the larger philosophical or political questions regarding how rights are defined. Institution building is associated with the formal representation of women not with concerns about how institutions deal with questions of distribution and regulate and mitigate the effects of complex inequalities in conditions of poverty.

The document appears as a negotiated text between World Bank economists and civil society women's rights activists trying to satisfy both constituencies. Although it places rights as a central structuring idea it evades the large questions of justice, agency, distribution, and diverse social formations. These questions which have concerned theorists of rights and global justice raise questions regarding the ethical principles of justice and how these might be theorized given social inequality, the different ethos of the public and private sphere and how the distribution of rights is to be adjudicated in conditions when there are marked differences say within families or cultural communities (Jeffries and Miller 1999; Okin 1999a; Cook 1993). These were questions of considerable concern to the feminist debate about rights, but there is little trace of the issues they raise in the Report.

Conclusion

Rights have been conceptualized morally, legally and tactically. Each approach gives a different emphasis to the demand for gender equality in education, but common to all three is the view that global social justice for gender equality in education is to be achieved by forms of institution building. The language of rights, however, is largely agnostic on the debate between thick and thin cosmopolitans, and this means that the remit of the institutions that will deliver global social justice for gender equality in education remains vague.

5 Capabilities and obligations in an unequal world

The institution building form of global social justice associated with an invocation of the language of rights was frequently inattentive to the complexity of particular settings where people were diverse and the demands of justice nuanced by different histories. A second version of the concern with intrinsic importance of gender equality in education that attempts to engage with these issues can be found in work on the capability approach developed by Amartya Sen and Martha Nussbaum. This has been applied to the field of education by a host of writers, policy makers and practitioners some of whom have been specifically concerned with gender equality.

The capability approach

The capability approach is a normative framework for the evaluation of individual well being and social arrangements (Robeyns 2005: 93). It is a critique of other approaches to evaluation which are concerned with the quantity or quality of resources or particular outcomes. In the capability approach the key ideas is that what should be evaluated are capabilities, that is people's freedom to achieve what they have reason to value. Sen defines capabilities as follows:

> A person's 'capability' refers to the alternative combinations of functionings that are feasible for her to achieve. Capability is thus a kind of freedom: the substantive freedom to achieve alternative functioning combinations (or less formally put, the freedom to achieve various lifestyles).
>
> (Sen 1999: 75)

The capability approach is therefore concerned with protecting and enhancing the freedoms that allow for a wide capability set. With regard to evaluating gender equality it differs from the approaches discussed in the previous chapters. Writers, like Sen, using this approach consider it is misleading to evaluate needs understood in terms of, for example, a fixed number of years in school specified by someone with little knowledge of a particular context. Evaluating rights to gender equality only in terms of whether they are laid down legally is also inadequate. The capability approach broadens the frame for evaluation suggesting more complex processes must be examined as gendered individuals are educated under conditions marked by gendered social arrangements.

The foundational idea behind this view is that, in making interpersonal comparisons for the sake of assessing questions of justice and forms of social arrangements, the focus should not be preference satisfaction or forms of resources. Preference satisfaction, associated with utilitarianism, is problematic because of difficulties with how one understands adaptive preference, for example that some women say they are happy with minimal or no education. Preference satisfaction as a means of comparison can be seen in human capital theory, in the assumption that the reason families educate their daughters is based on an assumed rate of return. Using this as a metric of justice raises the problem that the daughter, exercising adaptive preference, might assert it is appropriate not to be educated because she will be married, leave home and her parents will not see the benefit of their investment. Comparisons on the basis of resources or income earned through schooling in human capital theory are also problematic because they leave out so many important dimensions about what is valuable in a person's life in addition to income, for example relations with family and friends or feelings of social engagement. Comparisons based on access to social primary goods, as suggested by Rawls in his *Theory of Justice*, also have drawbacks. Social primary goods are basic liberties, freedom of movement and occupation, powers and prerogatives of office, income and the social bases of self-respect (Rawls 1971). Sen and Nussbaum criticized using these as a metric for equality because of the tendency to treat these as resources and not take account of reasoned reflections on how these might combine to provide valued actions for a person (Sen 1982; Nussbaum 2000: 88–9).

Instead of preference satisfaction, income or resources, Sen and Nussbaum argue that interpersonal comparisons should be made in terms of what a person is able to do or be, and evaluations should be made in relation to the freedoms that support the quality of life from which a person can develop reflection relating to what she or he has reason to value. Thus the capability approach urges that when making evaluations in education we should look not just at inputs like teachers, hours in class, or learning materials or outputs, earning from a particular level of education – be these earnings, that is a form of resources – or preference satisfaction – doing what is best for the family as assumed in human capital theory. Evaluations should look at the condition of being educated, the negative and positive freedoms that sustain this condition and the ways in which being educated supports what each and every individual has reason to value. This will vary considerably from case to case but may take in being able to support children with homework, read sacred books, participate in community activities or qualify for particular forms of employment.

Capabilities or the potential to achieve valued outcomes are distinguished from functionings, that is what is actually achieved. A capability is 'the opportunity to achieve valuable combinations of human functionings – what a person is able to do or be' (Sen 2005a: 153). For example, if one only evaluated functionings, say passing a school leaving examination at a certain level, one would be unable to distinguish between the following two girls, Saira and Anna, who both failed this crucial examination. Saira, despite attending a well-equipped school with ample support from teachers and parents, chose not to study for her exams reflecting rather that she valued time spent with her friends on social activities. Anna was unable to study because the teachers at her school had not been paid and had not come to work. She had inadequate access to learning materials to prepare for the examination because her government had not invested in these. In addition, her parents' income was so low that she had to engage in paid work to contribute to the survival of the household and undertake a large share of domestic work. The limited time she had to study was compromised by the widespread view in her community that girls were not intelligent. Saira and Anna had similar functionings, that is they both failed the school leaving examination, but making the interpersonal comparisons in relation to capabilities allows one to see Saira had the opportunity to achieve valuable combinations of human functionings, say schooling and going out with her friends, while Anna did not. Assessing only functionings might lead to a focus on motivation, IQ or teachers' skill and a failure to consider opportunities, social arrangements and questions of freedom. In making the evaluation in relation to capabilities one would need to be alert to how a girl's opportunity to achieve the education she values is constrained by social arrangements concerning teachers' pay and work, lack of resources to support learning, particularly for children who undertake employment, norms concerning the sexual division of labour in families and the appropriate education for women combined with decision-making processes that exclude girls from voicing concerns relating to their education (Unterhalter 2005d). Evaluating capabilities entails evaluating the combination of rights to education, in education and through education which Subrahmanian's analysis, discussed in the previous chapter, separated out (Subrahmanian 2005a).

Thus Saira had a different capability set from Anna. She could choose different functioning combinations, say working hard to pass her exams or not working hard and going out with friends. Anna's capability set was severely constrained. However hard she worked for her examinations her freedom to succeed was limited by her government's inability to pay or support teachers and to produce adequate learning materials. In addition aspects of her family's poverty, that is lack of income and decisions regarding how domestic work was organized, together with views in her community regarding girls' education, severely limited her capability set. There was no space for her to raise these concerns within or outside her family and have some sense that obligations to provide for her education would be met.

Martha Nussbaum (2000) expands the notion that in assessing human flourishing one needs to look to capabilities not preference satisfaction, resources or functionings. However, she puts Sen's idea to work in two distinctive ways. Firstly, she calls attention to 'capabilities to function in certain core areas' which she calls 'central capabilities and for which she develops a provisional list (Nussbaum 2000: 78–80).[1] Secondly, she considers that attention to a basic level of capabilities as signalled by her list is a necessary condition of justice (Nussbam 2000: 73–80). Unlike Sen, who has refused to provide a core list of capabilities for use in all contexts and to tie this tightly to a particular pronouncement on justice in this way (Sen 2005a), Nussbaum specifies that certain capabilities comprise a threshold with regard to justice:

> In certain core areas of human functioning, a necessary condition of justice for a public political arrangement is that it deliver to citizens a certain basic level of capability. If people are systematically falling below the threshold in any of these core areas, this should be seen as a situation both unjust and tragic; in need of urgent attention – even if in other respect things are going well.
>
> (Nussbaum 2000: 71)

Education, understood in a very wide sense, is part of Nussbaum's list of central capabilities. The list mentions education understood as formal instruction as one of the central capabilities. In addition, the list includes being able to use imagination and thought, to develop emotional attachments, and have the freedoms to sustain these. It also includes being able to develop a conception of the good through practical reason, develop the basis of self-respect, enjoy play and some sense of control of one's environment. While Sen leaves open the question of what form of education might reasonably be considered valuable to each individual living in conditions of freedom and enjoins only social arrangements that will make for a wide capability set, Nussbaum is quite prescriptive – albeit in very general terms – regarding the form and content of education linked to the central functioning capabilities.

However, both Sen and Nussbaum come to a similar conclusion regarding the intrinsic importance of gender equality in education. They come to this through slightly different routes. For Sen, gender inequality in education is intrinsically objectionable for three reasons. First, it has a bearing on the capability set, that is the freedoms to achieve capabilities. In the case of Saira and Anna, discussed above, Saira had a wide capability set constrained by relatively little gender inequality, although gender norms might have played a part in her decision not to study. She had the freedom to choose a combination of functionings. Anna, by contrast had her capability set constrained by some marked features of gender inequality which intersected with her family's poverty and the inadequacy of delivery of education in her country. Thus gender inequality in education and in the social relations and actions linked to education limits the opportunity to achieve valued functionings, while gender equality, by contrast, enhances it.

Second, Sen sees gender inequality as a key aspect of how individuals convert resources into capabilities. The idea of capability, Sen argues, allows us to see that resources are not enough. Two people with access to the same resources may not be able to achieve the same valued functionings because their capabilities vary (Sen 1980). For example, a teenage girl and boy from families with little spare income may attend a school which has no latrine or water. This is uncomfortable for both, but the physical differences between them mean that the girl is likely to be absent from school for several days a month when she is menstruating (Kirk 2005). She does not have the means to buy sanitary towels and when she cannot wash she is ashamed to appear in public. While they have access to the same resources, that is the same teachers and school facilities, the capability approach alerts us to the way in which gender differences, if not addressed, entail forms of inequality in their opportunity to use those resources (Unterhalter and Brighouse 2006 forthcoming). The capability approach also highlights how non-personal resources often marked by gender inequalities vary and affect schooling. For example, a girl who has to clean classrooms and cook food for a teacher in the time she might be doing homework requires additional resources and freedoms to help her progress with her learning. She has access to the same resources as boys and girls who do not have to perform this work – that is the lessons provided in the timetabled school day – but the capability approach shows us that she does not have the same capabilities, that is the same opportunities to achieve valuable combinations of what she wants to do. Possibly her valued doings and beings entail completing her homework, playing music and spending time socialising with friends and family. She lacks the freedom which opens up this range of alternatives. She attends school but has limited opportunities to convert this into functionings that are intrinsically and instrumentally valuable. If we evaluate only whether she attends school or not – as suggested by the basic needs and human capital approaches discussed in Chapter 4 – the ways in which gender inequalities limit her capacity to convert resources into capabilities are obscured. Attending to gender equality and the conversion of resources into capabilities highlights that what is wrong with gender inequality in education is not simply the amount of schooling provided as human capital theory argued. The capability approach highlights how some girls attend school and through routine discrimination based on gender, poverty or race divisions cannot achieve the same capability set as many boys and richer girls or children not subject to this form of discrimination. The implication is that poorer girls who are required to work to maintain the school in this way need more resources for their study, not less, as generally happens.

Third, Sen also considers that education is a basic capability that helps convert other capabilities into valued functionings or helps attain larger aspirations, for example human security. Gender equality in education helps enhance the way in which education itself contributes to enhancing other valued combinations of functionings. In a speech to the Commonwealth Education Ministers meeting in Edinburgh in 2003, Sen pointed out:

> ... widening the coverage and effectiveness of basic education can have a powerfully preventive role in reducing human insecurity of nearly every kind ... Women are often deprived of their due, thanks to illiteracy. Not being able to read or write is a significant barrier for underprivileged women, since this can lead to their failure to make use even of the rather limited rights they may legally have (say, to own land, or other property, or to appeal against unfair judgment and unjust treatment) ... Gaps in schooling can, thus, directly lead to insecurity by distancing the deprived from the ways and means of fighting against that deprivation ... empirical work in recent years has brought out very clearly how the relative respect and regard for women's well-being is strongly influenced by women's literacy and educated participation in decisions within and outside the family. Even the survival disadvantage of women compared with men in many developing countries (which leads to such terrible phenomenon as a hundred million of 'missing women') seems to go down sharply – and may even get eliminated – with progress in women's empowerment, for which literacy is a basic ingredient.
>
> (Sen 2003)

Here basic education reduces human insecurity and this has particularly powerful effects for women in widening their capabilities. Education is a form of capability because it enhances the opportunities of all to choose what they wish to do or be. Gender equality in education is intrinsically important because it enlarges capabilities generally.

Thus Sen argues for the intrinsic importance of gender equality in education, firstly, because it helps establish conditions in which a wider capability set is available to girls and boys; secondly, because it alerts us to differential conversion processes linked to gender and other social divisions with regard to how resources are utilized to establish the capability set; and thirdly, because of the importance of gender equality in basic education in preventing human insecurity and establishing conditions for capabilities and freedoms. His arguments are thus concerned with gender equality, education and opportunities, and not simply with particular outcomes linked to education. In this there is a key difference with human capital theory concerned with gender equality in education yielding specific rates of return, but with no concern with a wider concept of freedom. There is also a difference with the approach to gender equality in education linked in the libertarian tradition to rights which are morally 'self-evident' and not linked to other processes of social transformation or justice. I draw out below the ways in which Sen sees rights and capabilities as connected but separate.

Sen's focus on gendered processes constraining and enlarging capabilities in relation to education has similarities and differences with Nussbaum's analysis. Nussbaum's argument for the intrinsic importance of gender equality in education is opportunity based, liked Sen's, but has elements of an outcome oriented approach. However, her understanding of outcomes is different from that which emphasises social benefits and de-emphasizes the individual as in human capital theory. Her argument is that when establishing or evaluating social and political institutions their structure should be chosen with a view to promoting the threshold level of capabilities on her list. Gender equality in education is implicit in many of the capabilities on the list and thus forms part of the intrinsic threshold for justice she advocates (Nussbaum 2000). In specific work on gender equality in education Nussbaum has argued that education is key to women 'making progress on other problems in their lives' (Nussbam 2004: 319–20). In this work she enjoins governments to make women's education a higher priority, and calls on governments in rich and poor countries, corporations and citizens to devote more resources to it. Her article is a critique of the position that the demand for literacy for women is Western and undermines local forms of 'wisdom'. Nussbaum argues instead that literacy secures the possibility of work and movement outside the home, affords women opportunities to meet with others and develop networks of solidarity, and enhances access to the political and legal process locally, nationally and internationally. She also asserts the importance of learning for women involved in physical labour in cultivating 'mental space' and helping draw out the value 'of their own humanity' and capacities to question and inquire (Nussbaum 2004: 335–6).

The capability approach, Nussbaum argues, illuminates how actions need to be guided both by respect for the dignity of all humans – whether educated or not – and concern with how to attend to conditions that mar the chances of individuals, for example through lack of access to education which harms that dignity (Nussbaum 2004: 357). Nussbaum is here concerned with women and their capabilities and not with how gender equality can open a wider capability set, as Sen is. She is less interested in gender – as a verb or adjective – and conversion, and more interested in gender as a noun and women denied full opportunities or capabilities. Elsewhere, Nussbaum differentiates the demand for women's education based in capabilities from that based in rights, because she sees rights overly concerned with aspects of negative freedoms and thus insufficient to take forward the strong forms of provision nationally and internationally she associates with advancing women's education globally (Nussbaum 2005).

Sen (1997) has outlined how human capital and human capability are inter-related. The concept of human capital, he writes, with its stress on knowledge, skills and effort suggests how these can be converted into valued personal or economic functionings. But he draws out how the notion of human capability is wider, entailing not only a growth in productivity but an enlargement of wider freedoms. The instrumental importance associated with human capital might provide an analysis of what gender equality in education can achieve, for example that it enhances economic growth or national status, but it cannot explain why gender equality in education might be intrinsically important as the capability approach suggests because it expands 'human freedom to live the kind of lives that people have reason to value' (Sen 1997, 1959). This notion makes the importance of gender equality in education go considerably beyond its instrumental importance. Sen describes here policy directions linked to looking at human capabilities rather than human capital. These are concerned with social changes, not simply economic changes. Adapting these with regard to human capabilities, the implication is that policy makers and practitioners should take account of how gender equality in education is relevant to the wellbeing and freedoms of people. Instituting this will influence economic production and raise questions about the indirect role of gender equality in education on social change.

The capability approach to the intrinsic importance of gender equality in education differs both from the instrumentalism associated with human capital theory and basic needs and from the universalism associated with the rights-based approach. In human capital theory gender equality in education was efficient because it was seen to maximize a household or a nation's earning over several generations. For the capability approach this efficiency is not the reason gender equality in education is important. It is important because it widens opportunities, enables the realization of other capabilities and alerts us to human difference. Interpretations of basic needs came to associate the satisfaction of basic needs with the provision of a 'basic' commodity – commonly viewed as five years in school. The capability approach is more attuned to human diversity and it would be impossible to generalize that all capabilities could be addressed by a single form of school provision for girls and boys.

In the rights-based approach, gender equality was one dimension of the universalism that underpinned the moral and legal basis of rights. Rights apply to everyone either as an attribute of being human or because legal instruments dictate that they do. Nussbaum shares some of this universalism, although her capabilities express positive rather than negative freedoms including gender equality in education. Sen's version of the capability approach stresses the importance of establishing the conditions for capabilities as reasoned actions. Gender equality in education is not dictated morally or legally, but is a necessary condition to allow reflection on capabilities, the conversion of resources into capabilities for differently situated people and to enable the development of further capabilities. Thus, gender equality in education is part of the processes, the dialogues and the deliberation that underpin rights. What the rights-based approach dictates from assumptions about what is good or laid down in law like texts, the capability approach opens up to reasoned actions that take account of diversity.

The capability approach and the debate about rights: Sen and Nussbaum

Sen has set out elements of a theory of human rights, and sought to link the theory of rights with work on capabilities, freedom and agency (Sen 2004). Sen is concerned to specify, firstly, the kinds of statements entailed in declarations concerning human rights, the reasons why they are important and the duties and obligations they entail. He is thus working on the relationship between negative and positive freedoms, the question of rights and obligations and the contextual question which has been extremely troubling to feminist theorists because of the difficulties of realizing rights. He puts in a middle layer of analysis between the universalising architecture of arguments based on human rights and the critical riposte based on the specificity of particular conditions, relating to say the family or different cultural practice. Sen considers what from of action promotes human rights and whether they are promoted only by legislation or by other means. He discusses whether economic and social rights can be included as human rights.

Sen's argument is that statements about human rights are ethical demands. Ethical demands are based, not on existing legal rights as the legal positivism articulated in some policy documents discussed in the previous chapter suggested, but on the freedoms that form the basis of these rights:

> A pronouncement of human rights includes an assertion of the importance of the corresponding freedoms – the freedoms that are identified and privileged in the formulation of the rights in question – and is indeed motivated by that importance.
>
> (Sen 2004: 323)

Sen's analysis takes questions of agency and interaction seriously. He places a stress on freedoms and the importance of open public reasoning with regard to the specific content of rights.

Sen considers aspects of rights and freedoms pointing out that while freedoms are primarily descriptive characteristics of persons, rights entail claims on others, implied, but not necessarily entailed by freedoms. In contrast, to desire satisfaction in utilitarianism the importance of rights concerns not only 'the celebration of our own rights and liberties', it also enjoins us to take 'an interest in the significant freedoms of others' (Sen 2004: 328). This entails paying as much attention to the process dimensions of freedom, ensuring full and fair discussions and attention to very different voices, as to the opportunity dimensions. This link between rights and obligations of care and concern appears an implicit concession to the critiques of feminists like Okin regarding the public sphere of untrammelled negative rights and freedoms (Okin 1989). Human rights, Sen argues, generate reasons for actions by agents who are in a position to help in promoting and safeguarding underlying freedoms. Human rights thus entail much wider obligations than those that can be legislated for. In many cases they might be just as well promoted by discussion and appropriate action as by legislation. It follows from the analysis that rights entail very broadly based imperfect obligations on behalf of all other rights bearers. Thus economic and social rights can be considered as human rights even though there is no institutional body responsible for meeting those rights.

Sen's move in developing elements of a theory of human rights is to side step the question of which institutions will deliver rights. Implicit in this analysis is a commitment to equality that notes difference, but considers this does not undermine the ethical dimensions of rights or obligations. Gender equality rights are thus reflective of the general ethical egalitarianism entailed in the theory, but are also secured by aspects of process freedoms and imperfect obligations which take aspects of difference, agency and interaction seriously.

Gender equality in education can be thought of as a goal right which requires particular forms of action to fulfil the appropriate obligation. The effort to characterize this form of action guides the analysis. Difficulties concerning who specified need and by what process exposed the arbitrariness of considering needs in relation simply to commodities for girls. The lack of correspondence between some rights and institutional obligations and the lack of concern with context that was one of the key problems with some forms of the rights-based approach that limited its scope in relation to gender equality. Sen attempts to attend to these critiques.

He has also sketched what he considers the complementary but different terrain of rights and capabilities (Sen 2005a). Sen argues that evaluation on the basis of capabilities is important in identifying substantive opportunities which are crucial to establishing conditions based on rights, but the capability perspective may have little to say with regard to issues of process freedoms which are central to a theory of rights, because the capability approach does not of itself have much to say about fairness, equity and efficiency of processes. To illustrate this, Sen points out that women generally have greater longevity than men, but shows how it would violate our sense of process freedoms were women to be given less medical attention than men to limit their opportunities and make for equality in capabilities (Sen 2005a: 156).

The key point for this argument is that Sen sees concern with the process aspect of freedoms not necessarily entailed in the notion of capability and thus stresses how rights and capabilities are complementary to each other, but cannot be subsumed into each other. Indeed the attempt to do so yields some unsettling results. In some countries girls do better than boys at school. Some commentators, drawing mainly on human capital theory, have suggested that because girls achieve well at school no further attention to gender equality in education is required. This is the implication of the 'headline' message and some of the summary documents accompanying UNESCO's 2005 Global Monitoring report which concluded that as the overall gender gap in favour of boys is slowly closing, in many countries the gender parity gap in favour of boys in primary school is being replaced by a gender parity gap in favour of girls in secondary school (UNESCO 2005b). North points out there are problems with this conclusion in relation to the data themselves (North 2006b). In addition, it is important to draw out what is wrong with the underlying assumptions that drive this form of conclusion. The capability approach can highlight how gender inequality in the wider society might prevent women turning their successful schooling into valued combinations of functionings, but it cannot on its own say that the process of denying women continued good education on the grounds that they 'have enough' runs counter to our sense of fairness. We need a broader conception of human rights and a theory of justice to draw out how the issues are not just about equal amounts of schooling, but about equitable processes and ethical obligations. We thus need both an analysis based on rights and capabilities.

Drawing on Sen's analysis of human rights, gender equality is entailed in the ethical demand of human rights claims. Rights to gender equality in education entail process freedoms in formulating the content of that education, and opportunity freedoms in being able to have access to and progression through education in combination with other valued functionings. These rights to gender equality in and through education have moral standing whether or not at any particular time there is the institutional capacity to respond to this right or there are regulatory mechanisms that work. Part of the rights enjoyed by those with ample education entail obligations to ensure we secure rights for all others. Part of this obligation entails securing rights for children who do not have full moral agency.

Sen has clarified some of the 'reasoned actions' that must be taken in respect of these imperfect obligations. He distinguishes between 'compulsory action' involving perfect obligations, which require states or other institutions of global governance to give them effect and 'reasonable actions' associated with imperfect obligations. 'Compulsory actions' to ensure all children attend school are already a feature of many national states' legislation. A global government could require states to enforce gender equality in schooling and make it compulsory that school systems ensure no discrimination on the grounds of gender. But there is wide consensus that such a form of global government is neither practicable nor desirable. 'Compulsory action' associated with a form of global government is different from 'reasonable action'. The latter involves definite actions towards specific ends associated with imperfect obligations rather than actions specifically required by law.

Vizard (Vizard 2006: 87–91) expands these 'reasoned actions' suggesting that reasonableness entails balancing the following considerations which could contribute to establishing a framework for claims associated with rights and capabilities in international law:

- the fundamental importance of human rights being protected and promoted;
- special concern with actions and causal responsibility for violations;

- existing commitments, values and special relationships;
- the extent to which the actions of a particular agent can make a difference;
- pragmatic constraints and alternative actions that might have been performed;
- whether the range of pragmatic constraints can be altered by action.

This interpretation suggests there may be scope for work in international law on giving substance to the claims made for gender equality in education. For example, children attending school near the coffee plantations of Kenya live in extreme poverty, partly because of the low wages their parents earn linked to the current low global price for coffee. The harm caused to children who cannot progress with their schooling because they are too hungry to study takes gendered forms linked to girls' and boys' different food needs. Teachers at the children's school have perfect obligations to teach them and the government can take 'compulsory action' if they fail to fulfil this. But a wide range of people have imperfect obligations to the children and to ensure forms of gender equality. Their parents, teachers, education officials in their district, citizens of Kenya all have a mixture of perfect and imperfect obligations. People who drink the coffee, which the children's parents pick, and who live in political economies that profit from the coffee trade also have imperfect obligations. What actions should they take? All these diverse actors cannot do everything. 'Reasonable action' addresses the problem of the over capacious set of actions imperfect obligations can imply.

Vizard's specification of what 'reasonable actions' entail can be adapted to consider the issue of gender equality in this case. 'Reasonable actions' entail the protection and promotion of human rights. These are of fundamental global importance in assessing action. As 'reasonable actions' are associated with a process of allocating responsibility for human rights violations, special concern must be given to actions, such as the low price of coffee, which are implicated in limiting children's rights to education as they are too hungry to learn. Allocating causal responsibility for these violations merit consideration as part of 'reasonable action'. Pragmatic constraints with regard to resources to deliver gender equality in education, must be balanced with concerns for gender equality, but these constraints, such as teachers and education officials with inadequate understanding of gender issues, do not trump the importance of rights or reasonable actions to secure gender equality. Any assessment nationally or globally of what 'reasonable actions' entail must consider the extent to which the actions of agents, singly or collectively, to advance gender equality in education have been undertaken and what alternative actions have been performed. Thus 'reasonable global action' with regard to gender, education and the children on the Kenyan coffee plantations needs to take account of whether securing gender equality can be affected by collective action and appropriate institutions locally, nationally or internationally and whether such actions interfere with a range of commitments, values and special relationships. This approach does not prescribe a certain level or amount of education, but it does see the forms of association people make to discuss justice and the reasoned evaluation of actions they undertake as an important component of 'reasonable action' which becomes a key part of the stuff of global social justice

From her somewhat different approach to capabilities, Nussbaum (Nussbaum 2000: 96–100) is also concerned to show how rights and capabilities are complementary concepts. She believes capabilities provide a stronger basis than rights claims because they clarify the motivating concerns and the goals behind these and do not rest on ideas about political processes or pre-political identities. She thinks about rights as combined capabilities. This overcomes the problem that girls and women may have the right to education written in a Constitution but are effectively denied these rights by inadequate provision. Considering rights as opportunities to achieve valued combinations of capabilities one would be clearer that the legal positivist form of rights was a much less substantive demand than that based on the demand that opportunities to achieve capabilities were instituted. The argument based in capabilities, she points out, is also an argument based on spending more resources on the poor. Providing education only up to a certain minimum to fulfil a legal obligation may not provide the full combination of capabilities. As Janet Raynor has shown for Bangladeshi girls, they may have access to school but resources have not been provided to secure capabilities for play, control over environment, affiliation or valued outcomes from education (Raynor 2007 forthcoming).

Nussbaum, however, while considering that capabilities gives a stronger sense of the opportunities rights must secure, still argues for the importance of the language of rights (Nussbam 2000: 99–100). She stresses the language of rights signals that demands are justified and urgent claims. Rights in her view communicate more than the appeal to basic capabilities. Meeting basic capabilities, like basic education, might entail no further ethical demands. But rights language does suggest these demands and a sense of the 'terrain of agreement' on which the basis of the political justification for capabilities rests. In this, she echoes some of the feminist rights advocates discussed in Chapter 5 who strategized regarding how rights language would help widen demands made through policy and institution building.

The capability approach and gendered education

Sen and Nussbam's work has generated an interesting critical scholarship which illustrates and enhances their analysis with regard to education (Terzi 2005; Walker 2006; Walker and Unterhalter 2007). Some writings deal directly with questions of gender and education. Alkire, as part of a wider discussion of understanding freedom in Sen's capability approach, provides a case study of a woman's literacy project in Pakistan. A conventional cost-benefit analysis would have noted how the project was not financially viable and how the women did not gain access to employment, thus the rate of return from the project in human capital terms was low. However, evaluation based on the capability approach reveals how the women considered the project had led to improvements in how they were regarded and saw themselves (Alkire 2003). Other interview-based studies involving poor women, while similarly illuminating the approach in action, reveal some questions about the ethical individualism of the liberal underpinnings of the approach for women who see the world mediated through their immediate relationships (Raynor 2007; Uyan 2005).

Robeyns (2006) contrasts analyses to gender equality in education grounded in human capital theory, rights and capabilities and concludes that the human capital approach is fragmented and far too instrumental. While rights and capabilities are multi-dimensional and can account for non-instrumental aspects of education, rights are often utilized rhetorically and rather loosely in everyday talk. At a theoretical level rights require a prior moral criterion and must be rights to something. By contrast capabilities matter intrinsically, whether or not they matter instrumentally. She draws on work by Harry Brighouse to suggest that capabilities may be understood as the moral basis of rights (Brighouse 2004; Robeyns 2006: 82). This overcomes the problem with understanding rights either as merely legal and juridical or as immanent or 'self-evident'. Capabilities imply the 'reasoned actions' which may result in establishing the institutions associated with rights.

My own work over some years has moved from criticising the capability approach for its limited concern with the conditions in schools that might not promote capabilities, to consideration of how the capability approach might work together with an approach to rights and public deliberation to make the MDGs a site of strategic engagement by global civil society (Unterhalter 2003, 2005a, 2005b).

The emerging literature on the capability approach and education highlights a number of key issues for the debates about cosmopolitanism and global social justice with which this book is concerned. Firstly, it shows up how complex the task to institutionalize cosmopolitan concerns with political equality, democratic governance and social justice is, in a world marked by difference, inequalities, deeply entrenched forms of social division, and the consequences of ill thought out and sometimes opportunistic interventions. Nonetheless it also shows how the capability approach agenda resonates with aspirations articulated by people living in poverty. Clarifying some of the issues concerning capabilities, human rights and justice points to the potential for better policy and richer approaches to monitoring and evaluation. The capability approach appears to call particularly for more work on the moral basis of global social justice. Interventions to end gross insufficiency and procedures to establish appropriate forms of governance might be necessary as they develop human capital and rights, but they are not sufficient. This is not to say that the capability approach does not raise significant questions.

Critiques

The capability approach has been subject to a number of criticisms. The most relevant with regard to gender, schooling and global social justice are that it evaluates opportunities, rather than outcomes; that it fails to attend adequately to cultural relations; and that it calls for too much evaluative information that makes formulating any policy impossible. The thick forms of cosmopolitanism it rests on are viewed by some as unachievable.

In outline, the criticism of opportunity-based evaluation is that attending to opportunities with little or no consideration of outcomes may mean that while arrangements are made to attend to equalizing opportunities if there is no attention to outcomes the unjust status quo might persist, despite a widening of opportunities. For example, drawing on and adapting Anne Phillips' (1999) work on which equalities matter, it is possible that governments or international organizations put a great deal of resources into improving access to schools for the poorest girls and boys, making schools more welcoming for girls and training teachers to ensure they take account of the learning styles of different children. However, the structure of the labour market, the form of the political economy, and the history of political elites mean that virtually no women take significant political or economic decisions in either the government of the country or the international organizations concerned with promoting gender equality. The concern with opportunities – understood in a very narrow way – rather than outcomes thus results in a lack of concern with continued injustice. In defence of the capabilities approach it can be argued that the approach has a multidimensional understanding of opportunity as emerges in both Sen's notion of conversion, the sensitivity of the capability set to context, and Nussbaum's merging of opportunity and outcome in the discussion of capabilities and women's education. It is a misunderstanding of the approach to see it as limiting its concerns to only one narrow form of opportunity – say access to and participation in schooling.

Gerry Cohen (1993) makes a different critique of capabilities as opportunities. He argues that Sen's achievement in suggesting that capability is a better alternative than primary goods and welfare for what is distributed by egalitarians is twofold, and this duality is confusing. Cohen highlights how Sen uses capability to signal both opportunities and valued states. He writes that 'in progressing beyond Rawls, Sen proposed two large changes of view from actual state to opportunity, and from goods and welfare to … functionings' (Cohen 1993: 10). That is, Sen suggests egalitarian justice in relation to education is concerned, firstly, with the distribution not of completed levels of education and how this is supplied – actual state – but of opportunities for differently situated girls and boys to be educated, that is children's freedom to go to school and learn there in conditions that are appropriately attentive to gender and other inequalities – capabilities. For Sen, egalitarian justice is concerned not simply with education resources – primary goods – or the mental pleasure or desire satisfaction associated with being educated – welfare

– but with the condition of being educated – capabilities. Cohen argues that using the term 'capability' both for opportunities to be educated and for the condition of being educated is not satisfactory.

He suggests a neologism, 'midfare', as a better term for the state midway between a bundle of objective goods and utility. This separates out concerns with opportunities and conditions as a form of outcome. Capability, according to Cohen, is only one part of midfare. A person can have midfare without exercising capability or aspects of valued choices. One can become educated with little exercise of capability or freedom. A young girl who does not want to go to school, but who lives in a society where there is compulsory education will end up educated without exercising substantive freedom.

In response to Cohen, Sen distinguishes a functioning – being educated – from freedoms and the capacity to choose concerning a range of dimensions of education, that is capabilities. He emphasizes the significance of evaluating capabilities and not functionings. He is concerned to differentiate between capabilities and the social arrangements in which capabilities are exercised. The girl who is educated through compulsory schooling achieves a functioning, but she and her parents may have been excluded from the process of decision making about that education. This may have taken place because they lived in a society which barred people of their class or ethnicity from decision-making bodies. Information concerning the nature and content of schooling may not have been widely disseminated. The particular form of education the girl required, recognizing her language and health needs, was not made available to her. A war may have been raging and the daily traumas involved in the journey to school was not acknowledged. Evaluating capabilities, rather than functionings, allows all these aspects that constrain justice to become apparent (Sen 1993, 2005a). Noting only that the girl has completed school negates concern with the very troubling processes that have been intertwined with her education.

The critique that the capability approach fails to pay sufficient attention to culture has been made in a number of forms. Sometimes this is articulated as a general critique of western liberalism, sometimes as a specific comment on aspects of the approach. Frances Stewart (2005), while arguing for the importance of the capability approach's concern with individual wellbeing, has also noted the need to take account of how groups contribute to a person's wellbeing and the need to categorize group capabilities as well as individual capabilities. Thus, the capabilities of a particular women's group for example, and how these contribute to enhancing the capability set for education for young girls in a region, demand study in their own right and not just because they help facilitate the enlargement of a particular girl's capability set.

In my view Stewart's work does not negate the importance of capability-based evaluation, but highlights the importance of taking account of cultural and social processes, so key to schooling, when assessing the capability set. Sen also sees culture and history as important, but as his most recent works in this field illuminate he does not see 'culture' as fixed within certain boundaries where only a selected few are licensed to speak as cultural commentators. His work on India illuminates how he is interested in the heterodoxy of cultures, the ways in which they intermix different ideas, hold them up to critical examination, and are endlessly plastic and porous (Sen 2005b). Sen is also critical of the address to citizens through religious or other categories which tend to fix identities and obscure obligations owed through citizenship and human rights, not through cultural affiliation (Sen 2006 forthcoming). Nussbaum (2000, 2004), while frank about the importance of religion in her own life, is also troubled by the ways in which religious and cultural affiliations of people in the developing world come to be fixed and traditions viewed as unchanging.

The critique that the capability approach is too demanding in terms of the information required for evaluation linked to policy making is associated with the work of John Roemer (1996). A capability framework on gender equality in education requires consideration of information about conditions inside and outside school, complex local histories, and difficult processes of public deliberation. In conditions where urgent action is needed this is a demanding injunction. It requires access to and astute analysis of diffuse information sources. There are thus too many considerations and gathering the information is too expensive.

Some writers on the capability approach have looked at how capability frameworks for evaluation can be developed with local participation and yield important information for policy making and practice (Alkire 2003; Robeyns 2003). I have suggested how the approach can make use of historical and sociological analysis in order to deliver better policy (Unterhalter 2006b). Against these methods which point to alerting the approach to local complexities, we can set the work done by UNDP and the Human Development Reports which distil publicly available knowledge to yield capability informed analysis of global developments (Fukuda Parr 2003). The measures associated with this publication, most notably the Human Development Index, the Gender Development Index and the Gender Empowerment Measure (GEM) have all been attempts to consider what was feasible in relation to global measurement oriented towards information on capabilities. They speak to some of the concerns of the capability approach with multidimensionality as well as the need of global policy makers for streamlined information. Similar concerns were part of my work on a gender equality and education index (GEEI) (Unterhalter *et al.* 2005c; Unterhalter *et al.* 2005b; Unterhalter 2005b).

The thick cosmopolitanism associated with the approach has also been the basis of critique. Pogge (2002b, 2004) argues that a global consensus, say on education, will only be reached on the thin grounds of a minimal conception of rights and not Sen's thick notion of capabilities, agency and freedom. Pogge's 'institutional' understanding of human rights is an attempt to link rights with real institutions and to distinguish between acts that cause harm, for example forbidding girls to attend school under the Taliban, and acts that are only omissions, for example failing to ensure adequate clean water all the year round so that girls do not miss school on the days they menstruate (Unterhalter 2005d) He also makes the charge that positive obligations of assistance, for example for gender equality in schooling worldwide, are implausible. Vizard (2005: 20–1), however, points out that Sen emphasizes that the overall importance to achieve, say, gender equality in education cannot eliminate the special significance of negative freedom. Thus, campaigns to enrol girls in school cannot be aggressively taken forward, suppressing freedoms to criticize such a campaign in the press or demonstrate against its effects. She also shows how 'reasonable actions' to advance positive rights, for example through interventions, institution building and forms of dialogue, provide some means of avoiding the implausibility of completely open ended imperfect obligations.

The critiques of the capability approach are thus concerned with the metric of social justice, the complexity of the social settings in which global justice is feasible, the adequacy of regulatory mechanisms and the forms of information they draw on. However, with the exception of Pogge's suggestion of a very different orientation to thinking of global social justice, all the other critiques, it seems to me, can be accommodated within the flexibility and multi-dimensionality of the approach.

The capability approach in international policy: The Beijing Declaration

The capability approach has been important in framing policy that is significantly different from the instrumentalism of human capital theory and the overarching appeals to inherent human rights that talk primarily to an institutional and regulatory understanding of global social justice. Concern with freedoms forms part of the foundation for demands for gender equality in education in the Beijing Declaration of 1995. The Declaration affirms commitment to:

> Ensure the full implementation of the human rights of women and of the girl child as an inalienable, integral and indivisible part of all human rights and fundamental freedoms.
>
> (Beijing Declaration 1995)

The Declaration emphasizes empowerment linked with women's participation in decision making, in social development, equal sharing of work within the household and women's reproductive rights:

> Women's empowerment and their full participation on the basis of equality in all spheres of society, including participation in the decision-making process and access to power, are fundamental for the achievement of equality, development and peace; Women's rights are human rights;

> Equal rights, opportunities and access to resources, equal sharing of responsibilities for the family by men and women, and a harmonious partnership between them are critical to their well-being and that of their families as well as to the consolidation of democracy; Eradication of poverty based on sustained economic growth, social development, environmental protection and social justice requires the involvement of women in economic and social development, equal opportunities and the full and equal participation of women and men as agents and beneficiaries of people-centred sustainable development.
>
> (Beijing Declaration 1995)

The affirmation that women's rights are human rights draws out how socially situated women's demands for their rights are. The phrase also highlights how different the form of rights affirmed in the Beijing Declaration are to the form of rights affirmed in the EFA documents. The rights affirmed in the Beijing Declaration do not signal particular agents who must fulfil these rights in contrast to Jomtien and Dakar which outline very specific roles for governments, IGOs and partnerships with civil society. In the Beijing Declaration rights signal wide obligations to allow women full political, economic and social participation in all spheres. These obligations are both perfect and imperfect.

The sections of the Beijing Declaration that deal with education draw out opportunity and process dimensions and do not view education as simply limited to schooling. The declaration contains a commitment to:

> Ensure equal access to and equal treatment of women and men in education and health care and enhance women's sexual and reproductive health as well as education … Develop the fullest potential of girls and women of all ages, ensure their full and equal participation in building a better world for all and enhance their role in the development process. Ensure women's equal access to economic resources, including land, credit, science and technology, vocational training, information, communication and markets, as a means to further the advancement and empowerment of women and girls, including through the enhancement of their capacities to enjoy the benefits of equal access to these resources, inter alia, by means of international co-operation.
>
> (Beijing Declaration 1995)

This is the fullest statement on gender equality and education of any international Declaration, setting questions about the access of women and girls to education within a context of general social, political and economic development and most centrally within a framework of empowerment and capabilities that goes considerably beyond needs and rights. Unfortunately, it has been the vision that has been hardest to implement in the field of education.

Conclusion

This chapter has dealt with some of the key ideas in the capability approach and shown how the approach emphasizes different aspects of the demand for gender equality in education compared to those highlighted in the instrumental view of human capital theory and the intrinsic view relating to human rights. It has illustrated how a particular understanding of rights, linked to ethical demands in Sen's understanding of the capability approach, allows the approach to provide some of the normative framework that underpins rights and ethical demands. The chapter has also highlighted how the capability approach is dependent on other sources of knowledge and action. It is not a theory and does not suggest a particular epistemology, does not require particular ways of describing the world or demand prescribed forms of action. However, it is clear that reasoned actions concerned with a particular theory of justice need to be established in order to ensure the importance of process freedoms. What the procedures for doing this are on a global stage requires assessment of particular conditions and histories. The existence of international policy influenced by the capability approach, such as the Beijing Declaration, is an important starting point for making such an assessment. But it has been difficult to implement this vision in the work of the EFA movement. In trying to explore some of these difficulties some feminist critiques of the global social justice agenda on education are examined in the next chapter.

6 Power, meaning, and activism

Some problems for global social justice

Three problems in thinking about gender equality in education as a terrain for global social justice are articulated by the wider literature on gender, women, politics and education.

The first problem raised by feminist critics of social justice initiatives concerns questions of power. Sociological and anthropological studies which examine gendered relations in households, schools, the labour market, and the state call into question the certainties about social justice project formulated at a high level of abstraction in discussions of needs, rights or capabilities. Do these analyses of gendered power locally, nationally and internationally compromise the feasibility of institutionalizing a global social justice project for gender equality in education? In other words, does an acknowledgement of findings from empirical work regarding the nuance and complexity of gendered power and schooling present insurmountable obstacles for conceptualizing global social justice linked to gender equality in education?

The second problem concerns questions of meaning, identity and difference. These issues, considered by post-colonial and post-structuralist scholars in development studies, sociology and women's studies, are generally ignored in policy declarations and global social justice initiatives that deal with gender and schooling. But the issues have considerable salience given the multi-faceted inequalities these initiatives confront. Does consideration of difference and discourse so problematize the ideas regarding gender, schooling and global social justice that a global social justice project becomes unwelcome as well as difficult to achieve?

A third problem relates to feminist politics and women's organization. Feminist debates about empowerment and political action have suggested a range of different ways of 'doing politics'. These range from increasing the proportion of women in decision-making bodies to making political demands concerning what have been viewed as private matters of sexuality and family relations. They include political debates concerning sex work, reproductive rights, language and cultural representation. Does this reappraisal of politics present insurmountable challenges to the global social justice agenda focused on institutions and a key role for the state?

Gendered sites of power

The view of schools as sites where gendered power intersects historically with other processes of social division, such as race, ethnicity and age, and where contestation concerning these divisions takes place, raises questions for theory and practice in global social justice. Many sociological studies of schools indicate that far from these being spaces which fulfil needs, rights or capabilities, they establish complex social relations which sometimes confirm gender inequalities and sometimes contribute to their transformation (Skelton and Franics 2003; Aikman and Unterhalter 2005b). International and national policy pays insufficient attention to the gendered contexts in which policies are implemented.

Development assistance programmes of powerful G8 governments and UN organizations are difficult to disentangle from a geopolitics too often concerned with promoting a radical 'free trade' regime while taking limited action with regard to the most exploitative practices of economic globalization. Market liberalization generally undercuts the capacity of states to provide basic services to the poor with particular harsh effects for women, who carry out so much work in the care economy. For example, the establishment of special enterprise zones to entice multinational corporations to invest in poor countries are often accompanied by promises of tax exemptions and the waiving of minimum wage legislation. A consequence is continued low revenue for governments, which cannot tax multinationals to help provide for schooling. Low wages limit access to decent levels of health, housing and nutrition. The work of providing care for the sick, the preparation of food, and the maintenance of the household falls disproportionately on women, who have inadequate resources for support. The stark inequalities that contour so many features of global social relations raise key questions regarding how demands for gender, schooling and global social justice are implemented.

The significance of gendered power structures has been a key analytic concern for the theoretical and practical approach termed 'gender and development' (GAD), which emerged as a critique of WID in the late 1980s (see Chapter 3). GAD theorists noted how inequality needed to be challenged politically, for example through changing laws or redistributing income, and could not merely be ameliorated by a process of inclusion, welfare, or the belief in the greater efficiency of projects or programmes that included women. GAD grew partly out of poor rural and urban women's experiences of organization, debates about feminism in the third world, and feminist critiques in development studies (Sen and Grown 1988; Kabeer 1994). There was some resonance in this work with the approach of socialist feminists in Western Europe and the USA who campaigned for equal pay for all workers and for attention to the links between Marxist analysis of class relations and feminist analysis of gender division and the possibilities of egalitarianism. GAD focused on the sexual division of labour inside and outside the household, and on changing gendered structures of power. Some of its major aspirations were empowerment through restructured institutions, shifts in distribution, and changing forms of action to improve outcomes for the poorest (Kabeer 1999). Major GAD writers paid relatively little attention to issues concerning formal schooling, focusing instead on relations of production and macroeconomic questions (Kabeer 1994; Elson 1995).

Nonetheless, the GAD concern with power yielded some illuminating studies of gendered relations in households and the impact of macroeconomic polices on decisions about which children went to and remained in school (Vavrus 2003; Colclough *et al.* 2003; Leggatt 2005; Kingdon 2003). The extent to which women's schooling secured improved access to the labour market or merely confirmed the existing sexual division of labour in a particular industry, was much debated (Jayaweera 1999; Gibson 1996; Chen *et al.* 2005). Studies looked at how NGO networks and community organisations working on gender and change could exclude poor women and the difficulties women encountered in advancing their political demands, despite their access to education (Garrow 2005; Waylen 2004). Questions about education as the 'silver bullet' in relation to preventing infant mortality and decreasing fertility also emerged from this framework (Jeffery and Jeffery 1998).

Writings on gendered power influenced by GAD were a useful counter to some of the blanket claims of human capital theory regarding the instrumental benefits of investment in education, and assumptions that households make decisions about investment in human capital which paid little attention to labour market conditions and the sexual division of labour in the household. Empirical studies illuminated how complex household negotiations were, that entailed appeals to tradition and culture (Aikman 1999; Ames 2005). The abstract polarization of the debate about culture, rights and capabilities considerably underplays the complex meanings given by women and men to identifications based on culture within schooling. Furthermore, studies of difficulties in building institutions that tried to change gender relations showed how fragile these have been and how institutionalizing rights was not simply a matter of good drafting of documents or clear management (Goetz 1997; Rai 2003).

This empirical work on gendered sites of power raises the feasibility question for the theories discussed in the previous chapters and for all the three approaches to global social justice this book has identified. Any approach to a global agenda for gender and schooling should be assessed not only with regard just to the ethical ideas about social justice. How feasible implementing this ideal theory is, must also be a key dimension of thinking about justice (Brighouse 2004). Gendered power in schools, for example assumptions about what appropriate learning achievements are for girls and boys, how gendered structures of decision making and language result in gendered forms of learning and gendered forms of engagement with parents and community organisations, all illuminate how local conditions in a particular school setting make a global social justice agenda difficult to implement. This is the case whether such a project is conceived in instrumental, institutional or interactive forms. However, work on gendered power does not suggest that a global social justice agenda itself is not possible. Local conditions entail many contradictory processes, some of which might undermine a social justice agenda and some of which might make its achievement more feasible.

The conclusion that global social justice is not feasible has been a subtext in another stream in GAD research which has looked critically at donor initiatives and their failures to tackle injustice. Cecile Jackson (1998), for example, has noted how concepts of gender utilized in DFID poverty reduction policy in the late 1990s lost an engagement with injustice and meant little more as policy text or practice than 'including women'. Anna Robinson Pant's (2003) analysis of approaches to literacy work with women in Nepal highlighted how out of step the development assistance programme was with women's aspirations for different forms of literacy. Swainson (2000) has concluded that development assistance policy concerned with gender and education has often generated donor driven initiatives that promoted elite women or men who suffered few political or economic disadvantages. The implication in all these studies is that a global social justice agenda concerning gender and schooling is not just difficult to implement but undesirable given the ways in which such projects heretofore have been entangled with the unequal global politics of aid.

On the other hand some GAD scholars, like Diane Elson (1998), have written about the importance of 'talking to the boys' and getting involved in global policy making through global institutions. Some have indeed placed themselves in key positions drafting documents. Diane Elson was a member of the MDG task group on education, and Gita Sen, a key member of the Development Alternatives with Women for a New Era (DAWN) network which launched the GAD political manifesto in the 1980s, contributed to the work of the World Bank policy document on empowering women discussed in Chapter 4. An unresolved question for GAD theorists, therefore, is whether doing this policy work entails oversimplification and the possible 'betrayal' of GAD concerns with empowerment (Heward and Bunwaree 1999; Vavrus and Richey 2003).

The debate about how feasible it is to 'talk to' and change male bias in policy making is a key one for analysts of gender and education. Ambiguous partnerships with the state have been analysed as both facilitating and limiting the achievement of gender equality aspirations in education (Arnot and Dillabough 2000). Stromquist's (1995) important article argues that the state is necessary, but not sufficient to secure conditions for gender equality in education. Using the metaphor of 'romancing the state', she points out how feminists have 'sweet talked' the state to deliver education for women by offering 'good arguments' concerning how educated women are 'better' at productive work or motherhood, but have failed to take on direct political participation and wider demands for gender equality. Educators have romanced the state assuming the provision of access entails appropriate content and this has left many gendered processes of schooling unexamined. Intellectuals have also romanced the state confusing policy with action. Thus, critiques have been far less vociferous than they should have been giving the entrenched nature of gender inequalities and the inadequacy of policy alone to shift these. State engagement with gender equality is generally more symbolic than actual. Legislation has not been an effective instrument for social change and women activists have generally underestimated the ways in which education reproduces conventional gender identities. Stromquist (1995) concludes that change for gender equality in education needs to be encouraged from within the state, from outside the legislative process and from outside any particular national entity through international processes. She points to the necessity both to attempt to 'talk to' male bias in policy making and the formation of institutions, but also not to rely on this as the only form of politics for change.

The GAD literature has mainly been concerned with the ways in which gendered social relations intersect with education, but has paid little attention to gender within school or other education settings. In universities in Western Europe, North America and Australia research on gender and education developed side by side with GAD, but with few interconnections. Much of the existing academic literature was written after more than a century of compulsory primary schooling for girls and boys, extensive provision of secondary education for more than 50 years, and at least 20 years of expansion of higher education resulting in increased access for women and men. Hence questions of access have not been a major concern. For example the debate about whether girls flourished better in co-education or single sex schools, or disputes about whether the learning styles of girls and boys differed with regard to language and mathematics, assumed access was not an issue.

Moreover, much of the research in gender and education has stepped off from the direct experience of some key writers of feminist politics, their gendered experience as teachers, and issues that confronted them personally and politically concerning families and schooling (Weiner 1994; Leonard 2001; David 2003). A major focus has been how to analyse and explain the persistence of gender, class and race/ethnic inequalities, despite universal access and high levels of achievement by some girls. Much of this literature has been concerned with the gendered work of teachers and the gendered experiences of learners, considering schools and powerful discourses regarding gender and education as spaces that reproduce or reshape gendered social relations (Arnot *et al.* 1999; Skelton *et al.* 2006). These themes have been taken up in third world settings, but there are a very small number of empirically based studies that look at the nuance and complexity of gendered learning and teaching. Some examples are studies which explore gender-based violence in school (Leach *et al.* 2003; Mirembe and Davis 2001) and the gendered lives of learners and teachers (Vavrus 2003; Page 2005). This small literature stands in contrast to the large number of surveys underpinned by human capital theory or school effectiveness studies concerned with school quality that pay little attention to gender (Unterhalter 2005a). This points to an unfulfilled research project. The lack of more detailed research leaves it rather indeterminate whether a global social justice project for gender equality in education is absolutely undesirable, because it would always fail to address particular fine-grained instances of gendered power or only contingently undesirable in certain cases where initiatives for global social justice made conditions considerably worse.

Consideration of a supranational social justice project for gender equality in education based on the plans of large IGOs or INGOs has generally been written with some scepticism over its large ambitions, the ways in which demands for gender equality in education are translated into a universal project and the passivity often ascribed to women. Two main orientations colour this discussion. The first is the position that sees gender equality in education and the global justice agenda as only partially adequate to address the multiple forms of gender inequality women suffer. This is the source of Stromquist's earlier critique. In other work she has argued over many years that the injustices women suffer are multifaceted and are not all amenable to state regulation. She points out how there is a tendency in global policy formulation to view education systems as self-contained and therefore amenable to 'fixing' on very limited terms, for example through large-scale access programmes, without engaging wider questions of gender politics (Stromquist 1999, 2006). These criticisms can be levelled at the interventionist and institutional approaches to global social justice.

In a similar vein Jill Blackmore (2005) highlights how the discourse of rights used in relation to global social justice lends itself to co-option by neo-liberal policies that separate the social from the economic, promote niche markets of special interests, for example for elite groups of girls, that undermine wider notions of public good. She advocates a transnational feminist practice grounded in a theory of justice that deals with rights, recognition and redistribution and goes beyond the right of access to education and individual choice. The aim of such a politics is to demand that governments take responsibility for adequate funding and provision in schools. Elements of this vision can be seen in the interactive form of global social justice (see Chapter 9).

My own earlier work on this theme has considered the policy texts emerging in the 1990s from the World Bank and UNESCO. These stressed an essentialized and homogenized set of women's needs, rather than rights or the complexities of interlocking oppressions. I pointed to the challenge to build on some of the more emancipatory understandings available in the 1990s concerned with women's agency and collective action (Unterhalter 2000). I have subsequently argued for a strategic engagement with the MDGs as an opportunity for a wider dialogue and critique that could generate new forms of action (Unterhalter 2005d). This resonates with the argument this book is developing with regard to making connections between interventionist, institutional and interactive forms of global social justice to take on the challenge of wide aspirations for gender equality. Stromquist, Blackmore and I are all critical of aspects of how a global social justice agenda in education has thus far been articulated but we do consider that there are possibilities here for better politics and practice.

A contrasting view is developed by Anna Robinson Pant (2004). Noting the unequal power relations that characterize the conditions of the poorest women and girls in contrast to the cosmopolitan setting from which the programmes of the global social justice agenda emerge, she questions the premises of a global agenda. Instead, she argues for concern with local understandings. She makes a trenchant critique of the universal definition of 'gender equality' implicit in global policy statements arguing that this tends to downplay local understandings of gender and equality and, where these are considered at all, they are characterized as lower order 'cultural beliefs'. There is a general tendency in this policy work, she argues, to construct women as passive victims and not to look at the ways in which they might understand gender or schooling. Similar arguments are made by Andrea Cornwall (2001) with regard to the ways in which ideas about participation and partnership in development practice suggest a one size fits all notion of women's rights paying little attention to local nuance and complexity. Kate Greaney's (2006) detailed study of the implementation of a rights-based approach to education in Niger illuminated how little those charged with delivering the project shared an understanding of rights and gender equality with the global NGO that had planned it.

Some of this second group of writers are critical of the form in which any global ambitions might be formulated, while the first group consider that a global social justice agenda more engaged with the gender equality politics at global, regional, national and local level would yield better policy and practice. Thus, the feasibility argument takes a number of different forms. For the first group and some of the second it is framed in terms of whether better policy and practice are feasible given the different social formations engaged with a social justice agenda, for example women's groups, large IGOs and governments. For some of the writers, who focus on local understandings, no global policy or practice is ever desirable even were it feasible and suitably alert to local complexity. The assumptions of cosmopolitanism are seen to undermine the significance and importance of local specificity.

A number of empirical studies show how difficult the project is from both positions. Research in India on projects seeking to implement global social justice initiatives in education that intersect with local objectives, highlight that while interventions to get girls enrolled in school and women engaged in literacy campaigns may be relatively successfully achieved, broader dimensions of gender equality are much more difficult to achieve (Unterhalter and Dutt 2001; Page 2005; Oomen 2005). Frances Vavrus' study based in Tanzania (Vavrus 2003: 147–50) contrasts desire for the importance of education derived from global development strategies and decline for those who do not gain access to increased provision. A range of local processes intersect with global ambitions. Nonetheless, while there is much to critique there is also some possibility for better forms of action and research.

These studies suggest some ways in which concerns with rights or capabilities might be implemented through global social justice projects that go beyond interventions and institution building that are not alert to local complexities. Aspects of local conditions require full utilization of the multi-dimensionality that it seems the capability approach tries to express through some of its concern with human variability and the plurality of circumstances. Rights are not simply legal entitlements to political participation, as formally women have these in both India and Tanzania, but have not been able at either local or national level to secure a fairer distribution of resources amongst women and men, and between different socio-economic groups. They have not yet achieved recognition of gender relations within households that constrain what and how girls learn. The capability approach is particularly alert to how gender limits valued 'beings and doings'; it connects with a notion of human rights that suggests these limitations on capabilities also entail demands on others to support action for change. Thinking of rights interlinked with capabilities highlights how there are multiple injustices here. The works on India and Tanzania (Unterhalter and Dutt 2001; Vavrus 2003; Page 2005) do not suggest to me a global social justice project is not feasible. They indicate rather that if such a project were to take on the implication of rights and capabilities it would engage in much more transformatory politics than has been evident heretofore.

Who speaks for gender and schooling?

Global social justice policy declarations usually make claims on the basis of an assumed universal subject, for example the girl with inadequate schooling or subject to poverty and gender inequality. Post-structuralist and post-colonial critique considers this problematic. Post-structuralism questions the stability of definitions of gender paying particular attention to the fluidity and relational forms of gendered identifications and action, and the discursive practices in which they are located, which have profound consequences for political engagement. The implication of this analysis is that theories of global justice for gender equality in education lack appropriate nuance through their tendency to universalize. This has implications for the forms of transformational action they encourage.

Some writers have looked at how discourses, such as those associated with development as modernization form social practices and identities assigning particular gendered meanings that perpetuate colonial hierarchies (Parpart 1995, 2002). For example the use of universal categories of 'third world woman' are constructed and spoken by particular powerful discourses at a significant remove from the lives of particular groups of women and their shifting forms of local struggle (Mohanty 1988; Spivak 1999). These establish a hierarchy of those who have power to take decisions, accumulate wealth and those who are always relegated to the position where they are acted on and have no independent existence. These analyses question the hierarchies of value built into frames concerning rights which suggest that rationality and justice have their roots in histories of political emancipation in the West. As a consequence, different political histories are situated as 'other' and inferior, incapable of generating the notions on which a global social justice could rest (Escobar 1996; Sachs 2001). The implication of the post-structuralist and post-colonial orientation is that a single foundational idea concerning gender, schooling and global social justice like rights or capabilities is not simply limited by feasibility, but misguided in aspiration.

However, against this radical concern with the local and refusal of fixed meanings, a strand in post-colonial thinking continues to see the potential of transnational dialogues and of the interplay between positions as a theoretical and political opportunity. Alexander and Mohanty (1997: xxix) in considering how women have been positioned through colonial legacies, the interplay of old histories and new forms of capitalism allied with the state, and the links between feminist democracy and decolonization, point to the importance of the need to theorize transnational feminism which takes its orientation from feminist struggle This has been one strand in feminist post-development thinking.

The articles brought together in Kriemild Saunders' (2002) *Feminist Post Development Thought* engage with critiques of development linked to Western rationality, global hierarchies and the erasures or misrepresentations of culture, but some authors argue for improving some forms of development politics or practice, while others reject anything associated with 'development' as, in their view, this entails exploitation. Thus, although the appreciation of difference and relational forms of knowledge and action associated with post-foundational approaches are, not surprisingly, critical of a single global justice agenda, some writers adopt the position that the development of a global feminist agenda in gender equality and education is possible, yet could be done much better if it took some of the questions of empathy as seriously as efficiency. This analysis appears to me to resonate with the interactive approach to global social justice, which I have distinguished from interventionism and institutionalization.

Writers working on education within post-colonial or post-structuralist frames fall into two groups. On the one hand, there are those who see development associated with formal schooling actively disrupting indigenous knowledges and displacing the power women have gained through local networks that reproduce and sustain this knowledge. Modernization linked to schooling has rarely fulfilled the promise of economic growth or political improvements it has promised. Thus women have been left worse off (Smith 1999; Kolawole 1997). For these writers, implicitly, a global social justice agenda concerned with schooling entails further marginalization or these knowledges and an undermining of the power that preservation of and instruction in this knowledge affords women.

On the other hand, a group of post-colonial and post-structualist writers, while critical of the discourse of international development, are concerned with engaging in research to highlight the negative effects of development on women's and men's lives and thus contribute to a broader understanding in international development policy making and action. Frances Vavrus has been a key exponent of this view. She looks at the way Greene's 'feminist modern' figure appears in discourses of education that emerged in the 1990s. These cast education as a panacea for a wide range of social problems and situated the 'feminist modern' as a key provider of, and beneficiary from, education. The figure of the 'feminist modern' is accorded empowerment to change her circumstances, but only within certain parameters, defined by experts. These relate, say, to the acquisition of certain dispositions or certain concerns with the running of 'quality schools'. But the figure is not accorded empowerment with regard, say, to macro-economic decisions or foreign policy (Vavrus 2003: 25–44). Through detailed ethnographic study of gender relations in one area of Tanzania, Vavrus (2004, 2005) shows that despite this discourse, with its crude assumptions about women and society, macroeconomic relations and changing forms of the state have limited the forms of empowerment available to women. With a history marked by structural adjustment, the imposition of user fees for schooling, limited access to water, and changes in agricultural policy, families' decisions about sending daughters to secondary school have shifted over time. Decisions to keep girls from progressing to this level of education are not made on a simple calculation of household profit and loss as alleged by human capital theory, but on a complex assessment of the positioning of individuals in relation to national and global political economy. But Vavrus' conclusion is not that a social justice project to redress this is impossible. Her orientation to post-colonial theorizing prompts her to see the work in Tanzania as an unfinished project, an ongoing commitment to continue to research and act in a post-colonial way.

Similar conclusions are implicit in some of the work on gendered and sexualized identities of learners, written in response to the HIV epidemic. While oriented towards post-structuralism and questioning how children learn about and make gendered and sexualized identities, these writers consider questions of space – the circulation of ideas – and place – the formalization of certain boundaries – as part of a call for global policy, resources and appropriate practice to confront the pandemic (Pattman and Chege 2003; Kent 2004).

Much of the writing on gender, difference and discourse in relation to schooling and development, while critical of the discursive framings of policy and practice, is nonetheless optimistic. This optimism rests either on the basis of transnational feminist solidarities engaged with a project of constructing feminist selves and democratic forms or it considers there are gains to be made through critical scholarship examining gender relations, schooling and the effects of HIV and AIDS or structural adjustment. This research starts from another set of assumptions to that concerning the ethical individualism of rights and capabilities, but it reaches some similar conclusions regarding global social justice as an interactive project which requires deliberation, dialogue across difference and reasoned action to achieve substantive redistribution in complex conditions. But it arrives here by a route which is critical of global discourses, sceptical of policy frames, alert to colonial histories and meanings that overlay contemporary initiatives.

Doing politics differently

The third problem raised by feminist critics of global social justice questions the strategic planning and forms of organization used, highlighting how much these ignore the ways in which women's political activism has entailed concerns with empowerment and empathy. These are substantively different from the calculations of international relations which characterize work on global social justice.

The question whether women's movements engage a feminist politics has been much debated (Basu 1995; Molyneux 1998; Rai 2002). Part of the discussion is concerned with whether women's movements are to be analysed in terms of their membership, their objectives and the form of their actions. It must be stressed that not all women's movements are concerned with social justice issues. Some have engaged in vigorous action associated with destructive sectional identities and protection of exploitative relations. The ways in which transnational feminist formations concerned with aspects of justice engage relationally with local organizations and thus present a form of global social justice in process has been a question of abiding interest (Khanna 2001; Banaszak *et al.* 2003). This has looked at the expansion of political action by women beyond the realm of the state and struggles for representation in national and local government. The expanded political agenda has led to changes in states, in forms of representation and in the politicization of a range of social and economic issues from sexual harassment to land rights (Bhattacharjee 1997). But this literature has tended not to deal with questions of education and women's political organization, except in Latin America (Stromquist 1997; Eccher 2004)

Key debates in the feminist reshaping of politics have concerned, firstly, the dynamics of equality and difference and questions about the public–private divide. The tensions between the demand on the one hand that women have the same entitlements as men to take part in decision making and on the other that women have particular interests or perspectives that need to be represented in politics map onto particular contestations within education institutions (Lovenduski 2005; Unterhalter 2006a). Broadly, these divide as Nancy Fraser (1997) suggests between redistributional politics in which justice demands gender, like race, should disappear, and recognitional politics, where justice demands gender and race are required to be hypervisible, to redress past silencing. Concerns with difference often fragment further in attention to local multi-faceted experience and diversity.

Secondly, the politics of the public and the private concerns the ways in which women have been excluded from abstract notions of citizenship and political participation. Issues of embodiment, parenthood and the private realm of the household have been formally considered beyond the scope of the state, although much policy, often made with inadequate attention to gender relations has a direct bearing on these sites and these issues. This has been of major concern to women's political movements (Lister 1997; Yuval-Davis and Werbner 1999; Okin 1999a). Some searching reflection in education research has considered the ways in which a gendered politics of the family has been associated with marketization and privatization (Dehli 2000; David 2003). What are the implications of debates on equality, difference and the public–private divide for work on gender, schooling and global social justice?

Schooling conceived as a form of human capital lines up more closely with the views of social feminists concerned with difference and what sets women apart, than it does with views that are concerned to promote women's equal representation in decision making. Human capital starts from assumptions about the household as a gender neutral space and attributes to it particular 'rational' ideas concerning appropriate femininity, the labour market and the marriage market. These are believed to account for household decisions about education. Thus, policy drawing on human capital as a social justice vision is likely to stress the difference of girls in terms of rates of return from education. Human capital theory models the state on a vision of the household. It extrapolates from what is efficient for the household and concludes this is also efficient for the state. Analytically, this entails an abandonment of the public–private divide. The politics developed on the basis of human capital theory has thus both confirmed girls' difference, but simultaneously asserted the importance of state dictation to households with regard to schooling. However, as will be shown in the following chapters, the very inadequate education facilities states have been able to provide compromises this vision. These have fuelled demands for greater political will and quality schools to overcome 'household' recalcitrance. The assumption in human capital theory is that difference resides with girls. For households and nations they represent inefficiency in terms of rates of return. Human capital theory does not demand a different form of politics oriented to women's empowerment or particular forms of empathy. Rather it works with a politics steeped in utilitarianism relating to state action to secure better outcomes. The global social justice interventions associated with human capital theory, while concerned with women's difference, are not generally oriented to confronting or changing this.

Schooling, conceived of as a right or a capability, is more closely oriented to views about women's entitlements to equal representation in politics, equal participation in the labour market and in social and cultural practices. Policy drawing on rights or capabilities as a social justice vision is often likely to stress the equal rights of girls and boys, rights that cannot be rescinded even if girls do well at school in comparison to boys. But rights and capabilities pull in somewhat different directions with regard to the public–private divide. Rights in practice, despite some theorizations of the moral basis of rights that are more multi-dimensional, are generally thought of as justiciable and therefore demand a public sphere where justice is seen to be done. However, capabilities indicate only a space of evaluation, which could be public, private or somewhere between. The politics concerned with girls' schooling, rights and capabilities has thus been situated within broader demands concerning political, economic and social rights, often particularly concerned with the way lack of rights impacts on the private sphere. However, a problem for states and NGOs making demands in terms of rights has been the weak regulatory mechanisms to ensure equality, the lack of articulation between different organizations working with rights-based agendas, and the ways in which state and IGO policies are interpreted in households and communities that lack political power. Overcoming this points towards a politics concerned with empowerment and empathy.

Over some decades, concepts of empowerment and agency have been examined conceptually and empirically as a possible form to analyse some of the many dimensions of women's politics, particularly the politics of the poorest (Kabeer 1994; Lister 2004). Initial attempts to give empowerment conceptual coherence suffered from a number of difficulties. These included how best to specify the relationship of agency and empowerment to social context and theories of justice. In addition, there has been a problem with changing meanings of empowerment, as the language of choice and agency came to be associated with agendas about privatization and global restructuring, very different to those of the women's movement (Yuval-Davis 2003; Rai 2004).

The concept of empowerment centres analysis on the interface between generally poor and marginalized women and their capacities to exercise power particularly through self-expression, decision making, and distribution of resources. Rowlands (1997), developing ideas initially formulated by Naila Kabeer (1994), makes two intersecting distinctions. Firstly, she distinguishes between three different formations of empowerment: power over – the power to control and direct; power to – the power from within to reflect on information or take decisions; and power with – the power to work with others for change. Thus *power over* would entail a teacher having the power to take decisions about what should be included in a curriculum. *Power to* indicates the information and understanding she draws on to take these decisions, while *power with* denotes how she works with other teachers, parents, children and the education bureaucracy to implement these decisions. Rowlands also distinguishes between three different arenas in which empowerment occurs – the personal arena, close relationships such as the household and the collective arena (Rowlands 1997). While a woman teacher might have power over decisions about her own children's education in the household as she uses her salary to pay for their expenses, she might have only limited power over the allocation of resources in other arenas. Note that these different levels of describing power rely on a surrounding set of assumptions about gender equity to give notions of empowerment content. There is nothing in this theorization of empowerment that suggests what empowerment should be about.

Kabeer (1999) provides an approach to overcoming some of these difficulties suggesting three dimensions of empowerment which each indicate engagement with particular social structures and constitute a different meaning of choice from that advocated by advocates of the free market. Empowerment entails, firstly, access to resources; secondly, agency in decision making and negotiating power; and thirdly, achievements of outcomes of value. Kabeer argues that an adequate assessment of empowerment requires triangulation of measurement of all three dimensions. While this rigorous framework can be criticized for the rather sharp distinction between resources and agency on the one hand, and agency and outcomes on the other, a distinction that is often difficult to discern empirically, the approach does illuminate some interesting critiques of the simple WID stress on equality of resources. Mapping Kabeer's framework onto the field of education in order to explore questions of empowerment one would need to assess resources such as access to schooling up to a certain level. Access here includes retention, that is the capacity to retain access, and achievement, that is capacity to gain knowledge resources from schooling. Women's agency would need to be examined, for example, their participation in decision-making about education, in households, schools education ministries, or village education councils. Achievements that flow from education are not just narrowly defined notions of reading and writing up to a certain level, but more complex notions of well being (Unterhalter 2005d). Janet Raynor (2007 forthcoming) has explored this empirically in Bangladesh showing how the dimension of resources is much more easily fulfilled than that of agency or outcomes.

Ruth Lister (2004: 130), while writing more generally about poverty, provides an additional way in which empowerment or agency can be mapped. Her typology distinguishes everyday and strategic forms of action and personal and collective agency. This allows an analyst to see some of the differences between a single woman's daily determination to find the school fees for her children through long hours of work and denying herself food, a struggle she undertakes largely on her own – 'getting by' – and the same mother's long-term planning to educate all her children in this way – or use the earnings of some of the older children – with a view to them not experiencing the same levels of poverty – 'getting away'. These personal acts of resilience and strategy largely located within the private realm of the household are distinguished from those where the same mother might confront a local education official about the failure to pay a teacher's salary, thus compromising the quality of education the children receive – 'getting back' – and the woman's activism in a political party or feminist organization demanding the abolition of school fees, adequate and accountable funding for teachers' pay and human rights – 'getting organized'.

Lister concedes the typology separates out analytically what are frequently intermixed processes. Indeed the existence of a feminist organization might catalyse a woman's everyday or strategic personal planning, or vice versa. What the typology suggests, however, like Rowlands' and Kabeer's work, is that there are multiple locations for feminist action outside the state. Discussions of empowerment and agency do not of themselves say much about the equality and difference questions regarding the form and substantive demands of women's organizations. But the writing does help us see how human capital theory talks to only one arena of agency 'getting away'. Rights are important for resources and might help establish the context for getting back and getting organized. Rights to education might give a woman appropriate knowledge and the standing in her community to confront official neglect. They might provide access to the networks that will sustain organization. But the concept of capabilities is flexible enough to operate in all the different areas of empowerment and agency. Thus, capabilities entail reasoned action to support children in school – getting by – and plan for the education of all family members – getting away – as well as reasoned deliberation about where there have been failures of provision and how to secure these – getting back – and work with others to do this – getting organized. Sen uses the terms wellbeing and agency freedom and achievement to denote all these different areas (Sen 1980; Unterhalter 2005d). Working in all dimensions appears to provide the fullest basis for a feminist politics engaged with gender schooling and global justice.

The literature on women's political activism illuminates how institutional and interactive forms of global social justice need to engage on a multi-dimensional terrain. Aspects of empowerment, empathy and equality raise issues concerning the site, content and form of political action for gender equality in education and global social justice.

Conclusion

This chapter has looked at some critical perspectives on ideas for gender, schooling and global social justice. Analyses of gendered power raised the problem of the feasibility of a global social justice project concerned with gender and schooling. Seeing gender as a relational discourse situated within multiple formations of the post-colonial has questioned not only the feasibility of global social justice project, but its desirability and conceptual foundations. The question of equality and difference as raised by analysts of women's political movements and feminist organization questioned the nature of the institutions that might deliver global gender equality in schooling. If we put aside the views of those writers who consider all engagements in global social justice projects flawed because the contours of contemporary global political economy are inherently ordered in favour of the most powerful, there is a surprising consensus from some of the most critical quarters with regard to the possible feasibility and desirability of a global social justice agenda concerning gender and schooling. Many of the critical writers reviewed in this chapter considered a global social justice project for gender equality in education worth pursuing if questions of gendered power, relational forms of meaning making and the multiple sites of women's political activism can be engaged. With these critical concerns in mind I now want to look at accounts of what has and has not been achieved in global social justice work on gender and schooling. Thus far I have tried to map some of the ways in which ethical cosmopolitan ideas have been invoked and reworked in the context of debates about gender and schooling as global concerns. In Part III I consider how these ideas have been put into practice.

Part III

Schooling and global social justice

Interventions, institutions and interactions

Introduction

In Part I and Part II interventionist, institutional and interactiontist forms of global social justice for gender equality in education were distinguished. These divisions were drawn on the basis of differing approaches to cosmopolitanism and the locus of political action. Each rests on different analytical ideas about gender and contrasting understandings of the political basis for concern with gender equality in education.

Thus far I have dealt primarily with the ethical and conceptual language in which global social justice projects for gender equality in education have been framed. In the following chapters I turn to look at how the three approaches have been put into practice.

Interventionist approaches to global social justice, associated with addressing a basic minimum of need, or delivering education to girls to ensure efficient economic, political or social development, have been associated with the largest programmes and commanded the most extensive research. These deliver clear policy messages and entail very precise forms of action, for example enrolling girls in school or ensuring that they pass examinations. Programmes can thus be evaluated in relatively straightforward ways.

Institutionalist approaches to global social justice have been concerned with establishing legal, organizational and regulatory processes to address some of the gender dimensions of continuing inequalities in schooling. Thus they have the potential to use global funding mechanisms to remedy gender imbalances in the allocation of funds for education. Gender disaggregated data collection can help inform decisions about how resources are allocated. This approach to global social justice has some powerful advocates in the field of development assistance, but gender mainstreaming in education institutions has not yet realized its potential. Few instances of the instiutionalizing approach have been systematically researched. While concern with regulation suggests a clear policy line, putting this into practice nationally and globally has been difficult partly because of the depth of gender inequalities.

Interactionist approaches to global social justice have aimed to link diverse groups of civil society and state actors to mobilize globally for gender equality in education. While the approach talks to concerns with human diversity, empowerment, imperfect obligations, and different ways of engaging politically, economically and socially, this approach has been the hardest to implement, and many initiatives remain disconnected from each other. To the extent that they work with interventionist or institutionalist approaches, they generally do so in ways that do not argue strongly for the diversities this approach seeks to reflect. Lack of long-term research makes it difficult to come to conclusions about how to assess this approach. While it is more sensitive to the disparate actors and concerns which comprise a global social justice agenda on gender and schooling, it lacks a clear, prescriptive policy message.

In the chapters that follow, I look at initiatives associated with each of the three approaches, drawing out their achievements, identifying their main advocates, and assessing the nature of the difficulties they have encountered in putting a global social justice agenda into practice.

7 Interventions

'Get girls in'

Interventionist approaches to global social justice, gender, and schooling are largely concerned with providing schools for all children and ensuring that girls are enrolled. These initiatives have been particularly attentive to aspects of girls' difference that have made them 'hard to reach' and thus difficult to enrol in school. Interventions such as providing stipends or food for schooling have been rather less concerned with what girls learn in school and how they are taught, unless this has a bearing on access and enrolment. Thus, questions of the safety of the school and the quality of learning become second order concerns. Generally, as will be shown, interventionist approaches to global social justice elide with a form of thin cosmopolitanism that respects particular spaces for the nation, the state, and the family provided they accede to a minimal global demand that all girls have access to school.

Enrolling girls in school

Interventionist actions focusing on programmes to enhance girls' access to school have been a prominent feature of aid agencies' work with governments in countries with a low NER for girls or where there were significant problems with retaining girls in school for five years. For example in Mali between 1989 and 1999 girls' NER increased from 15 per cent to 36 per cent due largely to programmes which concentrated on community awareness raising about girls' education, building more schools and training more women teachers. This EFA agenda by the Ministry of Education received extensive support from USAID, Dutch development assistance and a number of other IGOs and INGOs (Ahouanmènou-Aguuey 2002: 3–4). Similar targeted interventions to reduce the primary gender gap nationally or in particular regions have been described in Laos, India, Bangladesh, Nepal, Malawi, and Uganda (Kwesiga 2002; Rose 2003b; Ramachandran 2003; Lee 2004; Bista 2004; Raynor 2005a).Virtually all of these have been associated with significant inputs from donor governments and UN agencies, although in India development assistance in this form was much contested.

By far the most successful intervention to increase enrolments take place when governments abolish various forms of user fees, employ more teachers with appropriate training, work closely with community groups to identify children out of school and provide support for families to send daughters to school. Herz and Sperling (2004: 45) identified four key areas that research evidence confirmed 'worked' as a means for governments to get girls to school. These were to make girls' schooling affordable by eliminating fees and offering scholarships to certain populations; to provide safe schools nearby every village; to make schools safer places where girls were encouraged to learn, and to provide quality education associated with educated and trained teachers, up-to-date books and a curriculum oriented to the contemporary world. The report of the Millennium Task Force on Education confirmed these recommendations calling for attention to the elimination of school fees, the provision of cash transfers to families who kept children in school, and the provision of school feeding programmes (Birdsall *et al.* 2005: 54–7). The report also detailed the significant improvements in girls' access achieved if women teachers were employed, if schools could be kept safe places for girls to study, if the distance to travel to school was decreased, and if school timetables were flexible to allow girls to work inside or outside their homes (Birdsall *et al.* 2005: 59–60).

All these interventions entailed steps governments could take either drawing on their own revenue base and resources within the country, or through utilizing development assistance in the forms of funding to compensate for the abolition of fees, to help finance building more schools, development of curriculum and training packages. Financing schooling that was provided free at the point of access and building schools in more rural settlements, generally required little knowledge of, and engagement with debates concerning gender that went beyond access issues. Generally, curriculum change and teacher training associated with interventionist forms of global social justice called for development assistance to help provide more training of women teachers and more images of women in textbooks (Sanou and Aikman 2005; Sales 1999).

Global bodies like the Millennium Task Force, which summarized existing knowledge of policy and practice, encouraged government action through pointing to successful interventions. These were presented as technical solutions which did not invoke complex discussions about gender or rights. In 2005, UNESCO's high level EFA group discussed whether a single intervention, for example the global abolition of school fees would inject a new dynamism with regard to girls' schooling in the face of the missed target on MDG 3 (North 2006a). The focus on free schooling worldwide as an achievable intervention had been a key demand of the GCE throughout 2005 (GCE 2005a, 2005b).

It can be seen how interventionist approaches to global social justice rest on thin cosmopolitanism by virtue of their commitment to non-interference with substantive issues of national policy. The strategies of development partners, be they bilateral or multilateral, or reflect the demands of sections of global civil society do not compromise or question the authority of the state. Uganda offers the prime example of a country where the interventionist approach to global social justice has melded well with the political programme of the government. Uganda instituted a package of free schooling, improved teacher training and considerable investment in curriculum and school development generally focusing on girls' access and participation. In the 1990s there was a huge expansion in primary enrolment. In 1997, the policy package for UPE was introduced. This provided free primary education for the first four children in any family and stipulated that these should not just be sons if there were also daughters. As a result of UPE, the numbers of children in schools increased at a great rate. From 2000, gender became a key concern within the Ministry of Education with the launching of the National Strategy for Girls. There were a number of initiatives at central and regional government level and within school districts to incorporate gender issues into teacher training and curriculum development, for example through specific focus on gender issues as part of initial training, as a requirement in lesson planning and as a feature of monthly teacher development discussions by school clusters (Unterhalter *et al.* 2005c; Burns 2004). A number of programmes working at district level took up gender as a key theme in their planning and practice often working closely with NGOs (Garrow 2005).

Development assistance helped finance this and supported technical assistance in various forms. From 1999–2003, the annual average amount of aid was US $47.2 million, although this translated into only US $1.3 per head (UNESCO 2005a: 416). Global interventions to assist the gender dimensions of education provision in Uganda can be compared with neighbouring Kenya, where before the elections of 2003, little aid flowed. Thus over the same period in Kenya the annual average amount of aid was US $23 million which translated into 70 cents per head (ibid.).

The tables in Appendix 3 show the increasing numbers of children in school in Uganda and how the NER among girls and boys virtually doubled over 10 years between 1990 and 2000 (Table 3.1, Appendix 3). The aggregated numbers are impressive, but the changes in regional differences are also telling. Table 3.2 (Appendix 3) charts increases in enrolment by district. In districts with a large gender gap in 1990 – Eastern, Western and Northern – this had narrowed considerably by 2002, although the size of the gap in the Northern Region was still a matter of concern.

Interventions and development assistance policy

Not all governments succeeded in developing co-ordinated packages of interventions. Malawi, with strong support from USAID, introduced free primary school education for all girls who did not repeat a class from 1991. Enrolments increased dramatically from 772,000 to 1.5 million between 1991 and 1996 (Kanjaye 2001). However, this high enrolment was not sustained because there were not sufficient teachers and infrastructure (Gibson 2005).

The interventions to boost the numbers of enrolments was only slowly linked to work on curriculum and teacher development.

USAID's focus on girls' education from 1990 was primarily concerned with interventions that were believed to work. The GABLE project in Malawi, which ran from 1991–8, was predicated on the instrumental view that increasing girls' enrolment in school would reduce fertility. It supported the Government in a range of interventions linked to the 'what works' agenda including building more schools, providing textbooks, training more teachers and supporting school mobilization campaigns and fee waivers for some girls (Anzar *et al.* 2004). In 1994, the new President announced he would make access to primary school free. Support was sought from USAID to help fund this. Opinions are divided on whether the huge influx of children into school and the scramble to train further teachers, build additional classrooms, and support learning was beneficial or not (Gibson 2005). In the late 1990s, GABLE developed a gender aware curriculum for use in schools and focused on girls' attainment in school as well as providing some scholarships for secondary school. But it did so in a climate of generally low quality school provision despite high levels of enrolment by girls (Anzar *et al.* 2004: 8–10). The programme to get girls into school was not associated with wider concern with gender linked to land rights, inheritance or political participation.

GABLE drew heavily on US technical assistance, evaluations by US researchers and was primarily carried out through very particular forms of contact with the government of Malawi. It was not an intervention concerned with institution building and it did not involve a broad dialogue with civil society critics of the government and promotion of voices clarifying meanings of gender and rights. Thus work with women's organizations or feminist activism was not a feature of GABLE, which focused on meeting basic needs for schooling. The catchword of GABLE was to 'get girls in' school. This highly focused but limited objective has been used again by USAID in the programme it developed in Mali and was a general feature of USAID's WID programmes, as a detailed evaluation of projects in contexts as varied as Morocco, Guatemala and Peru made clear (Brush *et al.* 2002: 5).

Interventions in Kenya and India

In Kenya when a new government was elected in 2003, one of their first actions was to abolish school fees with the result that 1.3 million children returned to school. There was a lack of classrooms, teachers and general support for the large numbers of newly enrolled children and the huge increase was not fully sustained (Kamau 2004). However, the initiative brought large-scale development assistance to Kenya with major programmes developed by bilateral and multilateral donors. Although countrywide enrolments increased with free primary schooling in some districts, conditions at the schools were not good and some parents continued to keep their daughters away. For example in the harsh conditions of Turkana district in the Rift

Valley in 2004, 60 per cent of children did not go to school – 28,000 boys were in primary school, but only 18,000 girls. Of the 3,000 children who proceeded to secondary school from this district in 2004 only 1,000 were girls (UNICEF 2005b). Interventions thus did not have immediate effects. They were a short-term form of action to address immediate gaps in school provision. They were not conceived to alter internal relations in families, communities or national states.

Interventions by governments and their development partners, for example the introduction of free schooling, have been necessary steps to begin to secure gender equality in education, but were not sufficient either to enhance education provision for children attending schooling or to challenge other aspects of gender and poverty which resulted in girls being kept out of school.

In India, the District Primary Education Programme (DPEP) was initiated in 1994, as a partnership between the Government of India and a number of international donors: UNICEF, the World Bank, the EU, DFID, and the Government of the Netherlands. DPEP identified 271 districts in 18 states with low levels of school enrolment by girls, scheduled caste and scheduled tribe children, yet high levels of motivation for schooling on the basis of previous education campaigns. A many-stranded approach to EFA was adopted which involved community mobilization to enrol children in school, teacher development, curriculum change, the establishment of devolved district and school governance with increased representation for women on village education committees and the mobilization of a women's empowerment programme. Under DPEP, 16,000 new schools were built and 3 million additional school places became available. Controversially, the programme promoted the development of alternative schools, where teachers, many of whom were women with lower qualifications than those required for teachers in standard government schools, were employed with lower pay and reduced opportunities for career development (Ramphal 2005).

There were falls in enrolment in some DPEP districts over the life of the programme, possibly associated with changing demographics within these districts and the decision of better off families to take children – often boys – to private schools. DPEP districts were associated with girls coming to comprise a greater proportion of children enrolled at primary school. Over the period from 1995–2001, girls increased as a proportion of children enrolled in DPEP districts from 45.6 to 47.5 per cent (Aggarwal 2002: 120).

DPEP was associated with a range of gender strategies which included gender training for education officials, the involvement of women in education management, discussions about gender in teacher development courses, the removal of material with gender bias from textbooks, the development of early childhood education programmes, and the mobilization and organization of women through a women's advocacy project Mahila Samakya (Aggarwal 2002: 119). DPEP was thus a combination of an interventionist and an institutional programme of the form discussed in the next chapter.

Interventions had multiple consequences. While increasing the level of girls' enrolment, they also contributed to forming new class and gender divisions between teachers and within communities. The institutional form of global social justice associated with the programme allowed women to participate in decision-making bodies on certain terms and engage in some economic and social and development projects that challenged aspects of gender inequality. But the programme placed some limits on what women could achieve (Unterhalter and Dutt 2001; Ramachandran and Jandhyala 2005). The fragility of institutional approaches to a more substantive global social justice in relation to a gender equality agenda are discussed more fully in Chapter 9.

DPEP provided some of the foundation from which the government developed *Sarva Shiksha Abhiyan* (SSA) in 2000 as a programme for universal elementary education (UEE). SSA was planned to ensure that all children in the 6–14 age group would complete elementary school by 2010 (Government of India 2001). Some of the interventions that had been used to secure girls' access to learning through DPEP were transferred to SSA. Shobha Bajpai, a village teacher in Madhya Pradesh in North India chronicled for the *Beyond Access* project newsletter *Equals* the changes she saw as a result of the work of SSA after 2000. Although approaches to curriculum, rules, examinations and teaching styles remained the same, and much of the gendered content of schooling was not challenged, nonetheless there were some important infrastructural changes that enhanced access:

> Without doubt some things are changing. The government have been funding school building and enhancement programmes. Nearly every village school has toilet facilities and work is in progress through SSA for those that don't. A number of surveys are underway to ensure that every child is counted and attending school. Efforts are being made to reach out to children who have dropped out of school through bridging courses that end in 5th and 8th class exams, and boarding hostels provide facilities for girls to attend these courses. Free textbooks are now available to Dalit and Adivasi boys and all girls from classes 6 to 8. Free uniforms are provided for all girls from class 1 to 8 and bicycles are provided for Dalit and Adivasi girls who live more than 1 km from school. Teacher training has been decentralized … Girls' enrolment and their completion of 5, 8, 10 and 12 years of schooling is gradually improving, and the exam results show that more children, and more girls are achieving at these stages … In 1986 when I joined Uda School there were no girls enrolled in Standard 8. In 1987 there were two. By 2003 girls made up 40 per cent of those completing Standard 8.
>
> (Bajpai 2005: 7)

Although this is an account of only one school, it is valuable, partly because the author is generally critical of socially sanctioned gender inequalities in the society and the way school reinforces this. Nonetheless she notes village level interventions that were being put into practice and were succeeding.

SSA drew on some development assistance from DFID, the World Bank and the EU, but the largest proportion of funding – 70 per cent – came from the Indian government. In 2002 the Indian Constitution had been amended to make elementary education, that is eight years of schooling, a fundamental right. This exemplifies the thin cosmopolitan argument where a national government takes leadership of education reform and development assistance supports locally determined priorities.

But thin cosmopolitanism had its limits. Not all governments succeeded in agreeing or instituting an interventionist approach to girls' schooling. As the tables in Appendix 1 show, in some countries girls access to and survival over five years in primary school barely increased between 1990 and 2002. Some of the reasons for governments' failures to increase access to school for all children and address particular discrimination against girls included episodes of war with attendant destruction of schools and disruption of teaching, heavy burdens of debt repayment which meant lack of investment in the education sector, inefficiencies in the bureaucracy so that teachers were paid only intermittently and schools had no equipment. High levels of poverty meant families could not afford the charges associated with schooling. When governments lacked resources and tried to transfer the costs of schooling to communities, families kept children out of school. A recent study of the level of government actions on gender and education in Commonwealth countries in Africa found that where there had been substantial interventions through a high level of policy engagement and action by governments, there had been improvements in girls' education over the decade. Patchy or inconsistent interventions by governments, sometimes with and sometimes without development assistance, resulted in unsustained gains (Unterhalter *et al.* 2005c). Thus thin cosmopolitanism, while protecting state autonomy, sometimes failed to support and sustain global social justice interventions.

Mobilizing for gender parity

The interventionist approach was evident throughout the 1990s and confidence that getting girls into school could be relatively quickly achieved was part of the thinking that set the target for MDG 3 earlier than all the rest. The target, set in 2000 was for gender parity in primary schooling by 2005. The gender parity target demanded no more than that there should be equal numbers of girls and boys in primary school by 2005. It therefore envisaged interventions on very limited terms to address a very minimal notion of need. Nonetheless this was an enormously ambitious target, and would have required an unprecedented global mobilization to meet it.

Unfortunately, the anticipated outcome did not materialize. UNICEF took the lead in trying to mobilize a global approach to interventions. But it was 2003 before it had identified where it would focus and how it would work. It identified 25 countries that met one or more of five criteria: low enrolment rates for girls, gender gaps of more than 10 per cent in primary school, more than 1 million girls out of school, included in the FTI for special accelerated funding, and hard hit by crises such as HIV/AIDS or conflict (see Table 3.3, Appendix 3). The initiative, termed 25 by 2005, was intended to accelerate progress on girls' education and help countries 'eliminate gender disparity' (UNICEF 2003: 4). But UNICEF was pulled in two directions by the logic of thin cosmopolitanism. The initiative stressed the urgency of the task of addressing girls' education. It was to be treated as in need of emergency action and staff would 'pull out all the stops' to scale up successful pilot projects (UNICEF 2003: 5). At the beginning of 2005, Carol Bellamy, then Executive Director, reflected on how the world had mobilized to provide humanitarian assistance in the wake of the tsunami and drew parallels with the destructive natural forces and the harm that would result from girls left out of school. She concluded that the time had passed for excuses why action could not be taken.

> If the world can mobilize so quickly and effectively against the forces of nature, it can surely mobilize quickly and effectively to make sure that every girl and boy will be in school before the year is out.
>
> (Bellamy 2005: 94)

But this confidence that interventions to get girls into school was like putting up tents and delivering water and that it would draw a generous global response as the tsunami had, was misplaced. By the end of the year the world had not mobilized fully as she had urged.

The 25 by 2005 initiative acknowledged that interventions were socially located and needed much negotiation. It noted the need to win the argument about the importance of girls' education in particular national and local settings and how success would depend on what could be negotiated with governments (UNICEF 2003: 4–5). UNICEF was clear it would involve itself at every level:

> The concept of accompanying a country involves long term support with a 'total resource package'. It means being there through thick and thin without being unduly obtrusive or trying to dictate. It means sharing and empathising with the vision and objectives of the country, and yet being constructive with support and advocacy for change where needed.
>
> (UNICEF 2003: 5)

This responsiveness to local conditions could not mesh with a forceful interventionist dynamic to 'get girls' into school.

Over and above this internal tension within the 25 by 2005 initiative, UNICEF lacked the financial resources to mobilize the huge numbers of staff needed to make its vision a reality. In 2004 Sarantu Yunusa, the

Basic Education Project Officer for UNICEF in the North East region of Nigeria, described the huge area she had to cover and how UNICEF had to wear 'a large hat of responsibility'. Despite support from central and local government, from head teachers, teachers, and from individuals contributing at whatever level they could, resources were limited. She saw the intervention as long term 'I am hopeful that in 20 years time things will be better for our daughters' (Yunusa 2004: 6). Thus, the confidence of the interventionist dynamic to meet the first target for MDG 3 had to be tempered by the realities of limited resources and the complexities of the task.

Connecting interventions and institutions

Generally, interventions tended to be successful when they were linked with an approach to institution building. But some of the difficulties of linking an interventionist with an institution building approach were evident in Bangladesh. The Programme to Motivate, Train and Employ women teachers in rural secondary schools (PROMOTE) was a large-scale project with an explicit focus on gender issues established in 1995 with EU funding. PROMOTE's goal was to:

> facilitate and accelerate a smooth transition to a more gender-sensitive and equitable society in rural Bangladesh by promoting girl-friendly secondary schools and high quality teaching in rural areas. The project purpose is to facilitate the employment of more and better-prepared women teachers in rural secondary schools.
>
> (PROMOTE 2001)

There was an institution building aim for the project to go beyond 'simple' interventions in education to secure conditions for a more generally gender equitable society. An impact study conducted in 2005 showed that where PROMOTE gender resource groups had been active in teacher training colleges there had been a growth in gender awareness, but that this had developed slowly over the 10 years of the project, and had not yet broadened from the groups specifically engaged with the project (Raynor 2005b). However, the evaluation concluded that good management practice could facilitate an understanding of equality.

> The most important findings indicated the need for a combination of good understanding of gender issues, good teamwork, support from Principals, and an overall commitment to promoting gender equality. In the absence of any or all of these, progress was likely to be hampered.
>
> (Raynor 2005b: 2)

While the evaluation had not looked at the ways in which gender resource groups in teacher training colleges could link with other civil society groups engaged with issues concerning women and gender, the limited opportunities for making these links seemed to isolate them unduly. The implication of this was that the institutional approach could only build very slowly towards success taking all constituencies with it. There was no 'quick win' using this approach in contrast with the spectacular gains the interventionist approach in Bangladesh had secured in increasing enrolments and training women teachers.

There is a puzzle at the centre of the accounts of differences in success between interventionist and institution building approaches. The constraints on governments with regard to interventionist approaches focused on access were partly external, linked to debt and 'internal' linked to infrastructure provision and capacity. The assumption in the 'what works' approach was that these difficulties were not insurmountable. In contrast, there was no agreement on how to develop institutional and interactive approaches to global social justice, how equality and quality connected and what the constraints on governments were in initiating these. The assumption at Jomtien and Dakar was that quality education for everyone would entail equality. But this assumption overlooked the existing gendered social relations in schools, bureaucracies and in the societies of which they are part. Good learning and teaching did not automatically entail either understandings about gender inequality, insights into how to change this, or approaches to building networks of support for change as the example from Bangladesh shows. Adequate learning and teaching linked to the prevailing curriculum does not necessarily address the intensity and force with which views about gender inequality are held or overcome the consequences of decades of gender inequality.

Fundamentally, the institution building approach on training gender groups in Bangladesh did not fully engage with the depth of norms of gender inequality and the range of resources these initiatives needed to effect transformation. This was a task that went beyond state provision and good project planning. Unlike the interventionists for whom the problems of providing for *access* were generally a problem of state capacity, and global assistance formulated in terms of eliminating gross insufficiency could address this relatively simply, the problems of linking quality and equality and working institutionally and strategically for change tended to be problems that arose because of inadequate links between state and civil society to drive and critique this agenda.

A global civil society voice to support change makers inside and outside government could play an important part in building knowledge about and commitment to gender equality in education, but building this level of mobilization has not been easy for global civil society to achieve. The ways in which donor governments understood their obligations with regard to development assistance to partner governments working institutionally for gender equality in education was not well articulated with an appreciation of issues concerning citizenship and global collaboration by women's movements. These more diffuse forms of network, inclusion in decision-making and intervention within and outside government did not proceed linearly in terms of what works unlike the simple forms of development assistance entailed by the interventionist approach.

The most dramatic social justice achievements of the period 1990–2006 used an interventionist approach to the problem of gender and schooling designed to address the problem of insufficiency and 'get girls' into and through school. This approach was relatively easy to resource from local and international revenues and could be achieved with or without civil society. It evaded many key problems concerning participation, democracy, process and the content of schooling. This was a response to gender equality in education seen in terms of meeting a narrowly delimited need. Issues raised by the multidimensionality of rights, strategic benefits from gender equality and education or wider issues about national and global citizenship were all outside the ambit of this approach. The achievements of the interventionist approach signal a global social justice agenda cast in terms of what was minimally necessary but not sufficient for gender equality in education to flourish.

Conclusion

This chapter has outlined some instances of interventionist forms of global social justice concerned with gender and schooling, highlighting how emphasis was primarily on girls and how social justice concerns were both taken forward, but also circumscribed by forms of the state. To the extent that civil society was engaged with these interventions it shared the understanding of gender as 'girls' and equality primarily as securing access to school. In the next chapter the achievements and limitations of interventionism are contrasted with initiatives associated with the institutional approach.

8 Institutionalizing gender equality in education

Building global and local institutions is a second approach to achieving gender equality in schooling. This has been associated with demands for global social justice gender equality and education that are grounded in rights and capabilities. Institutionalizing global social justice has both a thin and a thick cosmopolitan orientation. Linked to thin cosmopolitanism global affirmations of rights are urged through a politics of Declaration or through forms of regulation that do not demand particular interpretations or actions from nation states. Associated with thick cosmopolitanism this approach works to advance gender equality through rigorous change of global, national and local institutions. Aid for education has been linked with gender in a particular form of regulation.

A global financing initiative: the FTI

Throughout the 1990s adequate finance and resource were major obstacles to providing adequate schooling for girls and encouraging gender equality. Nonetheless, lack of finance provided an opportunity to regulate national and international institutions, through introducing forms of sanction and requiring particular approaches to management. This offered an opportunity to secure some attention to gender. At the World Education Forum at Dakar in 2000, donor countries had declared that 'no countries seriously committed to education for all will be thwarted in this goal by a lack of resources' (Dakar Framework 2000: 18). The FTI, launched by the Development Committee of the World Bank and the International Monetary Fund (IMF) at its spring meetings in 2002 came to comprise over 30 multilateral and bilateral agencies and regional development banks. It included low income countries and GCE in a partnership to accelerate the achievement of universal primary education.

The FTI aimed firstly to maximize co-ordination between development partners thus reducing transaction costs for governments which spent inordinate amounts of effort in negotiating separate aid agreements with different donors. Secondly, it aimed to facilitate sustained increases in aid to countries which could demonstrate they were able to use this effectively.

Thirdly, it intended to use aid to require countries to undertake a review of education policy and performance to ensure more coherent and evidence-based planning for UPE. Fourthly, it set out to motivate countries to locate aid within the context of reviewing the development of sustainable domestic financing for education. Fifthly, it aspired to establish an open global discussion about its progress (UNESCO 2004: 214). The FTI was thus a lever to regulate the development of EFA initiatives, but initially it gave no particular attention to gender.

Table 3.4 (Appendix 3) lists countries invited to be part of the FTI by the end of 2004 and highlights how many countries are at risk of not achieving UPE by 2015 had not yet been invited to join. Rose details how arbitrary benchmarks were identified as indicative of 'EFA success' and were used to monitor progress for the FTI (Rose 2005: 388). These included the percentage of girls of the relevant age group entering the first year of a primary cycle and completing five years of schooling. The benchmarks thus gave attention only to access and enrolment, paying no attention to the quality of education delivered and the extent of gender equality. Rose describes how the financing model used by the FTI gave no attention to gender in assessing teachers' salaries or costing the means to encourage girls to attend school (Rose 2005: 390–1). The potential to use aid as a form of regulation to encourage attention to gender equality was in danger of evaporation.

In 2005 a review of gender in the FTI was commissioned by UNGEI, described more fully in the next chapter. This concluded that the partnership had made inadequate use of its regulatory framework to promote the gender dimensions of the MDGs. Particular weaknesses were identified in country education plans that had been endorsed for support by the FTI, but which failed to pay any attention to gender other than increasing the numbers of girls enrolling in school (Seel and Clarke 2005). At an FTI partnership meeting in Beijing at the end of 2005 it was agreed that a more comprehensive approach to instituting gender equality should be adopted. This included explicitly including the UNGEI Secretariat in reviewing the FTI goals and guiding principles. Gender was also to be mainstreamed across the six steps used in the FTI's assessment and endorsement guidelines. This would entail the use of gender disaggregated statistics and the development of a clearly presented gender component of national education policies grounded in human rights. In addition, country readiness to progress to gender equality through responses to the Beijing Platform of Action or engagement with CEDAW would be reviewed (North 2006b: 2).

At the time of writing it is too early to say whether the decision of the FTI partnership to use its regulatory machinery to link the disbursement of aid with gender equality will result in a stronger institutional base for achieving global social justice, but it is evident that in the lifetime of the FTI there has been a movement away from understanding gender in minimal terms as interventions relating to girls' access to school. Accepting the UNGEI report signalled an orientation within the FTI to address policy on gendered institutions. Implicitly, there has also been some movement from the instrumentalism associated with addressing basic needs and WID to a greater concern with the intrinsic importance of gender equality in education framed through rights. It is not coincidental that this shift in emphasis at the FTI came at the end of a year of lobbying and public action in support of the gender components of the MDGs. The missed target for gender parity in education may have had some bearing on the decision taken. Thus, although the forms of transparency and global accountability of the FTI have been rigorously criticized (Rose 2005; GCE 2003c, 2003d; Actionaid 2003), what is clear is that at some levels the partnership was responsive to scrutiny.

The shift in emphasis in the FTI at the end of 2005 signals a change in orientation with regard to cosmopolitanism. The thin cosmopolitanism associated with interventionist forms of global social justice and the early processes of assessment for joining the FTI appear to be challenged by a thicker cosmopolitanism which is accompanied by ideas about rights. The authority of UNGEI is associated with a legal framework informed by the MDGs, CEDAW and the Beijing Platform of Action. The extent to which this thicker cosmopolitanism will be realized in FTI instruments and corresponding government actions remains to be seen.

Changing funding modalities from the late 1990s onward meant very dispersed groups carried responsibility for reviewing actions of the FTI. Much aid had previously been disbursed to discrete projects, largely dictated by donor histories and priorities in particular countries. This approach began to give way to direct budgetary support, that is the requirement that donors put a substantial amount of aid into the education budget for a recipient government. The rationale has been that such a budget is taken through the parliamentary process. Recipient governments therefore have to account for the receipt of these funds to their own citizens rather than the citizens whose countries gave the aid or to private donors. Global mobilization around the Make Poverty History campaign of 2005 sought to build connections between citizens in rich and poor countries to demand more aid, better public services and closer scrutiny of budgets. This approach to global social justice is discussed further in the next chapter where the fragility of the global civil society alliances to review budgets in this manner will be considered. Here, however, it is important to note how new forms of public accountability and shifts in approach to the institutional infrastructure have opened up possibilities concerning global social justice on gender and education that go well beyond minimum interventions.

Institutions and development assistance policy

The new institutional agenda with regard to gender and schooling signalled by the change in direction at the FTI in 2005 can be traced directly to the leadership of DFID, which held a key position on the FTI and within UNGEI. DFID's approach to development assistance, as it developed from the late

1990s under successive Labour governments, gave increasing prominence to institution building and strategic alliances.

DFID's policy objectives were tied to the MDGs which entailed concern with gender and the empowerment of women. Through its actions DFID aimed to 'promote sustainable development and reduce poverty'. Its mission statement defined its goals in terms of supporting

> long-term programmes to help tackle the underlying causes of poverty. DFID also responds to emergencies, both natural and man-made.
>
> (DFID 2004)

DFID thus saw itself engaged in action, not in promoting or protecting particular understandings of rights, unlike the Swedish International Development Cooperation Agency (SIDA), discussed in the next chapter. DFID was committed to taking strategic action through global multilateral institutions, national governments, INGOs, NGOs and civil society using a range of different approaches from direct budget support to developing research and building public opinion.

At the beginning of 2005 DFID published a strategy paper *Girls' education: Towards a better future for all* which was conceived as an attempt to get back on track the process that had led to the first target under MDG 3 – gender parity by 2005 – being missed (DFID 2005). In this policy paper DFID's strategic approach to the global social justice agenda relying heavily on a range of regulatory mechanisms and forms of institution building is evident.

DFID committed itself to make a financial contribution to girls' education, with a large expenditure of £1.4 billion over three years for general EFA programmes. The lack of a specific gender focus indicated a belief that strategic support for a whole education system would inevitably result in benefits for girls. This large amount was, like many other strategic gestures and commitments made in 2005 when Britain led the G8 and had the presidency of the EU, an attempt to jumpstart actions by other donors, by giving an ambitious lead. At the beginning of 2006 Gordon Brown, the British Chancellor of the Exchequer, made an even larger commitment pledging to give US $15 billion over the next decade for education around the world. This was four times the US $3.5 billion spent on education aid in the previous decade. The British gesture was partly to give concrete assistance, partly to lever greater commitments to aid from other G8 governments (*Guardian*, 10 April 2006). The ways in which the aid was to undergird institutional developments and elicit a global moral response was evident in the speeches made by the Chancellor in Mozambique where the package was announced. The aid was dependent on 'countries producing practical, financable and deliverable 10 year plans for education'. Some of it was to be used to double Britain's commitment to the FTI (UNGEI 2006). But in the Chancellor's words it was also a signal of the world's 'moral duty' to deliver education to children out of school. 'It is a perfectly achievable goal. It is not something you put down to dreamers or idealists' (*Guardian*, 11 April 2006). This global moral duty was framed through rights as the Chancellor's phrasing made clear 'it is one of the world's greatest scandals that today 100 million children do not go to school – denied one of the most basic rights of all, the right to education' (*Guardian*, 10 April 2006). This approach was echoed by Hilary Benn the International Development Secretary who commented during the same visit to Mozambique:

> Education is a basic human right, and to get every child into school we need more investment. Working with developing countries, through increased commitment from the UK, will help train more teachers, build more classrooms and give more children the best start in life.
>
> (UNGEI 2006: 1)

The connection between rights and institutional development are here made explicit.

The 2005 policy paper consisted largely of descriptions of strategic institutionalization to support a global agenda on girls' education including co-ordination work with UNICEF in the development of UNGEI, and engagement with the FTI. Therefore one year before the announcement of extra money in Mozambique DFID saw itself supporting and expanding the scope of existing institutions to promote a global social justice agenda, not simply delivering its own interventions. The policy paper made some bold commitments with regard to supporting governments to make education affordable, helping develop the learning environment in schools to enlarge girls' opportunities, supporting the scaling up of successful NGO initiatives in relation to provision, and demanding more resources from the international community and more co-ordination of effort (DFID 2005: 15–23). All of these may be seen as examples of institutionalizing rights and being generally agnostic on thick or thin cosmopolitanism.

The paper concluded that civil society has an important role to play in highlighting the problem of girls out of school, raising funds, and holding national and local leaders to account. DFID publicly acknowledged the support it provided to FAWE, the Association for Development of Education in Africa (ADEA) and the CEF, all of which had built up advocacy networks. These examples of alignments with civil society show how strategic alliances around EFA were important to DFID, rather than building a specific constituency concerned with gender. In 2005, FAWE, ADEA and CEF had different approaches to the prioritization of gender and women's issues. These ranged from central to marginal concern. DFID's strategic approach was not premised on building capacity to engage with the moral content of gender equality in education or the skill to participate in decision making on these issues as the interactive approach to global social justice suggested.[1] What was important for DFID was alliances that could work on institutionalizing EFA generally. These overrode concerns with building the capacity of civil society organizations to think through gender equality, rights or capabilities.

Gender was not mainstreamed for DFID and was notably absent from the announcements made by Brown and Benn in April 2006. But the policy paper did contain a vision of global social justice articulated through multilateral institutions and acted out by governments, which could be alternately supported and critiqued by civil society. Thus, DFID's approach to global social justice assumes connection between the institution building and the interactive approach this book has identified, but the form of articulation between the two is not well developed. Just as the DFID policy paper expressed a bifocal view of cosmopolitanism, concerned both with the autonomy of states and building the capacity of multilateral organizations to regulate and intervene, so it does not suggest a particular approach to engage wider questions of global justice.

The policy paper hovers between seeing the importance of girls' education instrumentally linked to economic and social development and intrinsically linked to the flourishing of individual girls and women. It opens with this passage:

> Women are at the heart of most societies. Regardless of whether they are working or not, mothers are very influential people in children's lives. Educating girls is one of the most important investments that any country can make in its own future. Education has a profound effect on girls' and women's ability to claim other rights and achieve status in society, such as economic independence and political representation … For all these reasons education has long been recognized as a human right. Past international commitments include addressing gender equality within the education system, the first step to eliminating all forms of discrimination against women.
>
> (DFID 2005: 2–3)

In contrast with any particular focus on democracy, human rights and equality, the DFID paper sets women in a guise that is familiar from earlier discussions of the instrumental approaches (DFID 2005). They are primarily mothers with a contribution to make to the lives of their children and the future of their countries. But the passage then makes some statements drawing on the intrinsic approach to gender equality and education in its narrowest forms using the language of rights – infused by WID – adopted in the World Bank paper discussed in Chapter 4, where education rights are seen as securing other rights. The significance of rights, according to the DFID paper, derives in a legal postitivist way from the Conventions that delineate them. Only in the last sentence of this passage is there a gesture towards rights, gender equality, and the elimination of discrimination that concedes some of the elements of analysis made in terms of rights and capabilities, that is that there are underlying capabilities which rights can and must protect and that gendered processes can constrain these.

DFID's achievements have been to use its leadership in relation to global development assistance to lever increased aid from the British government and from other G8 nations. It thus places rights and some aspects of the notion of the intrinsic importance of gender equality in education as a central explanatory framework for global social justice with regard to education. Furthermore, it emphasizes the importance of the progressive development of the institutions that already exist for delivery. The difficulties for this approach are that institutions are slow to change. While DFID itself, at a particular moment, has shown 'political will' to take forward initiatives for gender equality in education, the extent to which this is sustainable under different governments, with different geopolitical alignments, is not clear.

The significance of DFID's strategic stance on gender schooling and global social justice is threefold. Firstly, it positions the social justice agenda as a shared obligation between states, multilateral organizations and global and local civil society. Social justice is therefore not the obligation of one player, but of their collaboration. This places enormous significance on the second plank of this strategy, that is the regulatory machinery that will ensure the goals of social justice are met. These goals do not appear to entail obligations which are strictly enforceable, but rather obligations regulated by a global machinery comprising rational funding, some techniques for gender mainstreaming, and forms of measurement that identify where interventions are required. The strong reliance on regulation, rather than obligations to promote and protect gender equality in education identifies a third strand in DFID's policy, that is its general silence on distributive questions, the content and weight of responsibilities for gender equality in education in its programming, and the limited concern with interactive forms of global social justice.

Gender mainstreaming in education

The institutional approach to global social justice for gender equality in education opened the way for feminist engagement with institutions as a means to secure justice. Gender mainstreaming has been the shorthand term in use for approximately 10 years by activists working inside institutions to orient the values, policies, organizational processes and forms of evaluation so that these take due account of gender equality. It is thus a form of regulation that works both at the level of ideas and of organizational practices. The approach derives from a perception that an unexamined male bias concerning the nature of the public sphere and appropriate activities for women has coloured development practice (Elson 1995). In order to take initiatives for gender equality forward it is necessary both to innovate at the 'margins' and to change the character of powerful institutions – the mainstream – so that they place gender equality concerns at the centre of policies and practice.

In a widely circulating definition used by a UNDP training pack, gender mainstreaming was defined as a concern

> to strengthen the legitimacy of gender equality as a fundamental value that should be reflected in development choices and institutional practices. When gender equality is recognized as a strategic objective of development, gender equality goals influence broad economic and social policies and the programmes that deliver major resources. Efforts to achieve gender equality are thus brought into the mainstream decision-making criteria and processes and are pursued from the centre rather than the margins.
>
> (UNDP 2000: 7)

Some of the practices associated with gender mainstreaming were the increased involvement of women in decision making, consideration of gender issues in setting the goals and allocating resources in an organisation. Gender mainstreaming was seen as going 'beyond the participation of women in equal numbers as beneficiaries of initiatives to a form of participation that enable women a well as men to influence the entire agenda and basic priorities' (Jahan 1995: 13). The aspiration was to involve women in processes of setting agendas, accessing institutional resources and evaluating outcomes. A number of manuals with toolkits for training and checklist guides on gender mainstreaming for work in education have been developed by UNESCO and Oxfam (UNESCO 2004; Leach 2003). These were in addition to toolkits for gender mainstreaming in generic social development planning assembled by the United Nations Development Programme (UNDP) (UNDP 2000) and a Gender Management System (GMS) developed by the Commonwealth Secretariat for work on national gender plans (Commonwealth Secretariat 1999).

Gender mainstreaming has been criticized on a number of grounds. Sylvia Walby (2005) and Judith Squires (2005) have both looked critically at the assumptions behind the meanings of gender and the mainstream associated with gender mainstreaming pointing out how inattentive the process is to questions of difference and dissent. Within development practice, critiques have been not so much about meanings as about the ways in which gender mainstreaming has failed to tackle the networks of power within institutions (Miller and Razavi 1998; Goetz 1997). Some key bilateral and multilateral organizations engaged in delivering the MDGs have no systematic approach to gender mainstreaming. All too often those who have responsibility for mainstreaming gender in education departments are marginalized (Oddora Hoppers 2005). In field visits in India, Bangladesh, South Africa, and Kenya I have heard descriptions of a gender mainstreaming team housed in an office half a mile from the main education department without access to transport to attend meetings or computer facilities. I have seen an excellent plan for gender mainstreaming in an education department. The official instructed to implement it had previous experience only at school level as a counsellor. She was seen by her colleagues in the Education Department as 'lightweight', kept away from powerful officials and was unable to take the initiative forward. In Rwanda, an economist appointed to work on gender budgeting across all departments of government was initially viewed as primarily associated with the Department of Women and Girls, not with a mainstreaming initiative (Diop 2004). In Nepal, a rigorous gender audit of education took three years to report. All these instances show that a formal institutional commitment to 'do something' about gender mainstreaming does not always translate into practice that legitimates the significance of gender equality.

South Africa provides an illuminating example of this. Here the challenge was not large numbers of children out of school or of girls failing to do well in examinations, but findings from qualitative research that girls felt disempowered by schooling, faced high levels of gender-based violence, and women teachers found it difficult to contribute creatively to curriculum development or pedagogy (Chisholm 2001; Moletsane 2004; Unterhalter 2005b). Men and boys struggled to orient themselves to a new society and often drew on vocabularies of violent masculinity which gave a sense of power in an unsettled context (Morrell 2005; Reid and Walker 2005).

Shortly after the first democratic government took power in 1994 a Gender Equity Task Team (GETT) was appointed to undertake a year long investigation into the establishment of a permanent Gender Equity Unit in the Department of Education. This looked at correcting gender imbalances in enrolment, dropout subject choice, career paths and performance, single sex schools, sexism in curricula and teaching, and affirmative action strategies for promoting women into leadership. Developing a strategy to eliminate sexual harassment and violence was also in its brief (Wolpe *et al.* 1997: 4–5). GETT recommended to the Minister a gender mainstreaming approach, namely that a Gender Equity Unity (GEU) be established in the Department of Education in the Director General's office to give it status and authority. The GEU was to be supported by gender officers in each of the branches of the Department and by a similar structure at provincial level. It was assumed that presence at a senior level in the education bureaucracy would ensure a gender focus in all reform. Teacher training courses were to include material on gender and human rights and teaching about this in schools was to be considered within the new curriculum (Wolpe *et al.* 1997: 12–16).

The authors of GETT were influenced by the success of feminist bureau-crats – known as femocrats – in Australia who had developed gender reform in education from the 1980s (Blackmore 2004). They believed that placing feminists strategically in key positions in the Department of Education would allow for gendered practices in schools and the administration to be challenged and changed. However, this strategy had only limited success. In 2005, the lead author of the GETT report reviewed how difficult it had been to get these recommendations acknowledged (Wolpe 2005). The head of the GEU described how the strategic approach recommended by GETT had not fulfilled its potential. The GEU had not been located at a senior enough level within the Department. Its head, Mmabatho Ramagoshi commented critically that far from it being seen as a lynchpin to a cross-cutting strategic engagement with gender 'It is taken as one of the projects of the department and is lost within the bureaucracy' (Ramagoshi 2005: 133). Despite the vision of the GETT report, staff appointed at national and provincial level did not have adequate experience in gender. The short training courses they received were not adequate. In many provinces, they lacked a budget. Gender Focal Points in provincial ministries were not called to the major meetings where policy and planning decisions were taken and they had become officials with very limited roles, at worst 'events co-ordinators' for annual Women's Day meetings or similar (Ramagoshi 2005: 134).

While the far-reaching structural change envisaged by GETT had not happened, there had been some progress in schools with regard to heightened awareness of gender-based violence. Girls were being encouraged to discuss their education more openly.

In Australia, femocrats had managed to keep in touch with grassroots issues through constant engagement with the women's movement (Blackmore 2004). In South Africa, as in many parts of the world, there were not good connections between gender activists working on education and those campaigning on other issues of gender inequality. This lack of connection meant that in 2005 the Minister of Education, despite her own strong commitment to issues of gender and education, did not have an active constituency demanding change. She appointed a Ministerial Review Committee to look at what had happened since GETT, but the report itself became ensnared in bureaucratic delays. Gender mainstreaming through institutional change thus had many pitfalls associated both with conditions within education departments and the fragility of connections outside.

Despite these considerable difficulties, Naila Kabeer and Ramya Subrahmanian have written about the potential offered by gender mainstreaming to move institutional practice away from a targeted, yet limited interventions focused on girls to a wider more transformatory agenda about gender equality (Kabeer and Subrahmanian 1999). Kabeer has outlined additional processes that need to accompany a planning tool like the GMS, highlighting the importance of interlocking institutional arrangements, links with civil society and a range of incentives to make gender mainstreaming work (Kabeer 2003: 228–9). She stresses the importance of linking this approach to institutionalization with forms of popular mobilization to support gender equity goals and the development of an active citizenship supporting women's rights. The analysis highlights the intersection of institutional and interactive forms of global social justice suggesting the latter as enhancing the substance of democratization associated with the former.

A report written by Ramya Subrahmanian (2005b) for UNESCO and UNGEI in 2005 showed how this might be achieved. It set out to link what research had illuminated regarding what had not worked in general gender mainstreaming initiatives with an analysis of how small-scale projects for girls' education, often focusing on access, could be scaled up. The report identified three different forms of institutional change: firstly, targeted interventions mainly concerned with access; secondly, systemic reforms which took on issues of pedagogy, curriculum and quality; and thirdly, enabling conditions that would allow for change towards gender equality to be sustained. These included attending to forms of community mobilization, the establishment of women's groups with interests that went beyond education, and leadership training programmes for girls and boys focusing on issues of gender rights and gender-based violence (Subrahmanian 2005b: 33).

The report identified aspects of institutionalization where projects concerned with girls' schooling or limited gender change could be scaled up into wider gender programmes and systemic policies. These included targeted interventions by institutions to deal with gender issues and systemic reform within the education system that took gendered processes seriously and addressed changing the legal framework. Improved accountability by institutions could enhance gender equality effects. Partnerships 'upward' to global institutions and 'sideways' through networks with civil society and NGOs were also seen as important (Subrahmanian 2005b: 35). This report exemplified an attempt to use the analysis of institutions to embed systemic change and enhanced global accountability. It advocates links between the three forms of global social justice – interventionism, institutionalization and interactions – this book has identified.

The vision for gender mainstreaming in education institutions linked to a global social justice agenda is thus far untested. It may be that the forms of gendered power within organizations that have restricted the development of so many welllaid plans for gender mainstreaming, may similarly undermine any strategy for scaling up. On the other hand, it may be that the urgency of the drive to meet the MDGs, the critical mass of governments, multilateral organizations, and NGOs mobilized to advance demands for gender and schooling as a matter of global social justice will set an urgent pace to demand the implementation of insights of those who have worked on gender mainstreaming.

In assessing gender mainstreaming as a form of institutionalization for global social justice concerns with gender equality in education, it is necessary to distinguish the aspiration from the practice. All the accounts of gender mainstreaming in education thus far have highlighted difficulties rather than achievements. This does not prove that the approach cannot deliver significant gains for gender equality in education. But case studies that might illuminate how this happens have not yet been written. All the existing studies of the fragility of gender mainstreaming in education highlight how initiatives can become cut off from connection to local and global civil society and lose a dynamic of accountability and participation. A number of attempts at gender mainstreaming have gone no further than WID. Thus far there are no accounts of gender mainstreaming in education engaging in full discussions of rights and the intrinsic importance of gender equality. It therefore appears that the very protection institutions offer to global aspirations for gender equality in education run the risk of becoming empty formalized systems if a dynamic engagement with debates about rights, representation and interactive forms of global social justice is not maintained. Institutions, like interventions, are necessary but not sufficient to keep a global social justice agenda alive.

The fragility of the gender mainstreaming initiatives thus far documented suggest that the ethics of thin cosmopolitanism might concede too much in insisting on the autonomy of national, local and institutional spaces. Unless the mirror of the demands of thick cosmopolitanism, with its emphasis on positive freedoms, rights, capabilities and gender equality are constantly held up to institutions working within thin cosmopolitanism, the history and structures of institutions will offer their own legitimating approach to ideas that have potential to undermine a cosmopolitan project.

Monitoring girls in school

Part of the process of global institutionalization has entailed a struggle over how to monitor change in gender and schooling. After Jomtien it became evident how weak the informational base for the EFA movement was. In an influential intervention Stephen Heyneman (1997) castigated government officials and the staff of multilateral institutions on weak data gathering machinery though which progress could be tracked. Thereafter countries began to strengthen their Education Management Information Systems (EMIS) and multilateral organizations associated with the UN – UNICEF, UNESCO and UNDP – began to produce annual analyses of the data produced by governments and reviewed through the UN Institute for Statistics. From the late 1990s, gender-disaggregated data have become available on enrolment and progression through school, with data often available by district. While there are limitations with this data, as discussed below, the achievement in putting in place systems to collect gender-disaggregated data down to local community level should not be underestimated.

The reports of UN agencies, most notably UNDP's *Human Development Reports*, UNICEF's *State of the World's Children* and UNESCO's *Global Monitoring Report*, go some way to providing the information from which national progress could be assessed, but there are a number of serious limitations with this data. Amongst these are problems about what it measures, the quality of data, and how accountable these measures and data are.

The complex processes that take place in education, particularly with regard to its gender dynamics are not particularly amenable to analysis through 'simple' measures based on inputs and outputs to the system, such as enrolment rates and achievements in examinations. However, gross and net enrolment rates, intake rates, retention over five years in primary school, and transfer to secondary school have become the standard measures of efficiency used in international statistics. This form of monitoring carries within it the implication that gender equality in education is only about numbers of girls, access and efficiency.

The gender-related EFA index (GEI), developed by UNESCO for use in its Global Monitoring Reports (GMR) was an attempt to indicate the extent to which boys and girls were equally present at different levels in the education system – primary, secondary, and adult education. However, a country could have a GEI of 1, indicating complete equality between boys and girls, but still have low rates of access, retention, and achievement for girls and boys. For example, in 2003 Myanmar had a GEI of 0.949, with only 84 per cent primary NER, and Kuwait had a GEI of 0.966 with a primary NER of 83 per cent (UNESCO 2003: 288–9). Gender parity on its own can not tell much about gender equality in relation to accessing education, progressing through school, and living in a gender-equitable society after school.

In an attempt to bring together information on access, quality, and the gender gap, UNESCO developed the Education Development Index (EDI) from 2003 (UNESCO 2003: 284–92). The EDI constituents and related indicators were:

- *universal primary education*: net enrolment ratio;
- *adult literacy*: literacy rate of the group aged 15 and over;
- *gender*: gender-specific EFA index (GEI, the arithmetical mean of the Gender Parity Indices for the primary and secondary gross enrolment ratios and the adult literacy rate);
- *progression*: survival rate to grade 5.

There are several problems with the EDI with regard to gender. Firstly, its main gender component, the GEI, was concerned with parity, which gave insufficient insight into context. Men and women, or girls and boys, may have gender parity in literacy or access to schooling but have low levels of participation. Secondly, the EDI did not take account of gender in children's survival in schooling. It primarily considers gender in relation to access and not achievement. Thirdly, the EDI weighted each of its four components equally. Thus enrolments, and gender parity in enrolments were weighted equally with achievements. However, research in many countries showed that enrolling children in school was only the first hurdle. Ensuring attendance and completion were much harder tasks, and this has particularly been the case for girls, whose progress has been constrained by many factors linked to safety, hygiene, nutrition, and family responsibilities (Watkins 2000; Tomasevski 2004). Weighting access as equivalent to achievement underestimated the EFA challenge that confronts governments, but it was particularly serious because of its failure to adequately assess gender-related aspects of school achievement.

As regulatory mechanisms for monitoring, the GEI and the EDI gel well with the instrumental arguments for gender and schooling and interventionist approaches to global social justice. However they provide very little insight into the multi-dimensionality of rights and capabilities. The approach to monitoring, when utilized as a form of regulation for global social justice, has the potential for the developing institutions to address gender mainstreaming issues, but they have not been used this way. Rather, they have been used to locate gross insufficiencies outlined for example in EFA plans. They have been little used to regulate distribution in more complex ways. Thus, the approach to measurement has failed to support a platform for developing institutions to measure more complex dimensions of rights. The mechanism for monitoring have promoted a minimal interventionist objective to get girls into school and excluded consideration of wider meaning of gender, equality and education.

Over and above the reliance on an instrumentalist view of gender equality in education, this form of monitoring has a number of additional problems relating to data quality. EMIS is only as good as the relations of trust, truthfulness, and accuracy that underpin a system. In some contexts, local officials do not know the reasons why they collect data for EMIS. They may have difficulties in reaching areas that are socially or geographically distant to collect information; they may believe that underestimating or overestimating children on the school register may bring additional facilities to a locality. Carr Hill *et al.* (1999) emphasize the fragility of the data on which many national and international conclusions are based. District Household Surveys used in much development planning provide no data on people who do not live in households, because they are migrants or because they live on the street. Sampling which aims to include representatives of particular excluded groups may result in the least excluded members of those groups being surveyed, because they are the easiest for data collection teams to contact. In nomadic regions of Northern Kenya for example and conflict torn regions of Southern Sudan, it has been reported that social surveys contact only the most easily accessible groups within these regions, and thus distort the conclusions that come to be drawn.

When participatory activities are held in villages to identify children who are not at school, more robust data are assembled. However, there are difficulties in translating local mobilizing actions into official data on GER and NER, although in some countries this form of micro-planning is used by governments as well as NGOs. These activities were used with particular success in DPEP and subsequently in SSA in India. In Bangladesh in 1998 the Campaign for Mass Primary Education (CAMPE) ran large-scale surveys to assess which children were in school and their achievements in learning. Their conclusions offer a far less rosy picture of levels of access and achievement than official statistics (Chowdhury *et al.* 1999). With regard to gender, although these participatory processes use the same descriptive categories as EMIS and focus on gender as a noun, the *process* of data gathering has the potential to raise questions about the meaning of gender equity and equality and forms of engagement with state institutions (Ahmed and Chowdhury 2005).

Accountability is a key problem associated with monitoring as an approach to regulation and institution building. There has been a tendency for governments engaged in collecting EMIS data to see lines of accountability running upward from district officials to national departments and then to international monitoring publications. On the whole, governments have not disseminated EMIS data downwards so that national and regional patterns are discussed at village and district level. While this data may be available on websites or in government publications in this form it is not accessible to district education officials, teachers, or school management committees. UNDP has worked to develop national UNDP offices and to publicize country-based Human Development Reports. In some Poverty Reduction Strategy Programmes (PRSPs), regulating access to aid, there are mechanisms for the discussion of EMIS data at local level. Some NGOs affiliated to GCE have used official data as part of their campaigning and advocacy work (Elimu Yetu 2005). Some, like CAMPE, have conducted their own studies to challenge official presentations.

In much of this work gender categories have been taken from the official instruments. Thus what is monitored is the presence or absence of girls, not wider meanings of gender equality. As a result, NGOs, although trying to use EMIS to enhance accountability, have tended to work with instrumental views regarding gender and schooling. These forms of accountability have not yet been able to engage the potential of monitoring in relation to the multidimensionality entailed by rights and capabilities. Nonetheless, the initiatives that focus on the accountability of official statistics point to the potential for global civil society to engage strategically with monitoring as a form of regulation. This yields opportunities to identify where interventions should take place and to build strategic alliances for global social justice.

The achievements of the forms of monitoring instituted from the late 1990s by governments, IGOs and NGOs has been to secure gender disaggregated information and to circulate this through global publications like the UNDP *Human Development Reports*, the UNESCO *Global Monitoring Reports*, national census reports and the surveys and locally based participatory studies undertaken by NGOs. However, the difficulty with this form of monitoring is that as yet the means to understand gender in education in more complex and multi-dimensional forms that those of access and achievement have not been developed. Using this form of monitoring it can appear, as is the case in South Africa, that there are good levels of gender equality in an education system when qualitative research raises questions about this (Unterhalter 2005b).

Existing monitoring methods, therefore, talk largely to an instrumental understanding of schooling satisfied by a commodity of a set number of years in school and the presence of girls in the system. They invite an interventionist approach to global social justice and suggest there is no further cause for concern if girls and boys are enrolled and achieving at equal levels. That there might be gender-based violence in school, racial discrimination, failure to flourish or a dislocation between school and lives of value is not signalled by this approach to monitoring. It thus fails to affirm aspects of the intrinsic value of education except insofar as this may be minimally guaranteed by legal instruments. When this approach to monitoring is used in conjunction with processes of building civil society and enhancing democratic participation, however, it can stimulate discussion and alert people to hidden dimensions of their society. But it is often used as a form of counting by officials who are not aware of its significance and disengaged from any democratizing project (Page 2005). The form of monitoring associated with institutionalizing processes for global social justice might appear of minimal significance with regard to the debate about cosmopolitanism outlined in Chapter 2. Yet it is evident that forms of monitoring that mesh with descriptive and uni-dimensional meanings of gender, for example by concentrating on counting girls, evade the issues suggested by thinking about women's rights and global social justice. A complex meaning of rights and gender equality calls out for an approach to global monitoring to manage development that has some semblance of this multi-dimensionality.

Conclusion

The four approaches to institution building described in this chapter operate with a dynamic that pulls in two directions. On the one hand there is a pull towards a minimal concern with addressing the basic needs of getting girls into school and including women – as noted in the mechanisms the FTI has used to date, the elusiveness of a concern with gender and rights in DFID's commitment to institution building, the fragility of efforts for gender mainstreaming, and forms of monitoring girls' input and output from the education system. On the other hand there has been an orientation in the forms of institution building described to aspire to a more multidimensional understanding of gender equality as can be seen in the new direction regarding plans adopted by the FTI, selected passages of the DFID policy paper, the concern with accountability in gender mainstreaming as advocated by UNESCO and UNGEI, and the potential of monitoring strategies to be used to build local awareness. To date only initiatives concerned with basic needs and WID in institution building have been documented. The extent to which institutionalizing forms of global social justice are able to maintain a concern with rights and more complex meanings of gender equality awaits examination. But it is evident that institution building, given complex histories of gendered social relations in particular contexts, is only the first step on a very long journey to establish global social justice.

In contrast to the large numbers of girls attending school through interventionist programmes the achievements of the institutionalizing approach to global social justice for gender equality in education are ambiguous. A challenge for the institutionalizing approach lies in the strength of regulatory mechanisms. These could require that gender equality be placed more centrally in interventions. A second challenge concerns the identity of strategic partners. How much weight should be given to working with states, how much to civil society, how much to global bodies and how much to households and families, is by no means clear. What the status of feminist organizations should be in any strategic alliance also remains to be worked out. While the interventionist approach could 'work' regardless of the form of the body delivering the appropriate interventions, the institutionalizing approach implicitly depends on assumptions about global governance and areas of shared understandings and priorities. The power of the vocabulary of 'girls' and 'efficiency' associated with instrumentalism and interventionism entails that this has often become the default position used in developing institutions. The language of rights, participation and multi-layered understandings of gender equality still has to provide a policy vocabulary and approach to practice. In the next chapter, I look at the interactive approach as a complement to institution building for global social justice.

9 The interactive approach

Approaches to addressing gender and schools through interventionist and institutionalizing forms of global social justice appear necessary but not sufficient to bring about change. Gender inequality persists in diverse settings, and is often entrenched in language, everyday action, and deeply held conviction. Transforming institutions is a huge challenge. But engaging in discussion about issues that touch many private as well as public concerns is, if anything, a larger task. Concepts of rights and capabilities are multidimensional. They suggest some pointers to help guide new forms of practice that are concerned with change, but there are very few detailed descriptions of this in action. Many of these initiatives are fragile.

Rights as ethical obligations linked to capabilities provides an approach to look at equality, diversity, and changing contexts of schools. The philosophical ideas suggest that a single view of social institutions is not attentive enough to the range of different ways in which we exercise capabilities. Some social relations are within institutions, but some, for example those concerned with care, vulnerability, friendship, or difference are located in co-evolving networks. These are characterized, not only by institutional norms, laws and the kind of contracts linked with perfect obligations, but also by emotions, negotiations over language, and a very diverse range of relationships over time and space and different forms of affiliation, captured by the notion of imperfect obligations. Viewing society as formed both by institutions, structures, and looser forms of association, entails thinking about global justice differently. I have identified a nexus of ideas concerned with human diversity, and shifting sites of social negotiation. I consider this understanding of society links with a third form of global social justice, which I have termed the interactive approach. The term conveys the multiple sites in which global social justice is effected and the multiplicity of forms it takes. Imperfect obligations are not in themselves sufficient for global social justice. They complement and extend the perfect obligations that reside in institutions and interventions. But as the previous chapters have shown these perfect obligations are generally underpinned by too narrow a conception of social justice because achieving gender equality is not simply a matter of rational planning and mainstreaming policies. While these can help develop conditions for gender equality in schools, further forms of negotiation between differently situated people are necessary. The interactive forms of global social justice described in this chapter point to some of the ways in which this is being put into practice.

Interactions and development assistance policy

The Swedish government development assistance programme SIDA provides an illustration of policy and action on gender, schooling and global social justice that expresses aspects of the interactive form of global social justice. In the 1990s, SIDA, one of the largest contributors to overseas development assistance, both absolutely, and as a proportion of GNP, moved away from the direct delivery of projects to the adoption of a more facilitative role. From the middle of the decade, SIDA supported partner institutions in the south to develop and manage programmes, generally orientating all its work to poverty reduction. In 1996 gender equality was added as one of six additional goals for SIDA's work. Action plans were put in place in all partner countries to give this goal substance (SIDA 2002a).

Gender equality was here defined as 'equal rights of women and men to influence, participate in and benefit from development co-operation' (Lind 2006). Five years later an evaluation of how SIDA had mainstreamed gender was carried out with detailed studies of 12 projects in South Africa, Bangladesh and Nicaragua. These revealed how gender mainstreaming tended to be implemented largely in WID terms (SIDA 2002b). By contrast, SIDA had conceptualized gender mainstreaming in terms of rights and a strong concern with participation, agency and outcomes. Strategic work in the bureaucracy or with management, the establishment of institutions for their own sake, and specific interventions to get girls into school, were not the only concern. Policy and action focused on working with different kinds of organizations, with no predetermined idea of what the most appropriate form of practice was.

SIDA's approach to securing EFA goals has been concerned with development assistance and rights. The policy contains a strong statement about the intrinsic value of education as a human right. An aspiration for the education of girls is here mixed with a general orientation to human development:

> Education is a basic human right and is necessary for sustainable social and economic development. The education of girls is one of the most important determinants of development. Investment in basic education is indispensable for human development and pro-poor growth. A growing economy is, in its turn, a necessary, but not a sufficient condition for the preservation of sustainable development and education for all.
>
> (SIDA 2001: 11)

The formulation of the rights-based approach here, while acknowledging international Conventions and agreements, is an explicitly moral position in which rights are seen as central to 'promoting democracy, human rights, equality between women and men and sustainable development (SIDA 2001: 13). This linkage between different kinds of rights, democracy and a wide notion of development opens, even if it does not settle consideration of an ethical debate concerning the nature of rights, the weightings of different kinds of obligations, the importance of process and participation, and a consideration of the connection between rights and capabilities. Thus the formulation has a richer potential than policy couched simply in terms of attending to what works – the interventionist approach – or who one works with and the bureaucratic means that underpin this – the institutionalizing approach.

SIDA's view is that its work in education should facilitate partners to plan their own actions and interventions, promote dialogue, and support capacity development. The major concern is interaction, not achieving particular interventions or supporting certain forms of institution. Nonetheless a large proportion of SIDA funding has gone towards governments' EFA work and support for multilateral institutions. In 2004 it chaired the FTI and in 2005 it jointly chaired UNGEI with DFID. But SIDA has also been committed to assisting NGOs engaged with innovation in gender and education, to promoting democratic participation and to supporting organizations working to articulate the demand for education (SIDA 2001: 16–19).

In South Africa, while SIDA has given financial support to the Education Department, it also funded critical scrutiny of this Department's work through the publications of the Education Policy Unit at the University of the Witwatersrand and supported a conference, which took place in 2004, shortly after the elections, to critically assess progress in gender and education since the publication of the GETT report (Chisholm and September 2005). SIDA's engagement with rights, democracy and critical discussion has meant that SIDA officials were often candid about evaluations that highlighted where gender analysis in projects SIDA supported had been weak, and where understandings of gender equality, which focused entirely on girls or women were insufficient (Lind 2006). Thus SIDA's work linked to interactive engagement and debate, not simply the drawing up of plans.

SIDA has both supported national and multilateral initiatives for EFA, making use of the institutional approach to global social justice, and placed this in a wider context of interactive global social justice. Openings to take discussion, debate and examination of gender equality beyond institutions remain fluid. However, the difficulty for development assistance in this form is that institutions have their own dynamic. Conceding autonomy to a particular project, like the FTI, or an adult literacy scheme, means that processes to advance an interactive form of global social justice may not be clearly defined or readily available. For example, consideration of a more gender-responsive form of regulation within the FTI was initiated under

SIDA's chairmanship but not quickly completed. UNGEI was not easily able to realize the promise of a global social justice alliance concerned with gender and education. As described in the previous chapter the attempts by civil society in South Africa to make the process of gender mainstreaming, initiated by GETT, more responsive to their demands floundered, after the SIDA sponsored conference of 2004. Interactive forms of global social justice take a long time to be realized and outcomes are not certain. The thick form of cosmopolitanism SIDA articulates floats in a space where states, global institutions and NGOs have their own boundaries and objectives. While it appears SIDA does not concede the position of thin cosmopolitanism, that is it does not, as a matter of principle maintain it cannot advance demands concerning gender equality within a particular state, whose jurisdiction in these matters must be protected, it also does not advance its own agenda on matters concerning gender or human rights in open confrontation with non-cosmopolitan spaces, for example particular governments or organizations who are opposed to these interpretations.

Gender responsive budgeting in education: a wider view

A second form of interactive global social justice is evident in gender-responsive budgeting (GRB), although this has more commonly been associated with institutionalist responses. GRB is an approach to scrutinizing government budgetary practices which pays particular attention to their differential effects on men and women, girls and boys. It addresses the question: 'What is the impact of the government budget, and the policies and programmes that it funds, on women and men, girls and boys?' (Budlender and Hewitt 2002: 52). GRB has been used by governments, members of parliament and civil society groups to ensure that gender issues are considered and addressed in all government policies and programmes, and specifically in the budgets allocated to implement them. To the extent that GRB addresses the institutions that govern the allocation of funds it is clearly an important resource available to institutionalizing forms of global social justice. However, because of its concern to widen discussion about education finance, budgeting and forms of monitoring to take in not just those who sit in parliament but a very wide swathe of civil society it also has a resonance with interactive forms of global social justice.

A study of GRB in education published by the *Beyond Access* project highlighted a number of different initiatives civil society or government could consider (Beyond Access 2005b). Firstly, gender targeted expenditures are expenditures that set out to address specific needs or interventions, for example scholarships for girls, such as the Female secondary Stipend Programme in Bangladesh (Raynor 2005a). However, the work of the NGO Camfed in Africa shows how local discussion about scholarship programmes have become a means to open dialogue about the meanings of gender equality in education and the range of obligations citizens in many countries owe each other (Fancy 2004; Camfed 2003). Secondly, attention to gender in staff-related employment equity expenditures highlights the availability of training packages for women teachers to help in career development. While at one level this is an area of concern for institutionalizing forms of global social justice, particularly appropriate for consideration in changing the funding model of the FTI, at another level paying attention to the gender dynamics of teachers' employment and the limits on teachers' pay has been seen by civil society networks as an important area for discussion which keeps up popular pressure on institutions like the FTI and engages international networks of trade unions (Education International 2003; GCE and Actionaid International 2005).

A third form of GRB entails the scrutiny of general government expenditures for their gendered impact, for example the proportion of an education budget spent on higher education in which a small proportion of women are enrolled, compared with the proportion spent on early childhood education which has specific immediate benefits for large numbers of women (Beyond Access 2005b). It is here that the civil society networks associated with GCE have been particularly active in undertaking a review of budgets at national, provincial, district and school level (De Graaf 2005; CEF 2005).

The strengths of GRB as a form of interactive global social justice probably lie in its connection to institutionalizing forms, but rigorous evaluations of gender budgeting as a form of popular mobilization are yet to be undertaken. Nonetheless, if this interactive form of global social justice is seen to be complementary to institutional forms and if 'reasoned actions' and procedures to enhance global civil society's engagement with GRB can be set out, the approach appears to hold out considerable scope. GRB as a form of popular political action suggests a particular form of thick cosmopolitanism. Institutions do matter to effect redress and establish conditions for gender equality, but institutions are scrutinized by campaigns and popular discussion about public finance. These fluid and changing forms of political action express and examine imperfect obligations, but through some clearly established processes of negotiation with institutions transmute dialogue and critique into sustainable procedures for social justice.

Gender, indicators and the public

The limitations inherent in the forms of monitoring used as part of the institutionalizing approach to global social justice outlined in the last chapter prompted a discussion within the *Beyond Access* project of alternative ways to monitor gender equality in education. It was apparent, for example, how much monitoring enrolment and progression appeared to drive the policy on gender and schooling, rather than the other way round. *Beyond Access* worked to develop some alternative measures that engaged more fully with gender equality understood in terms of rights and capabilities. Initial conceptual work illuminated some of the key dimensions entailed in a richer measure of education equality that would take to some of the complexities of distribution beyond concerns for 'efficiency' (Unterhalter and Brighouse 2006 forthcoming). Subsequent work attempted to put some of these ideas into practice developing a number, termed the GEEI, that could be derived from existing data sources and used in monitoring progress on gender equality in education in particular countries. Each country or region could have a GEEI calculated and increases and decreases in GEEI could be tracked over time in ways that were similar to those utilized by the Human Development Reports and UNESCO's GMR (Unterhalter *et al.* 2005b).

But there are many problems with the GEEI as an expression of a richer notion of gender equality in education than that entailed by counting girls' and boys' enrolment or progression. The GEEI tables represent the inter-relationship between countries or regions as competitive creating a culture of winners and losers. The ranking of countries when the HDI is published is often accompanied by newspaper reports of 'We are the best'. This is quite at odds with notions of cosmopolitanism concerned with linkages between countries and their need of each other. Utilizing any form of measurement in this field relies on an arbitrary board of scorers, who usually have little experience of delivery, to judge performance. Establishing a numerical measure of performance tends to downplay the processes of working towards achievement suggesting the steps on the way to a particular score are not important, it is only achieving the score that is valuable. These were compelling reasons for *Beyond Access* not to proceed with work on a quantitative measure of gender equality in education. However, alongside these arguments it was also important to confront the absence of any way of tracking progress on gender equality in education through ideas located in rights and capabilities and not just a limited concept of need or WID. The development of the GEEI was therefore partly an attempt to address the distributional question in terms that went beyond access to school. The rationale was based on the view that it was important to work strategically to develop a methodology for measurement of a problem of global significance. The benefits of developing a somewhat better measure were seen to mitigate to some degree the negative dimensions associated with measuring performance (Unterhalter 2005c, 2005d). If *Beyond Access* could utilize the GEEI as a means to engage in dialogue with governments, IGOs and civil society while keeping open the tentativeness of the measure and the need to use it in conjunction with other forms of quantitative and qualitative research, it seemed that it might be useful as a form of interactive global social justice.

The first GEEI calculations were undertaken as part of commissions from the Commonwealth Secretariat, UNESCO and UNICEF to highlight the importance of greater mobilization in support of the MDGs (Unterhalter *et al* 2005c; Unterhalter *et al* 2005d; Unterhalter and McCowan 2005). Subsequently the measure was used by ASPBAE and Oxfam as part of campaign documents to report progress on the delivery of EFA (ASPBAE 2005; Beyond Access 2005c). To date, however, the GEEI does not appear to have been used as a monitoring mechanism beyond its initial concern with dialogue, discussion and the capability approach. But the fluid processes associated with the interactive form of global social justice mean that there is no in-built mechanism that means that the GEEI may not be used as a crude form of performance management, very different from the concerns which guided its design. The strength of the GEEI is that it goes a small way beyond the instrumental assumptions about monitoring associated with existing approaches. Its weaknesses are that it is not able to provide an approach to monitoring empowerment more fully. However, the development of the GEEI, like GRB, and UNDP's gender empowerment measure points to the potential to utilize some of the ideas associated with thick cosmopolitanism as a moral compass to assess the operations of existing institutions.

Building global partnerships

The global partnerships that have formed and reformed to take forward the gender equality in education agenda are a further instance of interactive global social justice. The *Beyond Access* project is one such partnership that has worked in overlapping and cross-cutting partnerships with governments, IGOs, NGOs, individual researchers, the media and education institutions (Aikman and Unterhalter 2005b; Unterhalter *et al.* 2005a). It has tried to engage with a fuller meaning of gender than those associated with the instrumental approach, with debates about rights and capabilities and with a very wide meaning of education entailing not just schooling.

AWID represents another approach to global networking and alliance building to advance discussion and demands associated with gender and rights. But education has not figured prominently in its concerns for reasons that are beyond the scope of discussion in this book (Leeson 2004). The Gender and Development Network which is associated with participation in the UN committees and sustaining the dynamic beyond Beijing remained largely detached from lobbying concerned with education until tentative links were made in 2005.

The UNGEI was launched in April 2000 at the Dakar conference as an attempt to build a global alliance to take forward the vision of Dakar. The history of UNGEI reveals some of the instabilities associated with the interactive form of global social justice; how difficult it has been to maintain concern with the intrinsic value of education, rather than the instrumental dynamic and how difficult global civil society has found it to work in dialogue with IGOs and governments on gender and schooling. This experience suggests that interactive forms of global social justice still need to be developed to take forward 'reasoned actions' to advance some of the apprehensions of thick cosmopolitanism. They themselves need clearer principles to underpin action.

The initial concept paper for UNGEI was developed in 1999 by a number of UN agencies. UNGEI was initially viewed as a 10-year programme to improve the quality and level of girls' education, a fundamental human right and an essential element of sustainable human development (UNGEI 2000). Initially it was thought UNGEI could bring together different parts of the UN co-ordinated by the UN Development Group.

In the initial concept document, UNGEI stood poised between concerns with rights and capabilities and more narrow assumptions about needs and human capital. The initial concept paper linked both of these sets of aims together:

> World leaders have emphasized in the recent International Conferences (Beijing, Copenhagen, Cairo, Rome, Vienna, ICPD+5, for example) and in other fora that without girls' education the goal of gender equality will never be reached and progress in national and economic development will be restricted. The broad social benefits of girls' education include increased family incomes; later marriages and reduced fertility rates; reduced infant and maternal mortality rates; better nourished and healthier children and families; lower childbirth-related death rates; greater opportunities and life choices for more women (including better chances to protect themselves against HIV/AIDS); and greater participation of women in development, and in political and economic decision-making.
>
> (UNGEI 2000: 3)

The objectives of the programme were primarily strategic with some orientation to intervention concerned with 'the elimination of gender discrimination and gender disparity'. The latter was understood not simply numerically, but to include policy and practice with many partners in a broad approach to education. However, the lack of a clear strategy beyond alliance building and the inadequacy of the monitoring tools made it difficult for UNGEI to orient itself. It was not able to put the more expansive moral meanings of the stance it had taken into action or open a space where a further clarification of questions concerning rights, distribution or obligations could take place. Without a single-minded interventionist approach or clear objectives regarding institution building or forming alliances it would inevitably come to be charged with 'not doing anything'.

One objective was to develop partnerships to help overcome the factors that impacted negatively on girls' education. In setting up UNGEI, it was acknowledged that much excellent work was being done, but that this was not sufficiently collaborative or strategic in its orientation. There were problems with a duplication of effort. Field-based initiatives by UN agencies, it was felt, should engage in joint programming, and collaboration in the collection of statistics (UNGEI 2000: 5). Work with governments was considered key and it was envisaged that UNGEI would 'make [governments] challenge and eliminate gender bias and discrimination through sound policy formulation, and emphasis on capacity development and sustainability' (UNGEI 2000: 8). The UNGEI remit also included 'broadening involvement in education, with a particular emphasis on family, community, civil society and NGO participation, strengthening social mobilisation, and expanding partnerships between and among UN entities and other organizations' (UNGEI 2000: 8). The emphasis was to be on country-level action with 'global efforts primarily for advocacy, partnership building, programmatic coherence, monitoring, and general guidance' (UNGEI 2000: 8).

However, strategic alignments without mass-based support were as difficult for a multilateral organization to achieve as they had been for governments and development partners. UNGEI lacked a plan on how its strategic orientation to institution building and advocacy was to be achieved. For nearly four years the organization failed to realize the global promise of institutionalizing social justice.

In launching UNGEI at Dakar in 2000, Kofi Annan laid out a remit for the initiative encompassing

> … an expanded and open partnership of the United Nations system, Governments, donor countries, NGOs, the private sector, and communities and families to demonstrably narrow the gender gap in primary and secondary education by 2005; to ensure that by 2015, all children everywhere – boys and girls alike – will be able to complete primary schooling.
>
> (Annan 2000)

The content and weighting to be given to the different strands of the moral underpinnings of global social justice articulated in the conferences of the 1990s was not addressed. Without this further specification, the strategic vision would be hard to sustain as pressures grew for visible delivery of programmes and results. In this climate UNGEI was pushed towards a more interventionist agenda.

The first annual review of the work on UNGEI in 2001 indicated that it had made virtually no connection to civil society and involved just a handful of UN agencies in an eclectic range of activities (UNGEI Task Force 2002). While the report described this as 'laying the foundations' (UNGEI Task Force 2002: 10), it appeared that much of the dynamism that had generated the initial concept paper was going untapped. In 2002 it was still difficult to identify what was the work of UNGEI and what was general input into ongoing UN initiatives, with very little advance of the debate on gender and education.

In June 2002, a consultation on the direction of UNGEI initiated by civil society groups took place in Geneva. Over 50 organizations took part. Thirty-five representatives from national and regional NGOs joined donors and other UN agencies. NGOs argued that they expected UNGEI to play a facilitative and monitoring role with regard to girls' education. They wanted the organization to give voice to their concerns in international fora (UNGEI 2002). They looked to UNGEI to work interactively with them, primarily in advocacy. INGOs indicated they wanted UNGEI to bring their voice to global planning meetings, to act as an honest broker in holding governments accountable, to share good practice, and to train a critical mass of gender advocates. They saw a key role for UNGEI to advocate for gender equality – broadly conceived – to be given a central place in countries' EFA plans (UNGEI 2002). The meeting drew up a detailed strategic plan stressing the need for UNGEI to have a proper structure and leadership. The NGO vision for UNGEI clarified an institutional and interactive remit. Global social justice was seen at this meeting as a process of building global democracy, not exclusively working through states, but widening participation in decision making. There is also evidence in the report of some concern that UNGEI provide the information for wider demands with regard to gender equality and education rooted in human rights.

This interactive vision for UNGEI had very little resource or political power behind it. The NGO representatives at the Geneva meeting did not have the capacity to develop a new role for UNGEI from within their organizations and had no mechanisms to take these visions down to national and district level in particular countries. Without a dynamic connection to civil society, and a grounding in local concerns, UNGEI, with its secretariat located in UNICEF, continued to drift, largely indistinguishable from some of the large UN agencies that constituted it.

One year later, in a critical paper about UNGEI for a UNESCO working group meeting on EFA, Cream Wright, head of education at UNICEF wrote how UNGEI had done some work to establish itself at the global level, but was virtually unknown at a regional or country level (Wright 2003). Wright's account of the history of UNGEI made virtually no mention of engagement with NGOs or civil society. He outlined that the initial vision for UNGEI encompassed the support it could provide to governments to make detailed plans concerning gender targets. In his interpretation, UNGEI had been conceived as a partnership with governments to help secure resources to tackle gender gaps in 52 countries with gender gaps of more that 5 per cent and to help support policy and planning on enrolment, curriculum, teachers, learner safety, reproductive health and ICT. Wright's analysis was that what was wrong with the original UNGEI vision was that not all of these areas were amenable to detailed planning with regard to gender. He advocated transforming UNGEI to make connections across development sectors, arguing that while measurement of access and achievement in education was still crucial, there was a need to make links with other development sectors and agencies working in health, nutrition and safety. Wright thus appeared to be suggesting UNGEI's remit become primarily interventionist with governments, rather than civil society. This entailed some elements of institutionalization. He placed emphasis on doing what was required to meet basic needs rather than attending to distributive questions or thinking through meanings and obligations entailed by the language of rights or diffuse interactive engagements with civil society.

Wright's paper was an attempt to assert UNICEF leadership over UNGEI. He argued that the origins of UNGEI in CEDAW with its stress on women's rights were often difficult for governments to agree to, but if UNGEI was seen as a form of technical assistance to governments it would win major support. UNICEF was in a position to provide leadership to this kind of partnership (Wright 2003). Wright's analysis was that girls' education was not just about redressing gender disparity in schooling, but also about

> focusing on the most pivotal group (girls) in order to help eradicate poverty, prevent and ameliorate the impact of HIV/AIDS, promote democratic decision-making and good governance, mitigate the impact of food deficits and malnutrition, as well as safeguard children from harmful practices like child labour and sexual exploitation.
>
> (Wright 2003: 7)

He thus outlined some of the multi-dimensionality of a rights-based approach, but the long list had little focus on gender equality. Thus, in clarifying a role for UNGEI linked to UNICEF's objectives, Wright was pointing away from the 'unstable' interactive advocacy role envisaged at the NGO consultation the year before. The vision of global social justice linked to participation and government accountability suggested by the NGOs was to be replaced by a vision of global social justice linked to joined-up policy – institutionalization – and good practice to remedy gross insufficiency – interventionism. While these were both strategic visions, Wright's was oriented more towards interventions to 'get girls in school' while the NGO approach was concerned with interactive processes to develop the moral and strategic basis for this, so that action was taken through a nuanced assessment of rights and obligations.

At the end of 2003, a Global Advisory Committee (GAC) was established for UNGEI. There were only four civil society representatives on this Committee with the largest presence being that of international donors – seven seats – and UN agencies – six seats. A loose group of partners, with no official standing with regard to decision making and policy direction, included a wider range of NGOs. Civil society representatives on UNGEI GAC differed in the extent to which they themselves were accountable to country and district level decision-making bodies.

In 2004 and 2005, UNGEI concentrated on developing communication, building a website and publicizing achievements through the Gender Achievements and Prospects (GAP) project which documented interventionist achievements at local level. At the end of 2005, it was working towards establishing a regional presence in South Asia (UNICEF 2005a). The UNGEI website presented the organization primarily in interventionist and institutionalizing terms concerned to narrow the gender gap in education worldwide and to co-ordinate country level activities. In a statement entitled 'About us' the organization described itself as concerned with influencing decision making and investments 'to ensure gender equity and equality in national education policies, plans and programmes' (UNGEI 2005: 1). The language of rights and the aspirations of civil society to hold governments and IGOs accountable had been replaced with a language in which attention to gender entailed efficient planning. Between the initial concept paper and the launch of the website there had been a shift from global social justice seen in interactive and institution building terms to a more limited interventionist orientation with some concern with institutionalisation.

The story of UNGEI suggests that whatever difficulties governments had in delivering on access or building institutions for gender equality in education, establishing an organizational base at a global level was at least, if not more, difficult. UNGEI, a latecomer among the UN initiatives, had no independent stature and no powerful voice. It was thus difficult to develop an identity independent from UNICEF. The attempt by civil society to give UNGEI a different character floundered for lack of resources and internal accountability processes. The compromise represented by the establishment of the GAC with limited civil society presence, was a compromise to achieve technical delivery, like gender plans, oversight of the inclusion of gender in the FTI, a multimedia website, and information sharing. These were of course important for building a global social justice project, but they were unable to provide leadership with regard to the thinking about rights and the connection with other domains of gender equality envisaged in the initial concept document.

That UNGEI survived at all over five years in the rootless cosmopolitan world of UN agencies was an important achievement. But its frequent changes of direction, its lack of connection with global civil society, the failure to make contact with the global women's movement, the frailties of its democratic processes all point to fragilities and unrealized aspirations associated with the interactive approach to global social justice. UNGEI, like many IGOs, indicates the difficulties of democratic institution building on a global stage. But the untapped potential of UNGEI appears to be to build links with global civil society, deepen dialogues about rights and capabilities, take the interactive global social justice project to a new stage, not ossify it in a particular institutional or interventionist form.

Conclusion

The third approach to the practice of global social justice for gender equality in education described in this chapter has been more diffuse than those concerned with interventions and institution building. While GRB and alternative forms of monitoring may be able to help address questions of distribution, there are as yet no robust studies that show their capacity to do this. The actions of SIDA and the work of UNGEI may have had the capacity to initiate discussion about the content and weight of claims about rights and obligations, and the connection between rights and capabilities, but these concerns have been largely submerged in the urgency to deliver places in school and institutionalize the global alliances through the FTI. The very limited debate on these issues currently taking place in global civil society does not augur well for the development of the interactive approach. The *Beyond Access* project may have raised issues regarding the meanings of gender equality in education with civil society organizations but these jostle for attention with more clearly formulated concerns articulated through campaigns like Make Poverty History to hold governments to account for non-delivery on the 2005 MDG target. Only in detailed work at country level does the interactive approach appear to have potential to ignite enthusiasm in workshops and network building. Thus, the potential of the interactive approach to global social justice remains at the time of writing largely unrealized, an idea rich in potential but waiting for institutional processes and organizational action to give it more substantive form.

10 Gender equality, global social justice and the promise of school

This book set out to examine some of the ways in which gender equality in education had been conceptualized and engaged as an aspiration of global social justice. It has partly been concerned with the ethical language in which understandings of gender, schooling and global justice have been framed and partly with some of the policy and practice which had put these ideas into action

Over time different meanings of gender, equality, education, and global social justice have been associated with different framings of the ethical debate and different forms of global action. A descriptive meaning of gender, that views the term as a noun denoting boys and girls, links with an approach to equality and education that means equal allocation of places in school and resources for education opportunities. This vocabulary has been associated with an analytical framework which regards gender equality in education as largely instrumental for wider political, economic and social benefits. Within this framework, global social justice is seen primarily in terms of interventions by governments, multinational organizations or aid agencies to address the most basic of needs for schooling in the poorest countries. Interventionist strategies in global social justice have been concerned to enrol girls in school, but have not considered it either ethically appropriate or institutionally desirable to raise wider questions about gendered processes of learning or wider social conditions of gender inequality in nation states. The interventionist approach thus fits with many of the concerns of thin versions of cosmopolitanism.

A second meaning of gender is concerned with the ways in which gendered power structures social relations and institutions. This framing has been associated with approaches to equality in education that have sought to challenge and change gendered relations in learning and teaching, the form of institutions and the outcomes of education. Equality has been concerned with changing the values and processes within institutions and confronting unequal forms of power in social relations. This has been associated with normative ideas about rights entailing legal and moral forms of equality and concomitant obligations to respect these. This framework has viewed global social justice largely in terms of building the institutional framework to deliver aid adequately and efficiently to monitor progress on internationally agreed goals and to promote gender equality within institutional settings. It has been concerned with appropriate procedures for global social justice. Questions about gender inequalities within global institutions have fallen within its ambit, although processes to address these have thus far remained undocumented. Indeed, all the instances of global institutionalization of gender equality in education highlight how difficult this is, and how much interventionism remains an easier option. This second approach is ambiguous on the debate regarding thin and thick versions of cosmopolitanism. Global institutions might seek to put in place values associated with thick cosmopolitanism or may elevate the importance and autonomy of local spaces, such as states, or local communities.

A third meaning of gender denotes human variability and is concerned with gender as a process of connecting and changing social conditions. This framing has been associated with approaches to equality in education that have sought ways of responding to demands of equality, difference and diversity within a single normative framework, paying attention to distributive questions, and the moral basis of rights and justice claims. This has been associated with the connection between rights and capabilities and the multi-dimensionality that capabilities signal with regard to evaluating valued freedoms. This framework has been concerned to connect institutions tasked to deliver global social justice regarding gender and schooling with processes of dialogue, critique and widening forms of action and obligation that go beyond institutional formation. At the time of writing, this orientation to a thicker form of cosmopolitanism has not been matched by substantive social processes to take forward this interactive form of global social justice, but there are indications of forms of development assistance, monitoring and alliance building that might promote this.

The three different forms of the ethical argument for global social justice, gender and schooling have had uneven effects on global action. Interventionist approaches have had the longest history, attract some of the most powerful global actors, and, focused on initiatives concerned with abolishing school fees or food for education, present the most straightforward programme to get girls into school. Institutional approaches, although more difficult to orient to wider gender equality goals, present global action as rational, fundable and monitorable. They thus appear as 'good sense' and are likely to underpin much global politics about gender and schooling in the next 10 years. Interactive approaches are currently the most fragile, their potential largely untested, and without significant big players to argue for what they can achieve. They are associated with a fragmented global civil society where the global women's movement has not yet made common cause with the EFA movement. Important alliances will have to be built if this form of global social justice is to realize its promise.

Approximately one-sixth of the world's population lacks adequate education and gender is implicated in the numbers affected, the institutions that perpetuate this and processes and possibilities for change. One single approach to global social justice cannot address the enormity of this challenge. Interventionist, institutional and interactive forms of global social justice all need to be mobilized in tandem if goals for gender equality and education are to be realized. One approach alone may go some way to address aspects of injustice, but too restricted a strategy limits meanings of gender, schooling or global social justice unduly. The most fruitful direction seems to be building a connection between all three approaches. This requires the development of political and social theory that can illuminate this task. Careful, critical documentation of actions taken to advance demands for gender equality and schooling worldwide are also needed, as is attention to new forms of policy and practice that express the importance of linking strategies. It is this combination of scholarship, politics and practice that is needed to engage with the complexity and ambiguities of a most pressing global challenge.

Appendix 1

Historical statistics

Table 1.1 Children and adults with little or no schooling by gender as a proportion of the world population, 2002–4 (Population 000)

	Girls/Women	*Boys/Men*	*Total*
Children without primary school	54,581	44,722	99,309
Youth and adults (over 15) with no schooling	574,598	329,441	904,038
Children leaving primary school after 5 years or less	144,155	110,951	214,621
Total (%)	773,332 (62)	485,114 (38)	1,217,962
World population	3,214,983	3,248,080	6,210,815
Children and adults with little or no schooling as a percentage of world population	24.03	14.94	19.6

Source: Calculated from UNESCO 2005a: 286, 317, 342; UNStats: 2005b

Table 1.2 Primary gross enrolment ratio by gender and region, 1965–2000 (GER girls (boys))

	1965	*1975*	*1985*	*1995*	*2000*
Arab States	41 (71)	56 (86)	70 (91)	77 (93)	86 (97)
East Asia and Pacific	83(116)	107(120)	110(124)	115(122)	109(111)
Latin America and Caribbean	80 (82)	97 (99)	105(108)	104(107)	122(125)
North America and West Europe	102(104)	100(100)	99(101)	100(102)	102(103)
South Asia	50 (88)	58 (92)	72(100)	81(103)	87(104)
Sub-Saharan Africa	37 (56)	55 (73)	67 (82)	64 (77)	76 (87)

Source: World Bank 2002b; UNESCO 1995; 33; UNESCO 2003: 234–5.

Table 1.3 Secondary gross enrolment ratio by gender and region, 1965–2000 (GER girls (boys))

Region	1965	1975	1985	1990	1995	2000
Arab States	12 (28)	24 (35)	41 (53)	38 (60)	54 (58)	71 (69)
East Asia and Pacific	28 (34)	43 (48)	57 (58)	42 (55)	63 (64)	81 (74)
Latin America and Caribbean	24 (26)	40 (38)	57 (51)	58 (48)	63 (57)	84 (78)
North America and West Europe	51 (59)	78 (80)	90 (88)	101 (96)	112 (109)	106 (107)
South and West Asia	10 (23)	16 (30)	21 (33)	21 (47)	47 (58)	45 (55)
Sub-Saharan Africa	4 (7)	8 (14)	16 (23)	14 (21)	26 (31)	24 (29)

Source: Derived from UNESCO 1976 pp. 144–91; 1983 pp. III 19–68; 1990 pp. 3.18–3.69; 1999 pp. II 262–3; 2003/4 pp. 350–1.

Table 1.4 Enrolment and retention by gender and school phase in selected countries, 1965–2000

Table 1.4.1 Africa and Arab states, 1965–2000

	1965	1970	1975	1980	1985	1990	1995	2000
Botswana								
Girls (boys) primary NER	45 (34)	–	70 (58)	82 (68)	94 (84)	98 (91)	83 (79)	86 (83)
Girls (boys) retention	–	67 (61)	–	84 (80)	91 (88)	98 (94)	93 (87)	92 (87)
Girls (boys) sec. GER	3 (4)	7 (8)	18 (16)	20 (17)	31 (29)	45 (40)	66 (60)	82 (77)
Burundi								
Girls (boys) primary NER	15 (36)	–	17 (27)	17 (26)	35 (47)	49 (57)	28 (31)	45 (59)
Girls (boys) retention	–	–	57 (57)	–	87 (87)	75 (74)	–	59 (68)
Girls (boys) sec. GER	1 (2)	1 (3)	1 (3)	2 (4)	3 (5)	4 (7)	–	9 (12)
Egypt								
Girls (boys) primary NER	60 (90)	44 (69)	56 (88)	65 (90)	–	79 (92)	88 (98)	90 (95)
Girls (boys) retention	–	74 (85)	81 (88)	88 (92)	–	–	97 (98)	99 (99)
Girls (boys) sec. GER	15 (37)	22 (46)	30 (56)	39 (61)	54 (77)	68 (84)	70 (82)	83 (88)
Gambia, The								
Girls (boys) primary NER	11 (26)	14 (30)	13 (27)	35 (65)	48 (77)	41 (59)	57 (72)	66 (71)
Girls (boys) retention	–	85 (92)	75 (95)	71 (74)	93 (97)	89 (85)	79 (81)	63 (75)
Girls (boys) sec. GER	4 (8)	4 (12)	5 (15)	7 (16)	10 (24)	10 (21)	19 (30)	31 (44)
Kenya								
Girls (boys) primary NER	40 (69)	76 (73)	79 (89)	89 (92)	–	74 (74)	–	69 (68)
Girls (boys) retention	–	–	–	62 (60)	–	–	78 (74)	–
Girls (boys) sec. GER	2 (6)	6 (13)	9 (17)	16 (23)	16 (26)	24 (31)	22 (26)	29 (32)
Lesotho								
Girls (boys) primary NER	114 (74)	88 (56)	139 (98)	78 (54)	84 (61)	84 (67)	76 (65)	82 (75)
Girls (boys) retention	–	–	63 (40)	68 (50)	70 (49)	83 (58)	66 (54)	74 (60)
Girls (boys) sec. GER	4 (4)	7 (6)	15 (12)	21 (14)	27 (19)	30 (20)	37 (25)	36 (30)

Table 1.4.1 continued

	1965	1970	1975	1980	1985	1990	1995	2000
Malawi								
Girls (boys) primary NER	32 (55)	–	50 (76)	38 (48)	41 (46)	47 (51)	100 (98)	–
Girls (boys) retention	–	–	33 (40)	40 (48)	54 (60)	57 (71)	44 (48)	47 (61)
Girls (boys) sec. GER	1 (3)	1 (3)	2 (5)	2 (5)	2 (6)	3 (5)	12 (21)	31 (41)
Mauritius								
Girls (boys) primary NER	77 (82)	–	84 (84)	93 (92)	98 (96)	95 (95)	96 (96)	95 (95)
Girls (boys) retention	–	–	–	–	97 (97)	98 (98)	99 (98)	99 (99)
Girls (boys) sec. GER	22 (40)	23 (33)	34 (41)	49 (51)	49 (53)	53 (53)	64 (60)	75 (79)
Morocco								
Girls (boys) primary NER	35 (78)	–	35 (58)	45 (71)	48 (73)	47 (67)	63 (82)	74 (82)
Girls (boys) retention	–	–	79 (78)	78 (79)	67 (60)	76 (75)	74 (76)	83 (84)
Girls (boys) sec. GER	12 (40)	7 (18)	12 (21)	20 (32)	27 (40)	28 (39)	33 (44)	35 (44)
Mozambique								
Girls (boys) primary NER	26 (48)	–	–	34 (39)	47 (56)	42 (55)	34 (45)	50 (59)
Girls (boys) retention	–	–	–	–	–	28 (37)	36 (52)	47 (56)
Girls (boys) sec. GER	2 (3)	–	2 (4)	3 (8)	4 (10)	6 (10)	5 (9)	9 (15)
Rwanda								
Girls (boys) primary NER	43 (64)	–	57 (66)	57 (62)	58 (61)	67 (67)	60 (58)	85 (83)
Girls (boys) retention	–	37 (42)	58 (58)	74 (69)	70 (68)	59 (61)	–	41 (39)
Girls (boys) sec. GER	1 (3)	1 (3)	1 (3)	3 (4)	5 (7)	7 (9)	–	14 (14)
Senegal								
Girls (boys) primary NER	29 (52)	–	35 (55)	30 (44)	39 (51)	41 (55)	48 (60)	60 (66)
Girls (boys) retention	–	71 (74)	–	82 (89)	–	–	81 (89)	65 (70)
Girls (boys) sec. GER	3 (10)	5 (13)	–	7 (15)	9 (18)	11 (21)	12 (20)	14 (21)
Swaziland								
Girls (boys) primary NER	–	66 (64)	75 (72)	81 (77)	80 (78)	91 (88)	94 (93)	94 (92)
Girls (boys) retention	–	67 (66)	75 (70)	–	78 (70)	78 (74)	89 (95)	76 (69)
Girls (boys) sec. GER	8 (9)	16 (21)	29 (35)	37 (39)	42 (43)	44 (45)	53 (53)	60 (60)

continued…

Table 1.4.1 continued

	1965	1970	1975	1980	1985	1990	1995	2000
Tanzania								
Girls (boys) primary NER	25 (40)	–	60 (79)	95(101)	56 (55)	50 (49)	48 (47)	48 (46)
Girls (boys) retention	–	–	82 (88)	90 (89)	87 (85)	81 (77)	84 (78)	80 (76)
Girls (boys) sec. GER	1 (3)	2 (4)	2 (5)	2 (4)	2 (4)	4 (6)	5 (6)	5 (6)
Uganda								
Girls (boys) primary NER	50 (83)	–	42 (61)	35 (43)	53 (60)	48 (58)	–	83 (92)
Girls (boys) retention	–	–	–	–	–	–	–	64 (63)
Girls (boys) sec. GER	2 (6)	2 (6)	2 (6)	3 (7)	8 (16)	9 (16)	9 (15)	12 (19)
Zambia								
Girls (boys) primary NER	46 (59)	–	86 (103)	81 (86)	85 (90)	78 (81)	74 (76)	65 (66)
Girls (boys) retention	–	–	77 (84)	82 (88)	84 (88)	–	–	75 (79)
Girls (boys) sec. GER	3 (8)	8 (17)	10 (20)	11 (22)	13 (23)	–	–	21 (26)
Zimbabwe								
Girls (boys) primary NER	92(128)	–	90 (106)	–	100(100)	86 (86)	79 (78)	80 (80)
Girls (boys) retention	–	–	–	–	–	81 (72)	–	–
Girls (boys) sec. GER	5 (7)	6 (9)	7 (10)	–	33 (50)	46 (53)	43 (52)	42 (47)

Table 1.4.2 Asia, 1965–2000

	1965	1970	1975	1980	1985	1990	1995	2000
Afghanistan								
Girls (boys) primary NER	5 (26)		5(30)	11 (46)	11 (23)	19 (34)	15 (42)	–
Girls (boys) retention				61 (62)			52 (39)	–
Girls (boys) sec. GER	1 (4)	2 (13)	2 (13)	4 (16)	6 (12)		11 (32)	–
Bangladesh								
Girls (boys) primary NER			60(106)	45 (67)	48 (64)	66 (76)	–	90 (88)
Girls (boys) retention				26 (18)			–	68 (63)
Girls (boys) sec. GER			11 (38)	9 (26)	11 (24)	13 (25)	–	47 (45)

continued…

Table 1.4.2 continued

	1965	1970	1975	1980	1985	1990	1995	2000
Indonesia								
Girls (boys) primary NER	65 (79)	–	67 (78)	83 (93)	95(100)	95 (99)	94 (97)	92 (93)
Girls (boys) retention	–	–	–	–	–	–	89 (88)	92 (87)
Girls (boys) sec. GER	7 (17)	10 (20)	15 (24)	23 (35)	42 (53)	40 (48)	48 (55)	56 (58)
Philippines								
Girls (boys) primary NER	111(115)	–	108(102)	92 (94)	96 (97)	96 (97)	–	93 (92)
Girls (boys) retention	–	–	–	–	79 (79)	–	–	83 (76)
Girls (boys) sec. GER	40 (42)	–	47 (65)	69 (60)	66 (63)	–	78 (77)	81 (74)
Korea (Rep.)								
Girls (boys) primary NER	99(103)	96 (96)	109 (99)	100(100)	95 (94)	100(100)	99 (98)	100 (99)
Girls (boys) retention	–	–	94 (94)	94 (94)	99 (99)	100 (99)	99 (98)	100(100)
Girls (boys) sec. GER	25 (44)	32 (50)	48 (64)	74 (82)	87 (91)	88 (91)	101(101)	94 (94)
Sri Lanka								
Girls (boys) primary NER	86 (98)	–	73 (80)	101(106)	100(100)	86 (89)	93 (92)	99 (98)
Girls (boys) retention	–	–	–	–	93 (92)	95 (94)	–	–
Girls (boys) sec. GER	34 (35)	48 (46)	49 (47)	57 (52)	67 (60)	77 (71)	78 (72)	

Table 1.4.3 Latin America and the Caribbean, 1965–2000

	1965	1970	1975	1980	1985	1990	1995	2000
Bolivia								
Girls (boys) primary NER	60 (86)	–	72 (88)	72 (81)	82 (90)	87 (95)	58 (63)	97 (97)
Girls (boys) retention	–	–	–	–	–	–	–	77 (79)
Girls (boys) sec. GER	15 (21)	20 (28)	26 (35)	32 (42)	34 (40)	34 (40)	–	78 (81)
Chile								
Girls (boys) primary NER	122(125)	–	97 (95)	–	–	87 (88)	86 (88)	88 (89)
Girls (boys) retention	–	81 (82)	76 (72)	–	–	–	100(100)	100(100)
Girls (boys) sec. GER	36 (31)	42 (36)	52 (45)	56 (49)	71 (65)	76 (70)	73 (66)	87 (85)

continued ...

Table 1.4.3 continued

	1965	1970	1975	1980	1985	1990	1995	2000
Cuba								
Girls (boys) primary NER	119(123)	–	–	95 (95)	91(91)	92 (92)	99 (99)	97 (98)
Girls (boys) retention	–	75 (67)	–	–	–	–	–	98 (97)
Girls (boys) sec. GER	24 (22)	23 (21)	42 (42)	83 (79)	88(82)	95 (83)	82 (78)	87 (83)
Costa Rica								
Girls (boys) primary NER	105(107)	88 (87)	92 (92)	90 (89)	84(83)	87 (86)	89 (86)	91 (91)
Girls (boys) retention	–	79 (76)	85 (78)	82 (77)	87(85)	84 (81)	–	95 (93)
Girls (boys) sec. GER	26 (22)	29 (27)	45 (40)	51 (44)	43(39)	43 (41)	56 (40)	63 (58)
Mexico								
Girls (boys) primary NER	90 (94)	–	–	120(122)	–	99(100)	100 (99)	100 (99)
Girls (boys) retention	–	–	73 (64)	–	–	82 (81)	86 (85)	91 (90)
Girls (boys) sec. GER	13 (21)	17 (26)	28 (41)	46 (51)	52(54)	55 (55)	61 (61)	77 (73)
Nicaragua								
Girls (boys) primary NER	69 (68)	–	86 (83)	74 (72)	79(74)	74 (71)	85 (82)	81 (80)
Girls (boys) retention	–	35 (31)	–	–	–	57 (51)	57 (51)	58 (51)
Girls (boys) sec. GER	12 (14)	17 (19)	25 (24)	45 (39)	55 (23)	45 (35)	53 (45)	58 (50)
Jamaica								
Girls (boys) primary NER	106(112)	–	90 (89)	97 (96)	95(92)	96 (96)	–	95 (95)
Girls (boys) retention	–	–	88 (88)	–	–	–	99 (93)	93 (88)
Girls (boys) sec. GER	49 (53)	45 (46)	63 (53)	71 (63)	63(56)	68 (60)	–	85 (82)
Trinidad and Tobago								
Girls (boys) primary NER	90 (97)	92 (90)	89 (86)	90 (89)	92(91)	91 (91)	94 (83)	92 (93)
Girls (boys) retention	–	–	–	87 (85)	–	96 (96)	97 (98)	76 (66)
Girls (boys) sec. GER	32 (37)	45 (40)	41 (36)	–	84 (78)	83 (80)	75 (72)	84 (78)

Source: UNESCO 1976: 144–78; World Bank 1979: 170–1; UNESCO 1980: 180–2, 196; UNESCO 1983: 19–55; World Bank 1985: 222–3; UNESCO 1987: 3.21–3.57; UNESCO 1990: 3.18–3.55; UNESCO 1993: 128; UNESCO 1995: 18–55, 134–6; UNESCO 1998: 3–45; 132–4; UNESCO 1999: II.263–331, II.419–450; World Bank 2002b, 2002c; UNESCO 2003: 328–35, 343, 344–51; UNESCO 2004: 302–9; UNESCO 2005a: 334.4

Table 1.5 Highest, lowest and median enrolments by gender and region (1965) tracked to 2000 (Girls (boys) Primary NER and Secondary GER)

	1965	1975	1985	1995	2000
Lesotho					
Primary	114 (74)	139 (98)	84 (61)	76 (55)	82 (75)
Secondary	4 (4)	15 (12)	27 (19)	37 (25)	36 (30)
Uganda					
Primary	50 (83)	42 (61)	53 (60)	–	83 (92)
Secondary	2 (6)	2 (6)	8 (16)	9 (15)	12 (19)
Burundi					
Primary	15 (36)	17 (27)	35 (47)	28 (31)	45 (59)
Secondary	1 (2)	1 (3)	3 (5)	–	9 (12)
Philippines					
Primary	111(115)	108(102)	96 (97)	–	93 (92)
Secondary	40 (12)	47 (65)	66 (63)	78 (77)	81 (74)
Bangladesh*					
Primary		60(106)	48 (64)	–	90 (88)
Secondary		11 (38)	11 (24)	–	47 (45)
Afghanistan					
Primary	5 (26)	5 (30)	11 (23)	15 (42)	–
Secondary	1 (4)	2 (13)	6 (12)	11 (32)	–
Chile					
Primary	122(125)	97 (95)	–	86 (88)	88 (89)
Secondary	36 (31)	52 (45)	71 (65)	73 (66)	87 (85)
Mexico					
Primary	90 (94)	–	–	100 (99)	100 (89)
Secondary	13 (21)	28 (41)	52 (54)	61 (61)	77 (73)
Bolivia					
Primary	60 (86)	72 (88)	82 (90)	–	97 (97)
Secondary	15 (21)	26 (35)	34 (40)	–	78 (81)

* Bangladesh became independent from Pakistan in 1971

Source: Derived from Table 1.4.

Table 1.6 Countries with girls' NER 90% and below, 2001

Uruguay	89.8	Malawi	81.0
South Africa	89.8	Namibia	80.7
Bulgaria	89.7	United Arab Republic	79.7
Lebanon	89.4	Lao PDR	79.4
Kazakhstan	89.0	Azerbaijan	79.1
El Salvador	88.9	Moldova Republic	77.8
Czech Republic	88.4	Equatorial Guinea	77.8
Kyrgyzstan	88.4	Gabon	77.8
Honduras	88.3	Swaziland	77.0
Egypt	88.3	India	75.7
Chile	88.3	Serbia & Montenegro	75.0
Turks & Caicos	88.0	Oman	74.9
Romania	88.0	Papua New Guinea	73.0
Latvia	87.9	Kenya	70.5
Mongolia	87.9	Gambia	69.7
Croatia	87.8	Madagascar	68.9
Slovakia	87.8	Nepal	66.0
Bahamas	87.6	Zambia	65.6
Lesotho	87.6	Mauritania	65.2
Bangladesh	87.5	Liberia	61.1
Colombia	86.3	Ghana	59.0
Morocco	85.1	Benin	58.1
Rwanda	85.1	Saudi Arabia	56.5
Thailand	85.1	Mozambique	55.9
Macao, China	84.8	Senegal	54.5
Turkey	84.8	Tanzania	54.5
Kuwait	84.3	Guinea	53.7
Armenia	84.2	Cote D'Ivoire	53.1
Togo	83.6	Pakistan	50.0
Cambodia	83.2	Burundi	48.0
Iraq	83.2	Chad	46.8
Zimbabwe	83.1	Ethiopia	40.8
Guatemala	82.9	Eritrea	39.2
Botswana	82.7	Guinea-Bissau	37.5
Nicaragua	82.2	Djibouti	29.6
Myanmar	82.0	Burkina-Faso	28.9
Ukraine	81.4	Niger	27.5

Source: UNESCO 2005: 287–93.

Table 1.7 Countries with percentage change[1] in girls' primary NER of more than 25%, 1990–2000

Countries	Girls' primary NER 1990	Girls' primary NER 2000	% gain in NER 1990–2000
Guinea	17	42	147
Mali	17	39	129
Eritrea	17	38	123
Chad	22	47	113
Mauritania	30	62	106
Ethiopia	21	41	95
Benin	31	57	84
Yemen	27	49	81
Kuwait	47	82	74
Nepal	41	67	63
Gambia	41	66	61
Morocco	47	74	57
Cote d'Ivoire	37	54	46
Senegal	41	60	46
Burkina Faso	20	29	45
Guinea-Bissau	32	45	41
Bangladesh	66	90	36
Cambodia	61	82	34
Guatemala	61	82	34
Laos	58	78	34
Niger	18	24	33
Togo	62	82	32
Rwanda	67	85	27
Suriname	80	100	25
Vanuatu	71	89	25
Barbados	80	100	25

Source: Derived from UNESCO 1993: 128–33; World Bank 2002b; UNESCO 2004: 328–35; UNESCO 2005a: 312–19.

Note

1   Percentage change is the difference between the NER in 2000 and 1990 as a fraction of the NER in 1990 expressed as a percentage. The formula used is thus $100(Y - X)/X$ where Y = NER in 2000 and X=NER in 1990.

Table 1.8 Countries showing decline in girls' primary NER, 1990–2000

Country	Girls' Primary NER 1990	Girls' Primary NER 2000	% decrease 1990–2000
Samoa	100	95	5
Namibia	90	85	6
Kenya	74	69	7
UAR	94	87	7
Zimbabwe	86	80	7
Iraq	96	86	10
Botswana	98	86	12
Kyrgyzstan	92	81	12
Myanmar	96	83	13
Iran	88	73	17
Zambia	80	65	19
Equatorial Guinea	89	68	23
Serbia & Montenegro	70	51	27
Angola	57	35	39

Source: UNESCO 1993: 128–33; World Bank 2002; UNESCO 2003: 328–35.

Table 1.9 Countries with less than 90% girls completing five years of primary school, 2000

Country	%	Country	%
Uruguay	89.7	El Salvador	70.0
Guyana	89.6	Cambodia	69.6
Panama	89.2	Niger	68.4
Sudan	88.4	Bangladesh	67.8
Vietnam	87.9	Ghana	65.2
Peru	86.1	Senegal	64.8
Djibouti	85.2	Sao Tome & Principe	64.7
Dominica	84.3	South Africa	64.2
Dominican Republic	83.8	India	63.5
Morocco	83.4	Iraq	63.3
St Kitts & Nevis	83.3	Colombia	63.0
Philippines	83.1	Lao PDR	62.7
Belize	81.5	Myanmar	60.5
Nepal	80.8	Ethiopia	59.0
Tonga	80.6	Burundi	58.8
Tanzania	79.9	Nicaragua	58.3
Togo	79.7	Mauritania	55.8
Swaziland	79.2	Guatemala	54.0
Mali	79.1	Mozambique	46.8
Ecuador	78.6	Cook Islands	46.8
Paraguay	78.4	Malawi	46.6
Bolivia	77.1	Rwanda	40.7
Zambia	74.8	Madagascar	34.4
Lesotho	74.2	Guinea-Bissau	33.8
Eritrea	73.7	Equatorial Guinea	31.3

Source: UNESCO 2004: 302–9.

Table 1.10 Countries with less than 80% of girls enrolled in primary school progressing to secondary school, 2001–2

Gambia	79.8	Comoros	59.6
Swaziland	79.6	Mozambique	58.4
Cambodia	79.3	Panama	58.0
Dominican Republic	78.6	Togo	57.8
Bahamas	77.9	St Vincent/Grenada	57.8
Tonga	77.6	Netherlands Antilles	57.3
Eritrea	77.6	Djibouti	57.0
British Virgin Islands	77.5	Zambia	55.6
Cape Verde	76.2	Benin	51.0
Syria	76.2	Mali	50.6
Nepal	75.9	Congo	46.0
Lao PDR	75.6	Guinea	45.5
St Lucia	74.6	Uganda	44.1
PNG	73.5	Mauritania	44.0
Turks & Caicos	71.1	Madagascar	43.7
Ecuador	70.8	Vanuatu	43.4
Kenya	70.4	Niger	40.6
Zimbabwe	70.2	Chad	39.0
Israel	69.3	Burkina Faso	38.7
Mauritius	68.4	Senegal	38.2
Lesotho	66.7	Cote D'Ivoire	36.3
Myanmar	65.8	Cameroon	25.4
Sao Tome	62.6	Tanzania	17.9
		Suriname	10.0

Source: UNESCO 2005a: 328–35.

Table 1.11 Countries where women comprise less than 33% of legislators, senior officials and managers

Countries	Percentage	Countries	Percentage
Argentina	25	Namibia	30
Austria	27	Belize	31
Bahrain	10	Pakistan	2
Belgium	31	Saudi Arabia	31
Bulgaria	30		
Croatia	26	Bangladesh	8
United Arab Emirates	8	Botswana	31
Chile	24	Cambodia	14
Hong Kong	26	Dominican Republic	31
Netherlands	26	Ecuador	26
Malta	18	Egypt	9
Korea, Rep. of	6	El Salvador	32
Singapore	26	Georgia	28
Czech Rep.	26	Honduras	22
Greece	26	Iran	13
Norway	30	Macedonia	27
Iceland	29	Malaysia	23
Israel	29	Maldives	15
Cyprus	18	Mongolia	30
Portugal	32	Occupied Palestine Territories	12
Denmark	26	Paraguay	23
Japan	10	Peru	23
Sweden	30	Romania	31
Italy	21	Sri Lanka	21
Finland	28	Suriname	28
Costa Rica	29	Swaziland	24
Switzerland	28	Thailand	26
Spain	30	Turkey	6
Ireland	29	Venezuela	27
Mexico	25	Yemen	4

Source: UNDP 2005: 302–5.

Table 1.12 Countries where education and gender equality present an enormous challenge

	Girls' NER below 90%	Girls' retention over 5 years primary school below 90%	Girls' progression to secondary school less than 70%	Women comprise less than one-third of decision makers
Bangladesh	87.5	67.8	n.i	8
Burundi	48	58.8	n.i	n.i
Cambodia	83.2	69.6	n.i.	14
Djibouti	29.6	85.2	57.0	n.i
El Salvador	88.9	70.0	n.i	32
Equatorial Guinea	77.8	31.3	n.i	n.i
Ethiopia	40.8	59	n.i	n.i
Eritrea	39.2	73.7	n.i	n.i
Ghana	59	65.2	n.i	n.i
Guatemala	82.9	54	n.i	n.i
Guinea-Bissau	37.5	33.8	n.i	n.i
India	75.7	63.5	n.i	n.i
Iraq	83.2	63.3	n.i	n.i
Lao PDR	79.4	62.7	n.i	n.i
Lesotho	87.6	74.2	66.7	n.i
Madagascar	68.9	34.4	43.7	n.i
Malawi	81	46.6	n.i	n.i
Mauritania	65.2	55.8	44.0	n.i
Morocco	85.1	83.4	n.i	n.i
Mozambique	55.9	46.8	58.4	n.i
Myanmar	82.0	60.5	65.8	n.i
Nepal	66	80.8	n.i	n.i
Nicaragua	82.2	58.8	n.i	n.i
Niger	80.7	68.4	40.6	n.i
Rwanda	85.1	40.7	n.i	n.i
Senegal	54.5	64.8	38.2	n.i
South Africa	89.8	64.2	n.i	n.i
Swaziland	77.0	79.2	n.i	24
Tanzania	54.5	79.9	17.9	n.i
Togo	83.6	79.7	57.8	n.i
Uruguay	89.8	89.7	n.i	n.i
Zambia	65.6	74.8	55.6	n.i

Source: Compiled from Tables 1.6, 1.8, 1.9 and 1.10.

Table 1.13 Countries with girls' NER below 60% by income poverty and level of debt service, c. 2001

Countries with Primary NER for girls below 60%	Girls NER c.2000	Population living below US $1 per day (%) 1990–2001	Total debt service as % of GDP 2001	Beneficiary of 2005 debt forgiveness package
Afghanistan	15.0			No
Angola	35.0		19.7	No
Benin	58.1		2.1	Yes
Burkina Faso	28.9	61.2	1.5	Yes
Burundi	48.0	58.4	3.3	No
Central African Rep.	45.0	66.6	1.4	No
Chad	46.8		1.5	No; considered close
Cote d'Ivoire	53.1	12.3	5.9	No
Djibouti	29.6		1.8	No
Eritrea	39.2		1.0	No
Ethiopia	40.8	81.9	2.9	Yes
Ghana	59.0	44.8	6.0	Yes
Guinea	53.7		3.5	No; considered close
Guinea-Bissau	37.5		11.7	No; considered close
Mali	36.0	72.8	3.0	Yes
Mozambique	55.9	37.9	2.4	Yes
Niger	27.5	61.4	1.3	Yes
Nigeria	33.0	70.2	6.2	Yes
Pakistan	50.0	13.4	5.0	No
Saudi Arabia	56.5			No
Senegal	54.5	26.3	4.6	Yes
Sudan	42.0		0.4	No
Somalia	7.0			No
Tanzania	54.5	19.9	1.6	Yes
Yemen	49.0	15.7	3.1	No

Source: UNDP 2003: 245–7; UNESCO 2004: 286–93; UNICEF 2004: 118–21.

Appendix 2

Millennium Development Goals

Table 2.1 Millennium Development Goals: targets and indicators

Goals	Targets	Indicators
1 Eradicate extreme poverty and hunger	1 Reduce by half the proportion of people living on less than a dollar a day	• Proportion of Population below US $1 (PPP) per day (World Bank) • Poverty Gap Ratio, US $1 per day (World Bank) • Share of Poorest Quintile in National Income or Consumption (World Bank)
	2 Reduce by half the proportion of people who suffer from hunger	• Prevalence of Underweight Children Under Five Years of Age (UNICEF) • Proportion of the Population below Minimum Level of Dietary Energy Consumption (FAO)
1 Achieve universal primary education	3 Ensure that all boys and girls complete a full course of primary schooling	• Net Enrolment Ratio in Primary Education (UNESCO) • Proportion of Pupils Starting Grade 1 who Reach Grade 5 (UNESCO) • Literacy Rate of 15–24-year-olds (UNESCO)
3 Promote gender equality and empower women	4 Eliminate gender disparity in primary and secondary education preferably by 2005, and at all levels by 2015	• Ratio of Girls to Boys in Primary, Secondary, and Tertiary Education (UNESCO) • Ratio of Literate Women to Men 15–24 years old (UNESCO)

continued …

Table 2.1 continued

Goals	Targets	Indicators
		• Share of Women in Wage Employment in the Non-Agricultural Sector (ILO) • Proportion of Seats Held by Women in National Parliaments (IPU)
4 Reduce child mortality	5 Reduce by two-thirds the mortality rate among children under five	• Under-Five Mortality Rate (UNICEF) • Infant Mortality Rate (UNICEF) • Proportion of one-year-old Children Immunized Against Measles (UNICEF)
5 Improve maternal health	6 Reduce by three-quarters the maternal mortality ratio	• Maternal Mortality Ratio (WHO) • Proportion of Births Attended by Skilled Health Personnel (UNICEF)
6 Combat HIV/AIDS, malaria and other diseases	7 Halt and begin to reverse the spread of HIV/AIDS	• HIV Prevalence Among 15–24-year-old Pregnant Women (UNAIDS) • Condom use rate of the contraceptive prevalence rate and Population aged 15–24 years with comprehensive correct knowledge of HIV/AIDS (UNAIDS, UNICEF, UN Population Division, WHO) • Ratio of school attendance of orphans to school attendance of non-orphans aged 10–14 years
	8 Halt and begin to reverse the incidence of malaria and other major diseases	• Prevalence and Death Rates Associated with Malaria (WHO) • Proportion of Population in Malaria Risk Areas Using Effective Malaria Prevention and Treatment Measures (UNICEF) • Prevalence and Death Rates Associated Tuberculosis (WHO) • Proportion of Tuberculosis Cases Detected and Cured Under Directly-Observed Treatment Short Courses (WHO)

continued ...

Table 2.1 continued

Goals	Targets	Indicators
7 Ensure environmental sustainability	9 Integrate the principles of sustainable development into country policies and programmes, reverse loss of environmental resources	• Forested land as percentage of land area (FAO) • Ratio of Area Protected to Maintain Biological Diversity to Surface Area (UNEP) • Energy supply (apparent consumption; Kg oil equivalent) per US $1,000 (PPP) GDP (World Bank) • Carbon Dioxide Emissions (per capita) and Consumption of Ozone-Depleting CFCs (ODP tons)
	10 Reduce by half the proportion of people without sustainable access to drinking water	• Proportion of the Population with Sustainable Access to and Improved Water Source (WHO/UNICEF) • Proportion of the Population with Access to Improved Sanitation (WHO/UNICEF)
	11 Achieve significant improvement in lives of at least 100 million slum dwellers	• Slum population as percentage of urban population (secure tenure index) (UN-Habitat)
8 Develop a global partnership for development	12 Develop further an open, rule-based, predictable, non-discriminatory trading and financial system. Includes a commitment to good governance, development and poverty reduction – both nationally and internationally	*Official development assistance* • Net ODA as percentage of OECD/DAC donors' gross national product (targets of 0.7% in total and 0.15% for LDCs) • Proportion of ODA to basic social services (basic education, primary health care, nutrition, safe water and sanitation) • Proportion of ODA that is untied
	13 Address the special needs of the least developed countries. Includes: tariff and quota free access for **least developed**	• Proportion of ODA for environment in small island developing States • Proportion of ODA for transport sector in landlocked countries

continued ...

Table 2.1 continued

Goals	Targets	Indicators
	countries' exports; enhanced programmes for HIPCs and cancellation of official bilateral debt; and more generous ODA for countries committed to poverty reduction	*Market access* • Proportion of exports (by value and excluding arms) admitted free of duties and quotas • Average tariffs and quotas on agricultural products and textiles and clothing
	14 Address the special needs of landlocked countries and small island developing States	• Domestic and export agricultural subsidies in OECD countries • Proportion of ODA provided to help build trade capacity
	15 Deal comprehensively with the debt problems of developing countries through national and international measures in order to make debt sustainable in the long term	*Debt sustainability* • Proportion of official bilateral HIPC debt cancelled • Total Number of Countries that have Reached their HIPC Decision Points and Number that have Reached their Completion Points (Cumulative) (HIPC) (World Bank-IMF)
	16 In cooperation with developing countries, develop and implement strategies for decent and productive work for youth developing countries	• Debt Service as a Percentage of Exports of Goods and Services (World Bank) • Debt Relief Committed Under HIPC Initiative (HIPC) (World Bank-IMF)
	17 In cooperation with pharmaceutical companies, provide access to affordable essential drugs in developing countries	• Unemployment of 15–24-year-olds, Each Sex and Total (ILO) • Proportion of Population with Access to Affordable, Essential Drugs on a Sustainable Basis (WHO) • Telephone Lines and Cellular Subscribers per 100 population (ITU)
	18 In cooperation with the private sector, make available the benefits of new technologies, especially information **and communications**	• Personal Computers in Use and Internet Users per 100 population (ITU)

Appendix 3

Selected interventions on gender and schooling

Table 3.1 Increasing primary NER by gender, Uganda, 1990–2000

	Number of girls 6–12 enrolled in school	Number of boys 6–12 enrolled in school	Total children 6–12 enrolled in school	Girls NER %	Boys NER %	Total NER %
1990	787,556	966,885	1,754,221	48	58	53
1995	988,076	1,092,206	2,080,282	52	58	55
1997	1,718,501	1,905,185	3,623,679	83	92	87
2003	2,916,551	2,894,087	5,810,638	99.9	99.7	99.8

Source: Uganda 2000, 2003.

Table 3.2 Increasing primary regional enrolment by gender in Uganda, 1990–2002

	Kampala	Central	Eastern	Northern	Western	Total
1990 Girls' Enrolment (%)	33,900 (52.4)	250,183 (50.6)	286,372 (44.2)	198,451 (35.6)	281,257 (43.6)	1,050,193 (44.4)
1990 Boys' Enrolment (%)	30,797 (47.6)	244,615 (49.4)	361,948 (55.8)	344,284 (63.4)	335,077 (54.4)	1,316,721 (53.6)
2002 Girls' Enrolment (%)	88,005 (51.8)	934,977 (51.2)	1,047,448 (49.5)	515,295 (43.5)	78,8401 (49.6)	3,101,020 (3,374,126)
2002 Boys' enrolment (%)	82,046 (48.2)	889,751 (47.8)	1,066,880 (50.5)	618,276 (54.5)	80,0844 (50.4)	3,172,248 (3,457,797)

Source: Derived from Unterhalter *et al.* 2005.

Table 3.3 The 25 countries selected for the UNICEF 25 by 2005 initiative

Afghanistan	Democratic Republic of Congo	Nigeria
Bangladesh	Djibouti	Pakistan
Benin	Eritrea	Papua New Guinea
Bhutan	Ethiopia	Sudan
Bolivia	Guinea	Turkey
Burkina Faso	India	Tanzania
Central African Rep.	Malawi	Yemen
Chad	Mali	Zambia
	Nepal	

Source: UNICEF 2004: 4.

Table 3.4 FTI countries by EFA status, December 2004

Fast track countries			Others at risk
Invited and endorsed	*Invited, not yet endorsed*	*Analytical*	*Not invited but at risk of not achieving EFA*
Burkina Faso (2002)	Albania	Bangladesh	Benin
The Gambia (2003)	Bolivia	D. R. of Congo	Burundi
Ghana (2004)	Ethiopia	India	Cameroon
Guinea Republic (2002)	Tanzania	Nigeria	Central African
Guyana (2002)	Uganda	Pakistan	Chad
Honduras (2002)	Zambia		Comoros
Mauritania (2002)			Djibouti
Mozambique (2003)			Equatorial Guinea
Nicaragua (2002)			Eritrea
Niger (2002)			Guinea-Bissau
Vietnam (2003)			Iraq
Yemen (2003)			Lebanon
			Madagascar
			Mali
			Morocco
			Nepal
			Senegal
			Sudan

Source: Rose 2005: 384.

Glossary

Adivasi   literally 'original inhabitants' of India. Indigenous minority ethnic groups in many states. Sometimes referred to as 'Scheduled tribes' because they are listed in the fifth schedule of the Constitution of India.

Civil society   non-state or private organizations (not comprising families and households) generally not concerned with commercial profit and oriented to public or community purposes. Includes work-based organizations, religious and community organizations, women's groups. NGOs are a form of civil society organization, but generally have a particular structure and may operate across national boundaries.

Dalit   literally 'the crushed' or 'the dispersed'. People without caste in India. Often excluded and discriminated against. Sometimes referred to as 'Scheduled Caste'.

EFA (Education for All)   the aspiration for expanding education provision worldwide in terms of the Jomtien Declaration (1990) and the Dakar Framework of Action (2000). Refers both to the general goal and to the movement of governments, IGOs, NGOs, activists, researchers and individuals who support the goal.

FTI (The Fast Track Initiative)   a partnership of governments, multilateral organizations and GCE formed in 2002 to make funds available on particular conditions for EFA.

GAD (Gender and Development)   a theoretical position in development research and a position in development policy and practice focused on analysing gendered structures in the political economy and gender relations in relation to development planning.

GCE (Global Campaign for Education)   a partnership of civil society organizations in 150 countries campaigning to advance EFA.

Gender gap   the lack of parity between the sexes in enrolment or progression ratios.

Gender parity   ratio of female to male values of a given indicator (enrolment or progression). A gender parity index of 1 indicates parity between the sexes.

Gender responsive budgeting   an approach to assessing financial plans to establish the impact of government budgets on women and men.

Global civil society   generally networks of civil society organizations making contact across national boundaries. Sometimes a shorthand for a particular orientation amongst civil society organizations that develops a critique of markets and the state.

Gross Enrolment Rate (GER) total enrolment at a specific level of education (primary, secondary, tertiary) regardless of age, expressed as a percentage of the population in the official age group corresponding to that level of education. GER may be more than 100 per cent if there are large numbers of overage or underage learners.

MDGs (Millennium Development Goals) policy and planning goals set out in the Millennium Declaration (2000) identifying eight goals the world should achieve to address poverty by 2015 (see Appendix 2 for full list of the MDGs).

Net Enrolment Rate (NER) enrolment of the official age group for a given level of education (primary, secondary, tertiary), expressed as a percentage of the population in that age group. May be difficult to calculate in countries where births are not officially registered.

NGO (Non-government organization) a voluntary, non-profit citizens' organization organized on local, provincial, national, regional or international level to deliver services, advocate for certain forms of social development, monitor policies, and represent citizens' concerns to governments and inter-government organizations. Some NGOs organize around specific issues such as education or human rights; some campaign on a broad front. They generally have more formal structures than some civil society organizations.

Out of primary school children children in the official primary school age range who are not enrolled in primary school.

Poverty Reduction Strategy Papers (PRSPs) describe a country's macro-economic, structural and social policies and programmes to promote growth and reduce poverty with associated financial needs.

Structural Adjustment Programmes (SAPs) policies intended to restore a sustainable balance of payments, reduce inflation, and create the conditions for sustainable growth. Typical measures include cuts in public expenditure and tight monetary policies.

Total debt service sum of principal repayments and interest paid in foreign currency, goods or services, on long-term debt, or interest paid on short-term debt, as well as repayments to the IMF.

UEE (Universal Elementary Education) a policy aspiration of the Government of India that all children in India will have enrolled in and completed eight years of elementary schooling.

UPE (Universal Primary Education) the aspiration that all children in the world will have been enrolled in and completed a primary cycle of schooling as defined in the country in which they live.

WID (Women in Development) a theoretical position in development research and a distinctive position in development policy and practice focused on including and noting women as part of economic and political assessments and the research that underpins this.

Notes

Preface

1 See Table 1.1 in Appendix 1.

1 Gender and Education for All: setting the scene

1 The High Level Group comprised 30 participants from four constituencies – Ministers of Education from developing countries, Ministers of International Development Co-operation/Foreign Affairs from donor countries, heads of multilateral/bilateral agencies and civil society representatives.
2 Established to provide additional funding for EFA and managed by Oxfam, ActionAid and Save the Children Fund.

2 Debating global social justice

1 Five years of school or the end of a primary cycle came to be associated with a minimally acceptable level through a particular interpretation of the basic needs approach as explained in the next chapter.
2 Nussbaum and Sen's ideas about global social justice and gender derive from their development of the capability approach as outlined in Chapter 5.

3 Schooling women and girls: a means, not an end

1 This was a catchphrase sometimes used on the United States Agency for International Development (USAID) funded project Girls' Attainment in Basic Literacy and Education (GABLE) in Malawi discussed in Chapter 8.

4 Gendered human rights in education

1 Utilitarianism is associated with approaches to justice concerned with maximizing welfare or desire satisfaction, which is different for different people (Kymlicka 2002). Rawls' theory of justice is particularly concerned with how to develop a theory of justice given particular forms of inequalities between people (Rawls 1971).

5 Capabilities and obligations in an unequal world

1 The most current version of Nussbaum's list of central capabilities are as follows: life; bodily health; bodily integrity; senses, imagination and thought; emotions; practical reason; affiliation; other species; play; control over one's environment.

8 Institutionalizing gender equality in education

1 Its funding of the *Beyond Access* project which did some of this work was limited to three years.

References

Actionaid (2003) *Fast Track or Backtrack?*, London: Actionaid. Available online at: www.campaignforeducation.org/resources/Apr2003/AA_Fast0403.pdf (accessed April 2006).

Ackerley, B. (2001) 'Women's human rights activists as cross-cultural theorists', *Feminist Journal of Politics*, 3: 311–46.

Ackerley, B. and Okin, S.M. (1999) 'Feminist social criticism and the international movement for women's rights as human rights', in I. Shapiro and C. Hacker-Cordon (eds) *Democracy's Edges*, Cambridge: Cambridge University Press.

Ackerman, J.M. (2005) *Social Accountability in the Public Sector: A Conceptual Discussion*, Washington, DC: World Bank.

Aggarwal, Y. (2002) *Progress Towards Universal Access and Retention*, New Delhi: NIEPA.

Ahmed, M. and Chowdhury, R. (2005) 'Beyond Access: Partnership for Quality with Equity', paper presented at *Beyond Access* Seminar 5, Dhaka, January 2005. Available online at: http://k1.ioe.ac.uk/schools/efps/GenderEducDev/Semi nar%20paper%20Manzoor%20Ahmed%20Rasheda%20Choudhury.doc (accessed December 2005).

Ahmed, N. (2003) 'Interview with Nashida Ahmed of BRAC, Bangladesh', *Equals*, 1, June: 5.

Ahouanmènou-Agueh, F. (2002) 'Retrospective Study on Girls' Education in Mali and the use of the simulation model for education management', Washington, DC: WID Technical Assistance Project. Available online at: www.usaid.gov/our_work/ cross-cutting_programs/wid/pubs/mali_0802.pdf (accessed December 2005).

Aikman, S. (1999) 'Schooling and development: eroding Amazon women's knowledge and diversity', in C. Heward and S. Bunwaree (eds) *Gender, Education and Development: Beyond Access to Empowerment*, London: Zed Books.

Aikman, S. and Unterhalter, E. (2005a) 'Introduction', in S. Aikman and E. Unterhalter (eds) *Beyond Access: Transforming Policy and Practice for Gender Equality in Education*, Oxford: Oxfam.

—— (eds) (2005b) *Beyond Access: Transforming Policy and Practice for Gender Equality in Education*, Oxford: Oxfam.

—— (2005c) 'Conclusion: policy and practice change for gender equality in education', in S. Aikman and E. Unterhalter (eds) *Beyond Access: Transforming Policy and Practice for Gender Equality in Education*, Oxford: Oxfam.

Alderman, H., Orazem, P. and Paterno, E. (1996) 'School quality, school cost, and the public/private choices of low-income households in Pakistan', Impact Evaluation of Education Reform Working Paper No. 2, World Bank Development Research Group, Washington, DC: World Bank.

Alexander, M.J. and Mohanty, C.T. (1997) 'Introduction: genealogies, legacies, movements', in M.J. Alexander and C.T. Mohanty (eds) *Feminist Genealogies, Colonial Legacies, Democratic Futures*, New York, NY: Routledge.

Alkire, S. (2003) *Valuing Freedom. Sen's Capability Approach and Poverty Reduction*, Oxford: Oxford University Press.

Ames, P. (2005) 'When access is not enough: educational exclusion of rural girls in Peru', in S. Aikman and E. Unterhalter (eds) *Beyond Access: Transforming Policy and Practice for Gender Equality in Education*, Oxford: Oxfam.

Annan, K. (2000) 'Meeting unmet promises', Speech at the launch of UNGEI , World Education Forum, Dakar, quoted in UNGEI, 2003, *A new global partnership meets an old global challenge*. Available online at: www.un.org/esa/coordination/ ecosoc/docs/UNGEI.pdf (accessed September 2005).

—— (2003) 'Foreword', in UNICEF, *The State of the World's Children 2004*, New York, NY: UNICEF.

Antrobus, P. (2004) *The Global Women's Movement: Origins, Issues and Strategies*, London: Zed Books.

Anzar, U., Harping, S., Cohen, J. and Leu, E. (2004) *Retrospective Pilot Study of USAID funded Projects in Malawi*, Washington, DC: Education Quality Improvement Programme. USAID. Available online at: www.equip123.net/ docs/e1-Malawi_Retrospective.pdf (accessed December 2005).

Arnot, M. and Dillabough, J. (eds) (2000) *Challenging Democracy: Feminist Perspectives on the Education of Citizens*, London: Routledge.

Arnot, M., David, M. and Weiner, G. (1999) *Closing the Gender Gap: Post-war Education and Social Change*, Cambridge: Polity Press.

Ashworth, G. (ed.) (2000) *Diplomacy of the Oppressed: New Directions in International Feminism*, London: Zed Books.

Asian South Pacific Bureau of Adult Education (ASPBAE) (2005) *Must Do Better: Asia Pacific School Report Card*, Mumbai: Asian South Pacific Bureau of Adult Education. Available online at: www.campaignforeducation.org/schoolreport/ AsiaPacific_School_Report_Card.pdf (accessed March 2006).

Bajpai, S. (2005) 'Talking with teachers', *Equals*, 15: 7.

Banaszak, L.A., Beckwith, K. and Rucht, D. (eds) (2003) *Women's Movements Facing the Reconfigured State*, Cambridge: Cambridge University Press.

Basu, A. (ed.) (1995) *The Challenge of Local Feminisms*, Nashville, TN: Westview Press.

Beck, U. (2006) *The Cosmopolitan Vision*, Cambridge: Polity Press.

Beijing Declaration (1995) *Fourth world conference on women Beijing Declaration* New York, NY: United Nations Division for the advancement of women. Available online at: www.un.org/womenwatch/daw/beijing/platform/declar. htm (accessed September 2005).

Beitz, C. (1999) 'Review article: international liberalism and distributive justice: a survey of recent thought', *World Politics*, 51, 2: 269–96.

—— (2001) 'Does global inequality matter?', in T.W. Pogge (ed.) *Global Justice*, Oxford: Blackwell.

Belew, R.T. and King, E.M. (1993) 'Educating women: lessons from experience', in E.M. King and M.A. Hill (eds) *Women's Education in Developing Countries: Barriers, Benefits and Policies*, Baltimore, MD: Johns Hopkins University Press.

Bellamy, C. (2005) 'Accelerating girls' education in South Asia in the post tsunami environment', keynote address to the UNICEF meeting, *2005 and Beyond. Accelerating girls' education in South Asia*, Kathmandu: UNICEF Regional Office for South Asia.

Beyond Access (2004) 'Children lobby governments for education', *Equals*, 6, June: 1, 9.

—— (2005a) 'Making it happen: political will for gender equality in education', *Education and Gender Equality Programme Insights*, Oxford: Oxfam.

—— (2005b) 'Gender responsive budgeting in education', *Education and Gender Equality Programme Insights*, Oxford: Oxfam.

—— (2005c) 'Girls' education in Africa', *Education and Gender Equality Programme Insights*, Oxford: Oxfam.

Bhattacharjee, A. (1997) 'The public/private mirage: mapping homes and undomesticating violence work in the South Asian immigrant community', in M.J. Alexander and C.T. Mohanty (eds) *Feminist Genealogies, Colonial Legacies, Democratic Futures*, New York, NY: Routledge.

Birdsall, N., Levine, R. and Ibrahim, A. (2005) *Toward Universal Primary Education: Investments, Incentives and Institutions*, London: Earthscan.

Bista, M. (2004) *Review of Research Literature on Girls' Education in Nepal*, Kathmandu: UNESCO. Available online at: http://unesdoc.unesco.org/images/0013/001386/138640e.pdf (accessed January 2006).

Blackmore, J. (2004) 'Gender Equity and Resourcing: Reflections from Australia', paper presented at *Beyond Access* Seminar 3, Oxford, April 2004. Available online at: http://k1.ioe.ac.uk/schools/efps/GenderEducDev/Blackmore%20version%202.pdf (accessed November 2005).

—— (2005) 'Feminist strategy rethinking of human rights discourses in education', in W.S. Hesford and W. Kozel (eds) *Just Advocacy? Women's Human Rights, Transnational Feminisms and the Politics of Representation*, Piscataway, NJ: Rutgers University Press.

Blaug, M. (1987) *The Economics of Education and the Education of an Economist*, Aldershot: Edward Elgar.

Boserup, E. (1970) *Women's Role in Economic Development*, New York, NY: St Martin's Press.

Braig, M. (2000) 'Women's interest in development theory and policy: from women in development to mainstreaming gender', *Development and Co-operation*, No. 3. Available online at: www.inwent.org/E+Z/1997-2002/de300-5.htm (accessed October 2004).

Braig, M. and Woelte, S. (eds) (2002) *Common Ground or Mutual Exclusion? Women's Movements and International Relations*, London: Zed Books.

Brighouse, H. (2002) 'What rights (if any) do children have?', in D. Archard and C.M. Macleod (eds) *The Moral and Political Status of Children*, Oxford: Oxford University Press.

—— (2004) *Justice*, London: Polity Press.

Brighouse, H. and Unterhalter, E. (2002) 'Primary goods, capabilities, and the millennium development target for gender equity in education', paper presented at the second Capabilities Approach Conference, St Edmunds College, Cambridge, September 2002. Available online at: www.st-edmunds.cam.ac.uk/vhi/nussbaum (accessed March 2005).

Brine, J. (2001) 'Education, social inclusion and the supranational state', *International Journal of Inclusive Education*, 5, 2–3: 119–31.

Brock, G. and Brighouse, H. (eds) (2005) *The Political Philosophy of Cosmopolitanism*, Cambridge: Cambridge University Press.

Brock, G. and Reader, S. (2002) 'Needs centred ethical theory', *The Journal of Value Inquiry*, 36, 4: 425–34.

Brush, L., Heyman, C. Provanik, S., *et al.* (2002) *Description and Analysis of the USAID Girls' Education Activity in Guatemala, Morocco and Peru*, Washington, DC: US Agency for International Development. Available online at: http://eric. ed.gov/ERICDocs/data/ericdocs2/content_storage_01/0000000b/80/27/a0/13.pdf (accessed November 2005).

Budlender, D. and Hewitt, G. (eds) (2002) *Gender Budgeting Makes More Cents*, London: Commonwealth Secretariat.

Burns, K. (2004) 'Uganda: Harriet Nambubiru talks to Kim Burns', *Equals*, 6, June: 7.

Butler, J. (2004) *Precarious Life: The Powers of Mourning and Violence*, London: Verso.

Camfed (2004) *Annual Review 2003–04*. Available online at: www.camfed.org/camfedannualreport2003-4.pdf (accessed November 2005).

Carnoy, M. and Samoff, J. (1990) *Education and Social Transition in the Third World*, Princeton, NJ: Princeton University Press.

Carr Hill, R., Hopkins, M., Riddell, A. and Lintott, J. (1999) *Monitoring the Performance of Education Programmes in Developing Countries*, Education Research Serials No. 37, London: Department for International Development.

Chabbott, C. (2003) *Constructing Education for Development: International Organizations and Education for All*, London: RoutledgeFalmer.

Challender, C. (2003) 'Pictures can make great changes', *Equals*, 2: 2–3.

Challender, C. and North, A. (2005) 'Going beyond access', *Equals*, 15, November/December: 1–3.

Chambers, R. (1984) *Rural Development: Putting the Last First*, London: Longman.

Charlesworth, H. (1993) 'What are "Women's International Human Rights?"', in R.J. Cook (ed.) *Human Rights of Women. National and International Perspectives*, Philadelphia, PA: University of Pennsylvania Press.

Chen, M., Vanek, J., Lund, F. and Heintz, J. (2005) *Progress of the World's Women: Women, Work and Poverty*, New York, NY: UNIFEM.

Chinkin, C. (1999) 'Gender, human rights and inequality', in A. Hurrell and N. Woods (eds) *Inequality, Globalization and World Politics*, Oxford: Oxford University Press.

Chisholm, L. (2001) 'Gender and leadership in South African Educational Administration', *Gender and Education*, 13, 4: 387–99.

—— (2004) *Changing class: education and social change in post-apartheid South Africa*, Pretoria: Human Science Research Council.

Chisholm, L. and September, J. (eds) (2005) *Gender Equity in South African Education 1994–2004: Conference Proceedings*, Cape Town: HSRC Press.

Chowdhury, A.M.R., Choudhury, R. and Nath, S.R. (1999) *Hope not Complacency: State of Primary Education in Bangladesh*, Dhaka: University Press.

Code, L. (2006) 'Vulnerability, particularity and "The States we're in"', conference paper presented at the Women and Politics Conference, University of Edinburgh,

February 2006. Available online at: www.sps.ed.ac.uk/gradschool/psafem/pdf/ VulnerabilityParticularity.pdf (accessed April 2006).

Cohen, G.A. (1993) 'Equality of what? On welfare, goods and capabilities', in M. Nussbaum and A. Sen (eds) *The Quality of Life*, Oxford: Clarendon Press.

Colclough, C. (2004) 'Towards universal primary education', in R. Black and H. White (eds) *Targeting Development: Critical Perspectives on the Millennium Development Goals*, London: Routledge.

Colclough, C. and Lewin, K. (1993) *Educating All the Children: Strategies for Primary Schooling in the South*, Oxford: Clarendon Press.

Colclough, C. and Manor, J. (eds) (1993) *States or Markets? Neo-liberalism and the Development Policy Debate*, Oxford: Clarendon Press.

Colclough, C., Al-Samarrai, S. and Tembon, M. (2003) *Achieving Schooling for All in Africa: Costs, Commitment and Gender*, Aldershot: Ashgate Press.

Commonwealth Education Fund (CEF) (2005) 'What is CEF'. Available online at: www.commonwealtheducationfund.org/home.html (accessed March 2006).

Commonwealth Secretariat (1999) *Gender Management System Handbook*, London: Commonwealth Secretariat.

Connell, R.W. (1995) *Masculinities*, Cambridge: Polity Press.

Cook, R.J. (ed.) (1993) *Human Rights of Women: National and International Perspectives*, Philadelphia, PA: University of Pennsylvania Press.

Cornell, D. (1993) *Transformations. Recollective Imagination and Sexual Difference*, New York, NY: Routledge.

Cornwall, A. (2001) *Making a Difference? Gender and Participatory Development*, Brighton: Institute of Development Studies, University of Sussex.

Dakar Framework (2000) *The Dakar Framework for Action*, Paris: UNESCO. Available online at: http://unesdoc.unesco.org/images/0012/001211/121147e.pdf (accessed December 2005).

David, M. (2003) *Personal and Political: Feminisms, Sociology and Family Lives*, Stoke on Trent: Trentham Books.

De Graaf, K. (2005) 'Public expenditure tracking in Tanzania at district level: effects on local accountability', paper presented at European conference of African Studies. Available online at: www.campaignforeducation.org/resources/Jul2005/ District%20PETs%20Tracking%20Surveys%20in%20Tanzania%20-%20report.pdf (accessed March 2006).

Dehli, K. (2000) 'Travelling tales: education reform and parental "choice" in postmodern times', in S. Ball (ed.) *Sociology of Education: Major Themes*, London: Routledge.

Delors, J. (1995) *The Treasure Within*, New York, NY: Oxford University Press.

Department for International Development (DFID) (2004) 'Mission statement', *DFID website*. Available online at: www.dfid.gov.uk/aboutdfid/missionstatement. asp (accessed November 2005).

—— (2005) *Girls' Education: Towards a Better Future for All*, London: Department for International Development.

Diop, N. (2004) 'Gender budgeting in education ministries: case study of the Rwandan Ministry of Education', paper presented at *Beyond Access* Seminar 3, Oxford, April. Available online at: http://k1.ioe.ac.uk/schools/efps/GenderEducDev/ Ngone%20Diop%20paper.pdf (accessed November 2005).

Doggett, R. (2005) 'Enabling education for girls in the Loreto Day School Sealdah, India', in S. Aikman and E. Unterhalter (eds) *Beyond Access. Transforming Policy and Practice for Gender Equality in Education*, Oxford: Oxfam.

Dollar, D. and Gatti, R. (1999) 'Gender inequality, income, and growth: are good times good for women?', The World Bank Development Research Group/ Poverty Reduction and Economic Management Network, Washington DC: World Bank. Available online at: http://siteresources.worldbank.org/INTGENDER/ Resources/wp1.pdf (accessed September 2005).

Doyal, L. and Gough, I. (1991) *A Theory of Human Need*, London: Macmillan.

Dubel, I. (2005) 'MDGs and gender equality: another fallacy of mainstreaming?', paper presented at WIDE workshop on the Millennium Development Goals, gender and human security Royal Tropical Institute, the Netherlands. Available online at: www.eurosur.org/wide/UN/NCDO_SID_WIDE_workshop_report. pdf (accessed January 2006).

Eccher, C. (2004) 'Gender and education, history of some struggles', paper presented at *Beyond Access* Seminar June 2004, UEA. Available online at: http://k1.ioe. ac.uk/schools/efps/GenderEducDev/Celita%20Eccher%20paper.pdf   (accessed October 2005).

Education International (2003) *Education for All. Is Commitment Enough?*, Brussels: Education International. Available online at: www.campaignforeducation.org/ resources/Apr2003/EI_EFA03_EN.pdf (accessed March 2006).

Elimu Yetu (2005) 'The challenge of educating girls in Kenya', S. Aikman and E. Unterhalter (eds) *Beyond Access: Transforming Policy and Practice for Gender Equality in Education*, Oxford: Oxfam.

Elson, D. (1998) 'Talking to the boys: gender and economic growth models', in C. Jackson and R. Pearson (eds) *Feminist Visions of Development: Gender, Analysis and Policy*, London: Routledge.

—— (1995) *Male Bias in the Development Process*, Manchester: Manchester University Press.

Escobar, A. (1996) *Encountering Development: The Making and Unmaking of the Third World*, Princeton, NJ: Princeton University Press

Fagerlind, I. and Saha, L.J. (1989) *Education and National Development: A Comparative Perspective*, 2nd edn, Oxford: Pergamon Press.

Fancy, K. (2004) 'Responses to the GMR 2005: a more conservative definition of quality', *Equals*, 15, November/December: 3.

Fast Track Initiative (2004) *Education for All. Fast Track Initiative Framework*, Washington: Fast Track Initiative on line at http://www.1.worldbank.org/ education/efafti/documents/FrameworkNOV04.pdf (accessed January 2006).

Fast Track Initiative (2005) 'Progress report'. Available online at: www1. worldbank.org/education/efafti/documents/FTI_statusreport_dec2105.pdf (accessed March 2006).

Forum of African Women Educationalists (FAWE) (2004) 'FAWE's vision'. Available online at: www.fawe.org/content/programmes.html (accessed December 2005).

Fine, B. (2001) 'Neither the Washington nor the post-Washington consensus: an introduction', in B. Fine, C. Lapavistas and J. Pincus (eds) *Development Policy in the Twenty-first Century*, London: RoutledgeFalmer.

Fine, B., Lapavistas, C. and Pincus, J. (eds) (2001) *Development Policy in the Twenty-first Century*, London: RoutledgeFalmer.

Fraser, N. (1997) *Justice Interruptus: Rethinking Key Concepts of a Post-socialist Age*, London: Routledge.

—— (2005) 'Reframing justice in a globalizing world', *New Left Review*, 36: 69–88.

—— and Honneth, A. (2003) *Redistribution or Recognition? A Political-philosophical Exchange*, London: Verso.

Freedman, J. (2001) *Feminism*, Milton Keynes: Open University Press.

Freeman, M. (2002) *Human Rights*, Cambridge: Polity Press.

Fukuda-Parr, S. (2003) 'Rescuing the human development concept from the HDI: reflections on a new agenda' in S. Fukuda-Parr and A.K. Shiva Kumar (eds) *Readings in Human Development*, Delhi: Oxford University Press, 117–26.

Fukuda-Parr, S. and Shiva Kumar, A.K. (eds) (2003) *Readings in Human Development: Concepts, Measures and Policies for a Development Paradigm*, New Delhi: Oxford University Press.

GADN (GAD Network) (2005) *Linking Women's Human Rights and the Millennium Development Goals: An Agenda for 2005*, London: The GAD Network.

Garrow, S. (2005) 'Multi-organizational partnerships: the alliance for community action in female education – Uganda', *Equals*, 15, November/December: 6.

Gasper, D. (2004) *The Ethics of Development. From Economism to Human Development*, Edinburgh: Edinburgh University Press.

Geisler, G. (2004) *Women and the Remaking of Politics in Southern Africa: Negotiating Autonomy, Incorporation and Representation*, Uppsala: Nordiska Afrikainstitutet.

Gibson, D. (1996) 'Literacy, knowledge, gender and power in the workplace on three farms in the Western Cape', in M. Prinsloo and M. Breier (eds) *The Social Uses of Literacy*, Amsterdam: Benjamins.

Gibson, S. (2005) 'Girls' education in Africa: an overview of "what works"', background paper for *Girls Education: Towards a Better Future for All*, London: DFID.

Gilligan, C. (1982) *In a Different Voice. Psychological Theory and Women's Development*, Cambridge, MA: Harvard University Press.

—— (1986) 'Remapping the moral domain', in T. Heller and M. Sostra (eds) *Reconstructing Individualism: Autonomy, Individuality and the Self in Western Thought*, Stanford, CA: Stanford University Press.

—— (1995) 'Hearing the difference: theorizing connection', *Hypatia*, 10/12: 120–7.

Global Campaign for Education (GCE) (2002) *An Action Plan to Achieve the MDGs in Education: Briefing for Amsterdam EFA conference*, Cape Town: Global Campaign for Education. Available online at: www.campaignforeducation.org/resources/Apr2002/Action0402.doc (accessed December 2005).

—— Briefing Paper prepared for the 2002 Annual Meetings of the World Bank and the IMF. Available online at: www.campaignforeducation.org/resources/Mar2003/Broken0902.pdf (accessed December 2005).

—— (2003a) *A Fair Chance: Attaining Gender Equity in Basic Education by 2005*, Johannesburg: Global Campaign for Education.

—— (2003b) *Report on Activities Hands up for Girls' Education*, Johannesburg: Global Campaign for Education.

—— (2003c) *Broken Promises: Why Donors Must Deliver on the EFA Action Plan*, Johannesburg: Global Campaign for Education. Available online at: www.oxfam.org/en/files/pp020923_broken_promises.pdf/download (accessed March 2006).

—— (2003d) *Window of Opportunity: Why Fast Track Funds Must be Released Now*, Cape Town: Global Campaign for Education. Available online at: www. campaignforeducation.org/resources/Mar2003/Window0303.doc (accessed March 2006).

—— (2004) *Big Book of the World's Biggest Lobby*, Johannesburg: Global Campaign for Education. Available online at: www.campaignforeducation.org/resources/ Aug2004/GCE_big_book_eng2.pdf (accessed March 2006).

—— (2005a) *Girls Can't Wait: Why Girls' Education Matters, and How to Make it Happen Now*, Johannesburg: Global Campaign for Education. Available online at: www.campaignforeducation.org/resources/Mar2005/b10_brief_final.doc (accessed November 2005).

—— (2005b) 'Educate to end poverty', statement prepared for World Summit, Johannesburg: Global Campaign for Education.

—— (2005c) 'Ensuring a fair chance for girls', in S. Aikman and E. Unterhalter (eds) *Beyond Access: Transforming Policy and Practice for Gender Equality in Education*, Oxford: Oxfam.

—— (2005d) *Missing the Mark: A 'School Report' on Rich Countries' Contribution to Universal Primary Education by 2015*, Cape Town: Global Campaign for Education. Available online at: www.campaignforeducation.org/schoolreport/ part1_overview.pdf (accessed March 2006).

—— (2005e) *UN Millennium Summit Delivers Rhetoric Without Commitment*, Johannesburg: Global campaign for Education. Available online at: www. campaignforeducation.org/resources/Sep2005/GCE%20Analysis%20of%20the% 20UN%20Millennium%20Summit%20Outcome[1].doc (accessed March 2006).

—— and Actionaid International (2005) *Contradicting Commitments: How the Achievement of Education For All is Being Undermined by the International Monetary Fund*, Cape Town: Global Campaign for Education.

Goetz, A. (ed.) (1997) *Getting Institutions Right for Women in Development*, London: Zed.

Government of India (2001) Basic Features of Sarva Shiksha Abhiyan. Available online at: http://ssa.nic.in/ssaframework/ssafram.asp#1.0 (accessed December 2005).

Gray, J. (1983) 'Classical liberalism, positional goods and the politicisation of poverty', in A. Ellis and K. Kumar (eds) *Dilemmas of Liberal Democracies*, London: Tavistock.

Greaney, K. (2006) 'Rhetoric versus realities: an exploration of the challenges of addressing gender equity through a rights-based approach to education in Niger', unpublished M.A. dissertation, London: Institute of Education, University of London.

Gulnara, M. (2003) 'Gender and education in Iran', background paper, *EFA Global Monitoring Report, 2003–04*, Paris: UNESCO.

Hadden, K. and London, B. (1996) 'Educating girls in the Third World: the demographic, basic needs and economic benefits', *International Journal of Comparative Sociology*, 37, 1–2: 31–46.

Hamilton, L. (2003) *The Political Philosophy of Needs*, Cambridge: Cambridge University Press.

Held, D. (2002) 'Cosmopolitanism: ideas, realities, deficits', in D. Held and A. McGrew (eds) *Governing Globalization*, Cambridge: Polity Press.

—— (2004) *Global Covenant*, Cambridge: Polity.

—— (2005) 'Principles of cosmopolitan order', in G. Brock and H. Brighouse (eds) *The Political Philosophy of Cosmopolitanism*, Oxford: Oxford University Press.

Herz, B. and Sperling, G.B. (2004) *What Works in Girls' Education*, New York, NY: Council on Foreign Relations.

Heynemann, S. (1997) 'Educational quality and the crisis of education research', in R. Ryba (ed.) *Education, Democracy and Development*, London: Kluwer.

Heward, C. and Bunwaree, S. (1999) *Gender, Education and Development: Beyond Access to Empowerment*, London: Zed Books.

Hill, M.A. and King, E.M. (1993) 'Women's education in developing countries: an overview', in E.M. King and M.A. Hill (eds) *Women's Education in Developing Countries. Barriers, Benefits and Policies*, Baltimore, MD: Johns Hopkins University Press.

Hossain, N., Subrahmanian, R. and Kabeer, N. (2002) 'The politics of educational expansion in Bangladesh', Brighton: IDS Working Paper No. 167.

Jackson, C. (1998) 'Rescuing gender from the poverty trap', in C. Jackson and R. Pearson (eds) *Feminist Visions of Development: Gender Analysis and Policy*, London: Routledge.

Jahan, R. (1995) *The Elusive Agenda: Mainstreaming Women in Development*, London: Zed Books.

Jayaweera S. (1999) 'Gender, education, development: Sri Lanka', in C. Heward and S. Bunwaree (eds) *Gender, Education and Development: Beyond Access to Empowerment*, London: Zed Books.

Jeffery, P. and Jeffery, R. (1998) 'Silver bullet or passing fancy? Girls' schooling and population policy', in C. Jackson and R. Pearson (eds) *Feminist Visions of Development: Gender Analysis and Policy*, London: Routledge.

Jeffries, A. and Miller, C. (eds) (1999) *Women's Voices: Women's Rights*, Boulder, CO: Westview Publishing.

Jensen, V. and Rajagopalan, R. (2004) 'Repair work: UNESCO designs a toolkit for gender equality', *Equals*, 5, March: 1–2.

Jones, P.W. (1992) *World Bank Financing of Education: Lending, Learning and Development*, New York, NY: Routledge.

Kabeer, N. (1994) *Reversed Realities*, London: Verso.

—— (1999) 'Resources, agency, achievements: reflections on the measurement of women's empowerment', *Development and Change*, 30, 3: 435–64.

—— (2002) *The Power to Choose Bangladeshi Women and Labour Market Decisions in London and Dhaka*, London: Verso.

—— (2003) *Gender Mainstreaming in Poverty Eradication and the Millennium Development Goals*, London: Commonwealth Secretariat.

—— and Subrahmanian, R. (1999) *Institutions, Relations and Outcomes: A Framework and Case Studies for Gender-aware Planning*, New Delhi: Kali for Women.

—— Nambissan, G. and Subrahmanian, R. (eds) (2003) *Child Labour and the Right to Education in South Asia: Needs Versus Rights?*, New Delhi: Sage Publications.

Kadzamira, E.C. and Rose, P. (2001) 'Educational policy choice and practice in malawi: dilemmas and disjunctures', IDS Working Paper No. 124, Brighton: Institute of Development Studies.

Kamau, N. (2004) 'The best gift the government gave Kenya: Taking forward free and compulsory education', *Equals*, 4, January: 2–3.

Kane, E. (2004) *Girls' Education in Africa: What do we Know about Strategies that Work*, Washington, DC: World Bank.

Kanjaye, H. (2001) *Girls' Education Project a Resounding Success*, Paris: UNESCO. Available online at: www.unesco.org/education/efa/know_sharing/grassroots_ stories/malawi.shtml (accessed December 2005).

Kent, A. (2004) 'Living life on the edge: examining space and sexualities within a township high school in greater Durban, in the context of the HIV epidemic', *Transformation*, 54: 59–75.

Kerr, J., Sprenger, E. and Symington, A. (eds) (2004) *The Future of Women's Rights: Global Visions and Strategies*, London: Zed Books.

Khanna, R. (2001) 'The ambiguity of ethics: specters of colonialism', in E. Bronfen and M. Kayka (eds) *Feminist Consequences: Theory for the New Century*, New York, NY: Columbia University Press.

King, E. and Hill, M.A. (eds) (1993) *Women's Education in Developing Countries: Barriers, Benefits and Policies*, Baltimore, MD: Johns Hopkins University Press.

Kingdon, G. (2003) 'Where has all the bias gone? Detecting gender bias in the intra-household allocation of educational expenditure', Centre for Study of African Economies, Oxford Working Papers. Available online at: www.csae.ox.ac.uk/ workingpapers/pdfs/2003-13text.pdf (accessed March 2006).

Kirk, J. (2004) 'Promoting a gender just peace: the roles of women teachers in peacebuilding and reconstruction', *Gender and Development*, 12, 3: 50–9.

—— (2005) 'Menstruation and body awareness: critical issues for girls' education', *Equals*, 15, January: 4–5.

—— (ed.) (2006) (forthcoming) *Women Teaching in South Asia*, New Delhi: Sage.

Klasen, S. (1999) 'Does gender inequality reduce growth and development? evidence from cross-country regressions', Policy Research Report on Gender and Development Working Paper No. 7, Washington, DC: World Bank.

Kolawole, M.E.M. (1997) *Womanism and African Consciousness*, Trentham, NJ: Africa World Press.

Krueger, A. (1968) 'Factor endowment and per capita income differences among countries', *The Economic Journal*, 78: 641–59.

Kwesiga, J. (2003) 'The national machinery for gender equality in Uganda: institutionalised gender politics?', in S. Rai (ed) *Mainstreaming Gender, Democratizing the State?*, Manchester: Manchester University Press.

Kwesiga, J.C. (2002) *Women's Access to Higher Education in Africa: Uganda's Experience*, Kampala: Fountain Publishers.

Kymlicka, W. (2002) *Contemporary Political Philosophy: An Introduction*, Oxford: Oxford University Press.

Leach, F. (2003) *Practising Gender Analysis in Education*, Oxford: Oxfam.

Leach, F., with M. Dunne, B. Chilesa, T. Maundeni, R. Tabulawa, N. Kutor, D. Forde and A. Assamoah (2003) *Gendered Experiences: The Impact on Retention and Achievement*, London: DFID.

Leach, F., and Little, A. (1999) *Education, Cultures, and Cconomics: Dilemmas for Development*, New York, NY: Falmer Press.

Leach, F., Dunne, M. and Humphreys, R. (2006) 'Gender violence in schools in the developing world', *Gender and Education*, 18, 1: 75–98.

Lee, Y. (2004) 'Developing gender policy from research in Lao People's Democratic Republic', *Equals*, 5: 5–6.

Leeson, R. (2004) 'Gender equality advocates speak: feminist issues and strategies in the future', in J. Kerr, E. Sprenger and A. Symington (eds) *The Future of Women's Rights: Global Visions and Strategies*, London: Zed.

Leggatt, I. (2005) 'Learning to improve policy for pastoralists in Kenya', in S. Aikman and E. Unterhalter (eds) *Beyond Access: Transforming Policy and Practice for Gender Equality in Education*, Oxford: Oxfam.

Leonard, D. (2001) *A Woman's Guide to Doctoral Studies*, Buckingham: Open University Press.

Lind, A. (2006) 'Reflections on mainstreaming gender equality in adult basic education programmes', *International Journal of Educational Development*, 26, 2: 166–76.

Lister, R. (2004) *Poverty*, Cambridge: Polity Press.

—— (1997) *Citizenship: Feminist Perspectives*, London: Macmillan.

Lovell, T. (2003) 'Nancy Fraser's project: an integrated conception of justice', paper presented at symposium University of Warwick, March 2003. Available online at: www2.warwick.ac.uk/fac/soc/sociology/gender/events/symposium/lovell/ (accessed March 2006).

Lovenduski, J. (2005) *Feminizing Politics*, Cambridge: Polity Press.

Machel, G. (1996) *The Impact of Armed Conflict on Children*, New York, NY: UNICEF.

McGrew, A. (2004) *Cosmopolitanism and Global Justice*. Available online at: www.ritsumei.ac.jp/acd/cg/ir/college/bulletin/e-vol.3/mcgrew.pdf (accessed October 2005).

McKay, S. and Mazurana, D. (2004) 'Where are the girls? Girls in fighting forces in northern Uganda, Sierra Leone and Mozambique: their lives during and after war', Montreal: Rights and Democracy ID21 (Institute of Development Studies, Sussex University) Insights September. Available online at: www.id21.org/zinter/id21zinter.exe?a=0&i=InsightsEdu3art6&u=442fbf4e (consulted November 2005).

McKim, R. and McMahon, J. (eds) (1997) *The Morality of Nationalism*, Oxford: Oxford University Press.

Mehrotra, S. and Jolly, R. (2000) *Development with a Human Face: Experiences in Social Achievement and Economic Growth*, Oxford: Oxford University Press.

Mgumya, L. (2004) 'How gender segregation at school undermines equal opportunities: a male viewpoint', *Equals*, 4: 5–6.

Millennium Project (2000) *Tracking the MDGs: Targets & Indicators*. Available online at: www.undp.org/mdg/tracking_targetlist.shtml (accessed October 2005).

Miller, C. and Razavi, S. (1998) *Missionaries and Mandarins: Feminist Engagement with Development Institutions*, London: UNRISD.

Miller, D. (1976) *Social Justice*, Oxford: Clarendon.

—— (1998) 'The limits of cosmopolitan justice', in D. Mapel and T. Nardin (eds) *International Society: Diverse Ethical Perceptions*, Princeton, NJ: Princeton University Press.

Mirembe, R. and Davis, L (2001) 'Is schooling a risk? Gender, power relations, and school culture in Uganda', *Gender and Education*, 13, 4: 401–16.

Mirsky, J. (2003) *Beyond Victims and Villains: Addressing Sexual Violence in the Education Sector*, London: Panos.

Mlama, P. (2004) 'Changing teaching for gender equality', paper presented at *Beyond Access* Seminar 2, February 2004, Nairobi.

Moellendorf, D. (2002) *Cosmopolitan Justice*, Boulder, CO: Westview Press.

Moghadam, V. (1992) 'Development and women's emancipation: is there a connection?', *Development and Change*, 23, 3: 215–55.

Mohanty, C. (1988) 'Under Western eyes: feminist scholarship and colonial discourse', *Feminist Review*, 30: 61–88.

Moletsane, R. (2004) 'Gender equality and teacher education in South Africa: a review of the history', paper presented at *Beyond Access* Seminar 2, February 2004, Nairobi.

Molyneux, M. (1985) 'Mobilisation without emancipation? Women's interests, the state and the revolution in Nicaragua', *Feminist Studies*, 11: 227–54.

—— (1998) 'Analysing women's movements', in R. Pearson and C. Jackson (eds) *Feminist Visions of Development*, London: Routledge.

Molyneux, M. and Razavi, S. (eds) (2002) *Gender Justice, Development, and Rights*, Oxford: Oxford University Press.

Morrell, R. (2005) 'Men, movements and gender transformation in South Africa', in L. Ouzange and R. Morrell (eds) *African Masculinities*, New York, NY: Palgrave Macmillan.

Moser, C. (1993) *Gender Planning and Development: Theory, Practice and Training*, London: Routledge.

Muito, M. (2004) 'Gender equity in the classroom: reflections from practice', paper presented at *Beyond Access* Seminar 2, February 2004, Nairobi. Available online at: http://k1.ioe.ac.uk/schools/efps/GenderEducDev/Muito%20paper. pdf (accessed December 2005).

Nakaweza, S. (2005) 'Talking with learners', *Equals*, 10: 6–7.

Noddings, N. (1984) *Caring: A Feminine Approach to Ethics*, Berkeley, CA: University of California Press.

North, A. (2006a) 'Missed target triggers call for bold steps – will they be enough?', *Equals*, 16, April: 1–3.

—— (2006b) 'What does the Global Monitoring Report say about gender? *Equals*, 16, April: 8.

Nussbaum, M. (2000) *Women and Human Development*, Cambridge: Cambridge University Press.

—— (2004) 'Women's education: a global challenge', *Signs*, 29: 325–55.

—— (2005) 'Beyond the social contract: capabilities and global justice', in G. Brock and H. Brighouse (eds) *The Political Philosophy of Cosmopolitanism*, Cambridge: Cambridge University Press.

O'Neill, O. (1993) 'Justice, gender and international boundaries', in M. Nussbaum and A. Sen (eds) *The Quality of Life*, Oxford: Clarendon Press.

—— (2000) *Bounds of Justice*, Cambridge: Cambridge University Press.

Obura, A. (1991) *Changing Images: The Portrayal of Girls and Women in Kenyan Textbooks*, Nairobi: African Centre for Technology Studies.

Odora Hoppers, C. (2005) 'Between "mainstreaming" and "transformation": lessons and challenges for institutional change', in L. Chisholm and J. September (eds) *Gender Equity in South African Education 1994–2004: Conference Proceedings*, Cape Town: HSRC Press: 55–73.

Okech J. (2005) 'Kenya: Working toward the goal', *African Women's Journal*: 30. Available online at: www.africafiles.org/article.asp?ID=7969 (accessed December 2005).

Okin, S.M. (1989) *Justice, Gender and the Family*, New York, NY: Basic Books.

—— (1990) 'Thinking like a woman', in D. Rhode (ed.) *Theoretical Perspectives on Sexual Difference*, New Haven, CT: Yale University Press.

—— (1999a) 'Is multiculturalism bad for women?', in J. Cohen, M. Howard and M. Nussbaum (eds) *Is Multiculturalism Bad for Women?*, Princeton, NJ: Princeton University Press.

—— (1999b) 'Reply', in J. Cohen, M. Howard and M. Nussbaum (eds) *Is Multiculturalism Bad for Women?*, Princeton, NJ: Princeton University Press.

—— (2003) 'Poverty, well-being, and gender: what counts, who's heard?', *Philosophy & Public Affairs*, 31, 3: 280–316.

Oomen, M. (2005) 'Crossing boundaries and stepping out of purdah in India', in S. Aikman, S. and E. Unterhalter (eds) *Beyond Access: Transforming Policy and Practice for Gender Equality in Education*, Oxford: Oxfam.

Page, E. (2005) 'Gender and the construction of identities in Indian elementary education', unpublished Ph.D. Thesis, Institute of Education, University of London.

Palazzo, L. (2005) 'Bolsa Escola, Brazil: enabling enrolment and empowerment', *Equals*, 11, March/April: 4–5.

Parpart, J. (1995) 'Post-modernism, gender and development', in J. Crush (ed.) *Power of Development*, London: Routledge.

—— (2002) 'Lessons from the field: rethinking empowerment, gender and development from a (post-?) development perspective', in K. Saunders (ed.) *Feminist Post-Development Thought*, London: Zed Books.

Pattman, R. and Chege, F. (2003) *Finding our Voices: Gendered and Sexual Identities and HIV/AIDS in Education*, Nairobi: UNICEF Eastern and Southern Africa Regional Office.

Peters, J. and Wolper, A. (eds) (1995) *Women's Rights Human Rights. International Feminist Perspectives*, New York, NY: Routledge.

Phillips, A. (1995) *The Politics of Presence*, Oxford: Clarendon Press.

—— (1999) *Which Equalities Matter?*, Cambridge: Polity Press.

Pogge, T. (2001) *Global Justice*, Oxford: Blackwell.

—— (2002a) 'Can the capability approach be justified?', in M. Nussbaum and C. Flanders (eds) *Global Inequalities*, special issue, 30, 2: 167–228, special issue of Philosophical Topics (appeared February 2004). Available online at: http://mora.rente.nhh.no/projects/EqualityExchange/Portals/0/articles/pogge1.pdf (accessed June 2004).

—— (2002b) *World Poverty and Human Rights*, Cambridge: Polity Press.

—— (2005) *World Poverty and Human Rights: Cosmopolitan Responsibilities and Reforms*, Cambridge: Polity Press.

Porteus, K. (2003) 'Pushing the "problems" underground? Left behind learners in South Africa', ID21 (Institute of Development Studies, Sussex University) Insights Education No. 2, September. Available online at: www.id21.org/insights/insights-ed02/insights-issed02-art03.html (accessed December 2005).

PROBE India (1999) *Public Report on Basic Education in India*, New Delhi: Oxford University Press.

Programme to Motivate Train and Employ women teachers in rural secondary schools (PROMOTE) (2001) *PROMOTE overview*, Dhaka: Programme to Motivate, Train and Employ Women Teachers in Rural Secondary Schools.

Psacharapoulos, G. (ed.) (1987) *Economics of Education Research and Studies*, Oxford: Pergamon Press.

—— (1994) 'Returns to education: a global update', *World Development*, 22: 1325–43.

Quisumbing, A. (1996) 'Modeling household behavior in developing countries: discussion', *American Journal of Agricultural Economics*, 78, 5: 1346–8.

—— Estudillo J.P. and Otsuka, K. (2004) *Land and Schooling: Transferring Wealth Across Generations*, Baltimore, MD: Johns Hopkins University Press.

Rahnema, M. and Bawtree, V. (eds) (1996) *The Post-Development Reader*, London: Zed Books.

Rai, S. (2002) *Gender and the Political Economy of Development*, Cambridge: Polity Press.

—— (ed.) (2003) *Mainstreaming Gender, Democratizing the State?*, Manchester: Manchester University Press.

—— (2004) 'Gendering global governance', *International Feminist Journal of Politics*, 6, 4: 579–601.

Ramachandran, V. (2003) *Getting Children Back to School: Case Studies in Primary Education*, New Delhi and London: Sage

Ramachandran, V. and Jandhyala, K. (2005) 'Tracing the journey: Mahila Samakhya from 1988 to 2005', paper presented at the UKFIET conference, September 2005, Oxford.

Ramagoshi, M. (2005) 'National Department of Education initiatives', in L. Chisholm, and J. September (eds) *Gender Equity in South African Education 1994–2004: Conference Proceedings*, Cape Town: HSRC Press.

Ramphal, A. (2005) 'Quality and equality in education: gendered politics of institutional change', paper presented at *Beyond Access* Seminar 5, Dhaka. Available online at: http://k1.ioe.ac.uk/schools/efps/GenderEducDev/Seminar%20paper %20Anita%20Ramphal.pdf (accessed December 2005).

Rawls, J. (1971) *A Theory of Justice*, Oxford: Oxford University Press.

—— (1999) *The Law of Peoples*, Cambridge MA: Harvard University Press.

Raynor, J. (2005a) 'Educating girls in Bangladesh? Watering a neighbour's tree?', in S. Aikman, S. and E. Unterhalter (eds) *Beyond Access: Transforming Policy and Practice for Gender Equality in Education*, Oxford: Oxfam.

—— (2005b) *A Study of Gender Awareness in Government Teacher Training Colleges*, Dhaka: PROMOTE.

—— (2007 forthcoming) 'Girls' education and capabilities in Bangladesh', in M. Walker and E. Unterhalter (eds) *Amartya Sen's Capability Approach and Social Justice in Education*, New York: Palgrave.

Raynor, J. and Unterhalter, E. (2007 forthcoming) 'Promoting empowerment? Contrasting perspectives on a programme to employ women teachers in Bangladesh, 1998–2005', in J. Kirk (ed.) *Women Teaching in South Asia*, New Delhi: Sage.

Reader, S. (2004) 'Need, capability and help', paper presented at fourth Capability approach conference, Pavia. Available online at: http://cfs.unipv.it/ca2004/ papers/reader.pdf (accessed September 2005).

Reid, G. and Walker, L. (eds) (2005) *Men Behaving Differently: South African Men since 1994*, Cape Town: Double Storey.

Robeyns, I. (2003) 'Sen's capability approach and gender inequality: selecting relevant capabilities', *Feminist Economics*, 9, 2–3: 61–92.

—— (2005) 'The capability approach: a theoretical survey', *Journal of Human Development*, 6, 1: 93–114.

—— (2006) 'Three models of education: rights, capabilities and human capital', *Theory and Research in Education*, 4, 1: 69–84.

Robinson Pant, A. (2003) *Why Eat Green Cucumbers at the Time of Dying? Women's Literacy and Development in Nepal*, Paris: UNESCO.

—— (2004) 'Education for women: whose values count?', *Gender and Education*, 16(4): 473–91.

Roemer, J. (1996) *Theories of Distributive Justice*, Cambridge, MA: Harvard University Press.

Rogers, B. (1980) *The Domestication of Women: Discrimination in Developing Societies*, London: Tavistock Publications.

Rose, P. (2003a) 'Can gender equality in education be attained? Evidence from Ethiopia', background paper for EFA Global Monitoring Report 2004. Available online at: http://portal.unesco.org/education/en/file_download.php/c122531 0d3b5f45162c7facca302092Can+gender+qaultiy+in+education+be+attained.+Ev idence+from+Ethiopia..doc (accessed June 2005).

—— (2003b) 'From the Washington to the post-Washington consensus: the influence of international agendas on education policy and practice in Malawi', *Globalisation, Education and Societies*, 1: 67–86.

—— (2005) 'Is there a "fast-track" to achieving education for all?', *International Journal of Educational Development*, 25, 4: 381–94.

Rowlands, J. (1997) *Questioning Empowerment*, Oxford: Oxfam.

Sachs, W. (2001) *The Development Dictionary – A Guide to Knowledge as Power*, New York, NY and London: Zed Books.

Sales, V. (1999) 'Women teachers and professional development: gender issues in the training programmes of the Aga Khan Education Service, Northern Areas, Pakistan', *International Journal of Educational Development*, 19, 6: 409–22.

Sanou, S. and Aikman, S. (2005) 'Pastoralist schools in Mali: gendered roles and curriculum realities', in S. Aikman and E. Unterhalter (eds) *Beyond Access. Transforming Policy and Practice for Gender Equality in Education*, Oxford: Oxfam.

Sarangapani, P. (2003) *Constructing School Knowledge: An Ethnography of Learning in an Indian Village*, New Delhi: Sage.

Saunders, K. (ed.) (2002) *Feminist Post Development Thought*, London: Zed Books.

Schultz, T.P. (1987) *Education Investments and Returns in Economic Development*, New Haven, CT: Yale University Press.

—— (1993) 'Returns to women's education', in E.M. King and M.A. Hill (eds) *Women's Education in Developing Countries: Barriers, Benefits and Policies*, Baltimore, MD: Johns Hopkins University Press.

Schultz, T.W. (1971) *Investment in Human Capital: The Role of Education and of Research*, New York, NY: The Free Press.

Seel, A. and Clarke, D.J. (2005) *Integrating Gender into Education for All Fast Track Initiative Processes and National Education Plans*, New York, NY: UNGEI. Available online at: www.ungei.org/resources/index_746.html (accessed January 2006).

Sen, A. (1980) 'Equality of What?', Tanner Lectures on Human Values, Stanford University reprinted in A. Sen (1982) *Choice, Welfare and Measurement*, Oxford: Blackwell.

—— (1993) 'Capability and well being', in M. Nussbaum and A. (eds) *The Quality of Life*, Oxford: Clarendon Press.

—— (1997) 'Human capital and human capability', *World Development*, 25, 12: 1959–61.

—— (1999) *Development as Freedom*, Oxford: Oxford University Press.

—— (2000) 'Consequential evaluation and practical reason', *Journal of Philosophy*, 97, 9: 477–502.

—— (2001) 'Global doubts as global solutions', Alfred Deakin Memorial Lecture, January 2006, Melbourne. Available online at: www.abc.net.au/rn/deakin/stories/s296978.htm (accessed January 2006).

—— (2003) 'Closing the Gap. Access, inclusion and achievement: The importance of basic education', speech to the Commonwealth education conference, Edinburgh. Available online at: http://education.guardian.co.uk/schools/story/0,,1072739,00.html (accessed June 2005).

—— (2004) 'Elements of a theory of human rights', *Philosophy and Public Affairs*, 32, 4: 315–56.

—— (2005a) 'Human rights and capabilities', *Journal of Human Development*, 6, 2: 151–66.

—— (2005b) *The Argumentative Indian: Writings on Indian History, Culture and Identity*, New York, NY, London: Allen Lane.

—— (2006 forthcoming) *Identity and Violence: The Illusion of Destiny*, New York, NY: W.W. Norton.

Sen, A. and Dreze, J. (1999) *The Amartya Sen and Jean Dreze Omnibus*, Delhi: Oxford University Press.

Sen, G. and Grown, C. (1988) *Development, Crises and Alternative Visions: Third World Women's Perspectives*, London: James & James/Earthscan.

Shapiro, I. and Hacker-Cordon, C. (eds) (1999) *Democracy's Edges*, Cambridge: Cambridge University Press.

Swedish International Development Cooperation Agency (SIDA) (2001) *Education for All: Human Rights and Basic Needs*. Available online at: www.sida.se/shared/jsp/download.jsp?f=EducationForAll+NY.pdf&a=2605 (accessed November 2005).

—— (2002a) *Perspectives on Poverty*. Available online at: www.sida.se/?d=118&a=1490&language=en_US (accessed November 2005).

—— (2002b) *Mainstreaming Gender Equality: Sida's Support for the Promotion of Gender Equality in Partner Countries*, Stockholm: SIDA.

Skelton, C. and Francis, B. (2003) *Boys and Girls in the Primary Classroom*, Maidenhead: Open University Press.

Skelton, C., Francis, B. and Smulyan, L. (eds) (2006) *International Handbook of Gender and Education*, London: Sage

Smith, L.T. (1999) *Decolonizing Methodologies: Research and Indigenous Peoples*, London: Zed.

Spivak, G.C. (1999) *A Critique of Postcolonial Reason: Toward a History of the Vanishing Present*, Cambridge. MA: Harvard University Press.

Squires, J. (2005) 'Is mainstreaming transformative? Theorizing mainstreaming in the context of diversity and deliberation', *Social Politics*, 12(3): 366–88.

Staudt, K. (2003) 'Gender mainstreaming: conceptual links to institutional machineries', in S.M. Rai (ed.) *Mainstreaming Gender, Democratizing the State?*, Manchester: Manchester University Press.

Stewart, F. (2005) 'Groups and capabilities', *Journal of Human Development*, 6, 2: 185–204.

Stewart, F. and Streeten, P. (1976) 'New strategies for development: poverty, income distribution, and growth', *Oxford Economic Papers*, 28, 3: 381–405.

Stromquist, N. (1995) 'Romancing the state: gender and power in education', *Comparative Education Review*, 39, 4: 423–54.

—— (1997) *Literacy for Citizenship: Gender and Grassroots Dynamics in Brazil*, Albany, NY: State University of New York Press.

—— (1999) 'The impact of structural adjustment programmes in Africa and Latin America', in C. Heward and S. Bunwaree (eds) *Gender, Education, & Development: Beyond Access to Empowerment*, London, New York, NY: Zed Books.

—— (2000) 'Voice, harmony, and fugue in global feminism', *Gender and Education* 12, 4: 419–33.

—— (2006) 'Women's rights to adult education as a means to citizenship', *International Journal of Educational Development*, 26, 2: 140–52.

Subbarao, K. and Raney, L. (1995) *Social Gains from Female Education*, Washington, DC: World Bank.

Subrahmanian, R. (2002) 'Engendering education: prospects for a rights-based approach to female education deprivation in India', in M. Molyneux and S. Razavi (eds) *Gender Justice, Development, and Rights*, Oxford: Oxford University Press.

—— (2005a) 'Gender equality in education: definitions and measurements', *International Journal of Educational Development*, 25, 4: 395–407.

—— (2005b) *'Scaling Up' Good Practices in Girls' Education*, Paris: UNESCO.

Summers. L. (1993) 'Foreword', in E.M. King and M.A. Hill (eds) *Women's Education in Developing Countries. Barriers, Benefits and Policies*, Baltimore, MD: Johns Hopkins University Press.

Swainson, N. (2000) 'Knowledge and power: the design and implementation of gender policies in education in Malawi, Tanzania and Zimbabwe', *International Journal of Educational Development*, 20: 49–64.

Swift, A. (2003) *How Not to Be a Hypocrite: School Choice for the Morally Perplexed*, London: RoutledgeFalmer.

Terzi, L. (2005) 'A capability perspective on impairment, disability and special needs', *Theory and Research in Education*, 3, 2: 197–223.

Tinker, I. (1990a) 'A context for the field and for the book', in I. Tinker (ed.) *Persistent Inequalities: Women and World Development*, Oxford: Oxford University Press.

—— (1990b) *Persistent Inequalities: Women and World Development*, Oxford: Oxford University Press.

Tomasevski, K. (2003) *Education Denied*, London: Zed Books.

Townsend, J. (1999) *Women and Power: Fighting Patriarchies and Poverty*, London: Zed Books.

Uganda (2000) *Uganda EFA Report*, Kampala: Ministry of Education and Sport. Available online at: www2.unesco.org/wef/countryreports/uganda/rapport_2/html (accessed May 2004).

—— (2003) *EMIS Databases for 2003 and Budget Planning Section*, Kampala: Ministry of Education and Sport.

Joint United Nations Programme on HIV/AIDS, United Nations Children's Fund and United States Agency for International Development (UNAIDS, UNICEF and USAID) (2004) *Children on the Brink 2004: A Joint Report of New Orphan estimates and Framework for Action*, New York, NY: UNICEF.

United Nations Development Programme (UNDP) (2000) *Gender Mainstreaming in Education: A Handbook*. Available online at: www.undp.org/gender/docs/RBEC_GM_manual.pdf (accessed March 2005).

—— (2003) *Human Development Report*, New York, NY: Oxford University Press.

—— (2005) *Human Development Report*, New York, NY: UNDP.

United Nations Educational, Scientific and Cultural Organisation (UNESCO) (1976) *Statistical Yearbook*, Paris: UNESCO.

—— (1980) *Statistical Yearbook*, Paris: UNESCO.

—— (1983) *Statistical Yearbook*, Paris: UNESCO.

—— (1987) *Statistical Yearbook*, Paris: UNESCO.

—— (1990a) *World Education Report*, Paris: UNESCO.

—— (1990b) *Statistical Yearbook*, Paris: UNESCO.

—— (1993) *World Education Report*, Paris: UNESCO.

—— (1995a) *World Education Report*, Paris: UNESCO.

—— (1995b) *Statistical Yearbook*, Paris: UNESCO.

—— (1998a) *Statistical Yearbook*, Paris: UNESCO.

—— (1998b) *World Education Report*, Paris: UNESCO.

—— (1999) *Statistical Yearbook*, Paris: UNESCO.

—— (2002) *Global Monitoring Report 2002: Is the World on Track?*, Paris: UNESCO.

—— (2003) *Global Monitoring Report 2004. Gender and Education for All. The Leap to Equality*, Paris: UNESCO.

—— (2004) *Global Monitoring Report 2005. The Quality Imperative*, Paris: UNESCO.

—— (2005a) *Global Monitoring Report 2006 Literacy for Livelihood*, Paris: UNESCO.

—— (2005b) *Summary Report: Progress towards EFA*, Paris: UNESCO. Available online at: http://portal.unesco.org/education/en/ev.php-URL_ID=43140&URL_DO=DO_TOPIC&URL_SECTION=201.html (accessed December 2005).

United Nations Girls' Education Initiative (UNGEI) (2000) *Concept Paper. The Ten Year UN Girls' Education Initiative*. Available online at: www.undg.org/documents/28-The_10-Year_UN_Girls__Education_Initiative__UNGEI_Concept_Paper_-_The_10-Year_UN_Girls__Edu.doc (accessed December 2005).

—— (2002) *Consultation with NGOs about UNGEI*. Available online at: www.undg.org/documents/423-Consultation_with_NGOs_about_UNGEI__Partnering_for_Girls__Education_in_relation_to_the_MDGs.pdf (accessed January 2006).

—— (2005) *What is UNGEI: About Us*. Available online at: www.ungei.org/whatisungei/index_211.html (accessed November 2005).

—— (2006) *UK government announces $15 billion to deliver education for all*. Available online at: www.ungei.org/infobycountry/247_643.html (accessed April 2006).

United Nations Girls' Education Initiative Task Force (UNGEI Task Force) (2002) *Summary of United Nations Girls' Education Initiative Activities, January–December, 2001*, New York, NY: UNICEF. Available online at: www.undg.org/documents/14-Summary_of_UNGEI_Activities__Jan_01_-_Dec_01__-_Summary_of_UNGEI_Activiti.doc (accessed December 2005).

United Nations Children's Fund (UNICEF) (2003) *State of the World's Children 2004*, New York, NY: UNICEF.

—— (2004) *State of the World's Children*, New York, NY: UNICEF.

—— (2005a) Kenya: regional disparities threaten progress towards education for all, Lokichoggio: UNICEF. Available online at: www.unicef.org/infobycountry/kenya_29919.html (accessed December 2005).

—— (2005b) *2005 and Beyond: Accelerating Girls' Education in South Asia*, report of meeting, Bangkok, February 2005, Kathmandu: UNICEF.

—— (2005c) *State of the World's Children*, New York, NY: UNICEF.

United Nations (1948) 'Universal Declaration of Human Rights'. Available online at: www.un.org/Overview/rights.html (accessed October 2004).

—— (2000) 'Millennium Declaration, 2000'. Available online at: www. unog.ch/ 80256EDD006B8954/(httpAssets)/12AFDD5AD2C8BBCDC1256FB600 52010A/$file/Millenium%20Declaration.pdf (accessed June 2005).

UNStats (2005a) *Millennium Development Goals: 2005 Progress Report*, New York, NY: United Nations. Available online at: http://unstats.un.org/unsd/mi/pdf/ MDG%20Chart%20No%20Text.pdf (accessed December 2005).

—— (2005b) *Global Population by Gender*, New York, NY: United Nations. Available online at: www.geohive.com/global/pop_gender.php (accessed March 2006).

Unterhalter, E. (2000) 'Transnational visions of the 1990s: contrasting views of women, education and citizenship', in M. Arnot and J. Dillabough (eds) *Challenging Democracy: International Perspectives on Gender, Education and Citizenship*, London: Routledge.

—— (2003) 'The capabilities approach and gendered education: an examination of South African complexities', *Theory and Research in Education*, 1, 1: 7–22.

—— (2005a) 'Fragmented frameworks: researching women, gender, education and development', in S. Aikman and E. Unterhalter (eds) *Beyond Access: Developing Gender Equality in Education*, Oxford: Oxfam Publishing.

—— (2005b) 'Gender equality and education in South Africa: measurements, scores and strategies', in L. Chisholm and J. September (eds) *Gender Equity in South African Education 1994–2004. Conference Proceedings*, Cape Town: HSRC Press.

—— (2005c) 'Mobilization, meanings and measures', *Development*, 48, 1: 110–14.

—— (2005d) 'Global inequality, capabilities, social justice and the Millennium Development Goal for gender equality in education', *International Journal of Education and Development*, 25: 111–22.

—— (2006a forthcoming) 'New times and new vocabularies: theorising and evaluating gender equality in commonwealth higher education', *Women's Studies International Forum*, 29, 6

—— (2006b forthcoming) 'The capability approach and gendered education: some issues of operationalisation in the context of the HIV/AIDS epidemic in South Africa' in S. Alkire, F. Comim and M. Qizilbash (eds) *The Capability Approach: Concepts, Measures and Application*, Cambridge: Cambridge University Press.

—— and Brighouse, H. (2003) 'Distribution of what? How will we know if we have achieved Education for All by 2015?', paper presented at the Third Conference on the Capabilities Approach: University of Pavia, September. Available online at: http://cfs.unipv.it/sen/3rd.html (accessed September 2005).

Unterhalter, E. and Brighouse, H. (2006 forthcoming) 'Distribution of what?', in M. Walker and E. Unterhalter (eds) *Sen's Capability Approach and Social Justice in Education*, London, New York, NY: Palgrave.

Unterhalter, E. and Dutt, S. (2001) 'Gender, Education and Women's Power: Indian state and civil society intersections in DPEP (District Primary Education Programme) and Mahila Samakhya', *Compare*, 31, 1: 57–73.

Unterhalter, E. and McCowan, T. (2005) 'Girls' education and the millennium development goals: what do the indicators show us?', paper presented at UNGEI Technical Meeting, Bangkok, February 2005.

Unterhalter, E., Aikman, S., Challender, C. and North, A. (2005a) 'Translating frameworks: reflections on the beyond access project for gender equality in education', paper presented at UKFIET Conference, Oxford, September.

Unterhalter, E., Challender, C. and Rajagopalan, R. (2005b) 'Measuring gender equality in education', in S. Aikman and E. Unterhalter (eds) *Beyond Access: Developing Gender Equality in Education*, Oxford: Oxfam Publishing.

Unterhalter, E., Kioko-Echessa, E., Pattman, R. *et al.* (2005c) *Scaling Up: Developing an Approach to Measuring Progress on Girls' Education in Commonwealth Countries in Africa*, London: Commonwealth Secretariat.

Unterhalter, E., Rajagopalan, R. and Challender, C. (2005d) *A Scorecard on Gender Equality in Girls' Education in Asia, 1990–2000*, Bangkok: UNESCO.

Unterhalter, E., Ross, J. and Alam, M. (2003) 'A fragile dialogue? Research and primary education policy formation in Bangladesh, 1971–2001', *Compare*, 33, 1: 85–100.

Uyan, P (2005) 'A search for universalism: reconsidering the capability approach in Turkey', unpublished Ph.D. thesis, Politics and International Relations Department, Bogazici University, Istanbul.

Vavrus, F. (2003) *Desire and Decline*, New York, NY: Peter Lang.

—— (2005) 'Adjusting inequality: education and structural adjustment policies in Tanzania', *Harvard Educational Review*, 75, 2: 174–201.

Vavrus, F. and Richey, L. (2003) 'Women and development: rethinking policy and reconceptualizing practice', *Women's Studies Quarterly*, XXX1(3 and 4): 6–18.

Vizard, P. (2005) 'Sen vs. Pogge on poverty and human rights', paper presented at the Fifth International Conference on the Capability Approach, UNESCO, Paris, 13 September 2005.

—— (2006) *Poverty and Human Rights: Sen's 'Capability Perspective' Explored*, Oxford: Oxford University Press.

Walby, S. (2002) 'Feminism in a global age', *Economy and Society*, 31, 4: 533–57.

—— (2005) 'Gender mainstreaming: productive tensions in theory and practice', *Social Politics*, 12, 3: 321–43.

Waljee, A. (2005) 'Transition or transmission? Gender and education in Tajikistan', paper presented at UKFIET Conference, Oxford, September 2005.

Walker, M. (2006) *Higher Education Pedagogies*, Maidenhead: Open University Press.

Walker, M. and Unterhalter, E. (2007 forthcoming) (eds) *Amartya Sen's Capability Approach and Social Justice in Education*, New York: Palgrave.

Walzer, M. (1983) *Spheres of Justice*, Oxford: Martin Robertson.

Watkins, K. (2000) *The Oxfam Education Report*, London: Oxfam International.

Waylen, G. (1995) *Gender in Third World Politics*, Boulder, CO: Lynne Rienner Publishers.

—— (2004) 'Putting governance into the gendered political economy of globalization', *International Feminist Journal of Politics*, 6, 4: 557–78.

Weiner, G. (1994) *Feminisms in Education: An Introduction*, Buckingham: Open University Press.

Wichterich, C. (2000) *The Globalized Woman*, London: Zed Books.

Wiggins, D. (1985) 'Claims of need', in T. Honderich (ed.) *Morality and Objectivity*, London: Routledge.

—— (1998) *Needs, Values, Truth*, Oxford: Blackwell.

Wolfensohn, J. (2001) 'Foreword', in *World Bank Engendering Development: Through Gender Equality in Rights, Resources and Voice*, Oxford: Oxford University Press.

Wolpe, A. (2005) 'Reflections on the Gender Equity Task Team', in L. Chisholm and J. September (eds) *Gender Equity in South African Education 1994–2004: Conference Proceedings*, Cape Town: HSRC Press.

Wolpe, A., Quinlan, O. and Martinez, L. (1997) *Gender Equity in Education: A Report by the Gender Equity Task Team, Department of Education, South Africa*, Pretoria: Department of Education.

World Bank (1979) *World Development Report*, New York, NY: Oxford University Press.

—— (1984) *World Development Report*, New York, NY: Oxford University Press.

—— (1985) *World Development Report*, New York, NY: Oxford University Press.

—— (1995) *Priorities and Strategies for Education: A World Bank Review*, Washington, DC: World Bank.

—— (2001) *Engendering Development*, New York: Oxford University Press.

—— (2002a) *Engendering Development: Through Gender Equality in Rights, Resources and Voice*, Oxford: Oxford University Press.

—— (2002b) *Genderstats. Database of Gender Atatistics*, Washington, DC: World Bank. Available online at: http://genderstats.worldbank.org/ (accessed December 2005).

—— (2002c) *Edstats. World Bank Database of Education Statistics*, Washington, DC: World Bank. Available online at: http://devdata.worldbank.org/edstats (accessed December 2005).

World Conference on Human Rights (1993) *Vienna Declaration and Programme of Action*, New York, NY: United Nations General Assembly. Available online at: www.unhchr.ch/huridocda/huridoca.nsf/(Symbol)/A.CONF.157.23.En?Open Document (accessed October 2005).

World Conference on Women (1995) *Beijing Declaration*, New York, NY: United Nations. Available online at: www.un.org/womenwatch/daw/beijing/platform/declar.htm (accessed June 2005).

World Declaration (1990) 'World Declaration on Education for All', in World Education Forum, *The Dakar Framework for Action*, Paris: UNESCO.

Wright, C. (2003) *Understanding UNGEI as an EFA Flagship, Issues of Leadership and Co-ordination in Girls' Education*, Preliminary document for the Fourth meeting of the Education for All Working Group, 22–23 July, Paris. Available online at: www.unicef.org/girlseducation/flagship.doc (accessed November 2005).

Young, I.M. (2002) *Inclusion and Democracy?*, Oxford: Oxford University Press.

Yunusa, S. (2004) 'Viewpoint: quality education for girls benefits boys too', *Equals*, 6, June: 5–6.

Yuval-Davis, N. (1997) *Gender and Nation*, London: Sage.

—— (2003) 'Human security and the gendered politics of belonging', paper presented at symposium on Justice. Equality sand Dependency in the 'Post Socialist' condition, Centre for the study of Women and Gender, University of Warwick, online at http://www2.warwick.ac.uk/fac/soc/sociology/gender/news2/pastevents/symposium/yuval/ (accessed January 2006).

Yuval-Davis, N. and Werbner, P. (1999) *Women, Citizenship and Difference*, London: Zed Books.

Zoll, M. 'The compensation debate: improving care to African orphans and vunerable children by compensating female care workers for their unpaid labour', paper prepared for Panel Discussion on *The Burden of HIV and AIDs Care on Women and Girls*, London, March 2006.

Index